HOSPITALS

— AND —

HEALTH

SYSTEMS

WHAT THEY ARE
AND HOW THEY WORK

CHARLES R. MCCONNELL, MBA, CM

Human Resource and Editorial Consultant, Ontario, New York

JONES & BARTLETT
LEARNING

World Headquarters
Jones & Bartlett Learning
5 Wall Street
Burlington, MA 01803
978-443-5000
info@jblearning.com
www.jblearning.com

Jones & Bartlett Learning books and products are available through most bookstores and online booksellers. To contact Jones & Bartlett Learning directly, call 800-832-0034, fax 978-443-8000, or visit our website, www.jblearning.com.

Substantial discounts on bulk quantities of Jones & Bartlett Learning publications are available to corporations, professional associations, and other qualified organizations. For details and specific discount information, contact the special sales department at Jones & Bartlett Learning via the above contact information or send an email to specialsales@jblearning.com.

Production Credits

VP, Product Management: Amanda Martin
Director of Product Management: Cathy Esperti
Product Manager: Danielle Bessette
Product Assistant: Tess Sackmann
Director of Project Management: Jenny Corriveau
Senior Marketing Manager: Susanne Walker
Manufacturing and Inventory
    Control Supervisor: Amy Bacus
Composition: codeMantra U.S. LLC
Project Management: codeMantra U.S. LLC
Cover Design: Kristin E. Parker
Text Design: Kristin E. Parker
Director of Rights & Media: Joanna Gallant
Rights & Media Specialist: Merideth Tumasz
Media Development Editor: Shannon Sheehan
Cover Image (Title Page, Chapter Opener):
    © sudok1/Getty Images
Printing and Binding: McNaughton & Gunn
Cover Printing: McNaughton & Gunn

Library of Congress Cataloging-in-Publication Data
Names: McConnell, Charles R., author.
Title: Hospitals and health systems: what they are and how they work / Charles R. McConnell.
Description: Burlington, MA: Jones & Bartlett Learning, [2020] | Includes bibliographical references and index.
Identifiers: LCCN 2018044200 | ISBN 9781284143560 (pbk.: alk. paper)
Subjects: | MESH: Hospital Administration | Hospitals—history | Delivery of Health Care | United States
Classification: LCC RA971 | NLM WX 150 AA1 | DDC 362.11068—dc23
LC record available at https://lccn.loc.gov/2018044200

6048

Printed in the United States of America
23 22 21 20 19   10 9 8 7 6 5 4 3 2 1

Contents

Chapter 6 Health Benefits Coverage and Types of Health Plans 53

Peter R. Kongstvedt

Chapter 7 Reimbursement: Following the Money 83

James Gillespie, Kendall Cortelyou-Ward,
Reid Oetjen, and Timothy Rotarius

Chapter 8 Is Bigger Better? Hospitals and "Merger Mania" 101

Cristian H. Lieneck

Chapter 9 The Health System Emerges 119

Meghan Gabriel, Kendall Cortelyou-Ward,
Timothy Rotarius, and Reid M. Oetjen

Chapter 10 Mergers, Acquisitions, and the Government . . . 135

Nancy J. Niles

Chapter 11 Structure, Organization, and Portals to Care.... 147

Claudia Neumann and Ashish Chandra

Chapter 12 Direct Patient Care: The Hospital Team........... 157

Charles R. McConnell

Chapter 13 Staffing Shortages: Then, Now, and Continuing....... 177

Susan Young and Laura Reichhardt

Chapter 14 The Physical Facility 193

Camonia R. Graham-Tutt and Lisa K. Spencer

Chapter 15 Business Activities and the Business of Medicine 203

Randall Garcia and Ashish Chandra

Chapter 16 Unions in Healthcare Organizations 213

Charles R. McConnell

Preface

Upon initial consideration, this book, when proposed, was envisioned as becoming a new edition of *Hospitals: What They Are and How They Work*. This fundamental explanation of the composition and operation of the institution long regarded as occupying the center of what we had seen as our healthcare "system" was intended as a comprehensive introduction to the hospital primarily for persons interested in pursuing careers in health care. *Hospitals: What They Are and How They Work* has appeared in four editions to date, the first two by original author I. Donald Snook and the third and fourth editions edited by Donald J. Griffin with sections provided by a team of contributors.

However, in consideration of all that health care has experienced in recent decades, it appeared that a straightforward new edition of *Hospitals: What They Are and How They Work* could not adequately address the present-day reality that more and more the individual hospital does not stand alone in providing care for the population. Certainly, there remain a significant number of free-standing hospitals, but this number is diminishing as more and more individual hospitals are brought together in healthcare systems. In recent years, there have even been hospitals and relatively new "systems" combining to comprise even larger systems. This present volume, *Hospitals and Health Systems: What They Are and How They Work* recognizes the reality of organizing for the delivery of health care today; in most instances, one must think beyond the boundaries of the individual institution and accept the fact that patient care may today be delivered in settings that are considerably different from the traditional hospital.

Thus *Hospitals and Health Systems: What They Are and How They Work* addresses so much change that simply designating it as a fifth edition of *Hospitals: What They Are and How They Work* would be misleading. However, the basic intent of this volume remains as that of its predecessor volumes: to provide individuals who may be considering employment in health care a solid grounding in the arena in which they may find themselves pursuing careers.

Yet regardless of the label attached to a specific entity involved in providing health care—hospital, healthcare system, clinic, group practice, urgent care center, or whatever—the quest to enhance the quality of patient care has forever been the guiding principle for healthcare professionals since the first hospitals opened their doors. With the increasing complexity of systems of healthcare delivery, and the seemingly growing presence of economic and regulatory factors, healthcare workers are continuously expected to do more with less.

But regardless of how one refers to the individual arena in which some form of care is delivered, that care is provided by people: healthcare professionals, paraprofessionals, and vital support staff—together the folks who collaborate in the provision of quality patient care. Whether individual hospital, clinic, free-standing surgical center, group practice, or other care delivery alternative, those who work in healthcare must conscientiously work together in delivering quality healthcare services.

This text makes a determined effort to simplify some of the growing complexity of the hospital or health system; however, there are some elements that even when viewed "simply," such as reimbursement for care and managed care and its variations—require careful study.

The healthcare environment is volatile in a number of dimensions. With the passage of the Patient Protection and Affordable Care Act (PPACA) on March 23, 2010, the country's healthcare system underwent a dramatic shift to expand access to care for millions of otherwise uninsured Americans, while simultaneously attempting to reduce the cost of health care.

Yet healthcare costs continue to climb, and what now remains of the PPACA makes it clear that health care in the United States is highly politicized to the extent that the two major political parties are unable to agree on a workable approach to the problem.

The first three chapters of *Hospitals and Health Systems: What They Are and How They Work* provide a condensed history of hospitals overall and United States hospitals in particular. These chapters take us up to the mid-1960s and the advent of Medicare and Medicaid, which truly were, as the Chapter 4 title claims, major game changers for health care in this country. From there, the advent of managed care and the numerous and sometimes complex means of providing care are addressed, followed by the sometimes equally complex means of paying for care. There follows examination of mergers and affiliations and other combinations leading to a focus on the creation and operation of health systems.

Chapters 12–16 actually provide an abridgement and update most of the contents of the fourth edition of *Hospitals: What They Are and How They Work*. Thus a new book rather than a fifth edition of an existing volume, given that most of what is contained in the pages that follow is new. *Hospitals and Health Systems: What They Are and How They Work* is a determined effort to present a current picture of what is probably the most volatile and changeable industry in the country. Yet the evolution of health care in the United States will continue unabated as further advances and organizational changes accrue; this we can count on.

Charles R. McConnell
August 2018

About the Author

Charles R. McConnell is an independent healthcare management and human resources consultant and freelance writer specializing in business, management, and human resource topics. For 11 years, he was active as a management engineering consultant with the Management and Planning Services (MAPS) division of the Hospital Association of New York State (HANYS) and later spent 18 years as a hospital human resources manager. As an author, coauthor, and anthology editor, he has published a number of books and has contributed numerous articles to various publications. He is in his 38th year as editor of the quarterly academic and professional journal, *The Health Care Manager*.

Mr. McConnell received an MBA and a BS in Engineering from the State University of New York at Buffalo.

Contributors

Ashish Chandra, MMS, MBA, PhD, University of Houston-Clear Lake, Houston, TX.

Camonia R. Graham-Tutt, PhD, CHES, University of Hawaii West Oahu, Kapolei, HI; and Lisa K. Spencer, DHA, MPH, University of Hawaii West Oahu, Kapolei, HI.

Claudia Neumann, University of Applied Sciences for Health Care Professions (HSG), Germany.

Cristian H. Lieneck, PhD, FACMPE, FACHE, FAHM, CPHIMS, Associate Professor, School of Health Administration, Texas State University, San Marcos, TX.

Danielle N. Atkins, MPA, PhD, College of Health and Public Affairs, University of Central Florida, Orlando, FL.

James Gillespie, PhD, JD, President, Center for Healthcare Innovation in Chicago, IL.

Kendall Cortelyou-Ward, PhD, Department of Health Management and Informatics, University of Central Florida, Orlando, FL.

Laura Reichhardt, MS, APRN, NP-C, Hawaii State Center for Nursing, Honolulu, HI.

Meghan Gabriel, PhD, University of Central Florida, Orlando, FL.

Nancy J. Niles, MS, MPH, MBA, PhD, Rollins College, Winter Park, FL.

Peter R. Kongstvedt, MD, FACP, American College of Physicians, AcademyHealth, George Mason University, Fairfax, VA.

Randall Garcia, BS, MHA/MBA, CG Consultants, Houston, TX.

Reid M. Oetjen, PhD, University of Central Florida, Orlando, FL.

Robert R. Kulesher, PhD, MBA, Professor, Health Services and Information Management, College of Allied Health Sciences, East Carolina University, Greenville, NC.

Susan Young, DHA, MSA, RN, Assistant Professor of Health Care Administration, University of Hawaii West Oahu, Kapolei, HI.

Timothy Rotarius, MBA, PhD, Department of Health Management and Informatics, University of Central Florida, Orlando, FL.

CHAPTER 1

Hospitals: Origins and Growth from Early Times to 1900

Charles R. McConnell

CHAPTER OBJECTIVES

- To overview the development of hospitals through the ages from ancient times up to the beginning of the 20th century.
- To address the transitioning of hospitals from housing for the dying to houses of healing.
- To overview the early development of nursing as a healing occupation.

KEY TERMS

Almshouses

American Medical Association (AMA)

Hippocrates

Pennsylvania Hospital

▶ The Earliest Years of Hospitals

This introductory chapter explores the various ways in which human beings have sought and received medical care in a more or less organized setting when they experienced illness or injury and examines how organizations and institutions developed over time to provide such care. Hospitals as such—though the term "hospital" was likely not actually attached to the earliest facilities—date back to early civilization and the initial development of the most rudimentary means of caring for the ill and injured. According to medical anthropologists, there were such

1

organized institutions existing more than 4000 years ago in Mesopotamia, and hospitals existed in Egypt and India even in antiquity. In the great river valleys of the world that were favorable for settlement, families became clans and then tribes and these became empires and civilizations that rose and fell. Hospitals and medicine played an ever-expanding part in the history of the world and have always been intertwined with the political and economic affairs of society and the prevailing social norms of the day. As Christianity and Islam became widespread, hospitals were established in both Christian and Muslim countries (Chilliers & Retief, 2005). During the early years of Christianity, the outreach of the church in general included caring for the sick, feeding the hungry, and caring for the destitute.

To Welcome and Care for Visitors

The term *hospital* seems to have evolved beginning with the Latin word *hospes*, originally meaning a visitor or a host who receives visitors. This led to the Latin word *hospitalia*, a place for strangers or guests. Medieval Latin gave us the term *hospitale*, and then Old French shortened this to *hospital*. The term *hospital*, in fact, derives from the same origins as *hotel*.

Written accounts and archeological conclusions provide a window into the medical care of the time of the great civilizations of Egypt, China, Persia, Greece, and Rome (Risse, 1999). The historian Herodotus described the Egyptians as particularly healthy people with good health practices and gifted physicians. Early medical practices in Egypt and in many other ancient societies were integrated into religious practices, services, and ceremonies. Transcripts identifying certain religious deities with specific healing abilities have been found dating as far back as 4000 BCE. The temples of Greek and Roman gods such as Saturn, and later Asclepius in Asia Minor, were recognized as healing centers. Such centers provided refuge for the sick and offered pleasant vistas, salty air, hot and cold baths, and prescribed medications such as salt, honey, and water from sacred springs—though not always for everyone; there is evidence to suggest that the best of such services usually went to the wealthy or socially prominent. Around 100 BCE, the Romans established hospitals (known at the time as "*valetudinarian*") for the treatment of their sick and injured soldiers. Providing care for the legions was of paramount importance, as the power of Rome depended on its great army (Risse, 1999).

Ancient Greek writings also describe temples and other healing places. Certain gods were named for their healing powers. Aelius Aristides, a wealthy Roman orator, had purportedly visited a Greek temple to seek healing from the goddess Isis (Risse, 1999). **Hippocrates**, long considered the father of medicine, advocated a rational, nonreligious approach to the practice of medicine. Hippocrates began the practice of auscultation (the act of listening to sounds of organs within the body), performed surgical operations, and kept detailed records of his patients in which he described diseases ranging from tuberculosis to ulcers (Risse, 1999). In the Asclepieion of Epidaurus (Risse, 1999), three large marble slabs that date from 350 BCE preserve the names, case histories, complaints, and cures of about 70 patients who came to the temple with medical needs. These are reported to be among the very first medical records. The surgeries listed in these records, such as lancing of an abdominal abscess or removal of foreign material, could have taken place while the patient was sedated with some soporific substance such as opium that was used at the time (Risse, 1999).

A Growing Concern for Illness

During the early years of Christianity in the Near East, sickness was a source of constant anxiety. Growing population densities and resultant sanitation issues in areas such as Rome and Mesopotamia were responsible for epidemics of infectious diseases that kept mortality rates high during this period (Chilliers & Retief, 2002). The rise of commerce with the Far East along over the Silk Road brought people into frequent contact with foreign populations, and two separate disease pools— east and west—came together with grave consequences for the entire region. Many diseases, such as smallpox, measles, and plague routinely devastated populations. The Byzantine Empire, for example, succumbed to famine and civil unrest brought about by extensive migrations from rural to urban centers where both endemic and epidemic diseases decimated the cities (Chilliers & Retief, 2002).

As it had become in Rome, the practice of medicine in Persia also became widespread. The Persians are credited with preserving the early Greek texts until the time of the Renaissance, and without their efforts, much valuable information would have been lost (Chilliers & Retief, 2002). Three kinds of medicine are described in a passage of the *Vendidad*, one of the surviving texts of the *Zend-Avesta*, not found until the early 1700s: medicine by the knife (surgery), medicine by herbs, and medicine by divine words. According to the *Vendidad*, the best medicine was healing by divine words (Chilliers & Retief, 2002).

The Nursing Tradition Emerges

The establishment of the first hospital in Europe is generally credited to Saint Basil the Great of Caesarea, a Cappodocian Father who lived during the 4th century. Known as the Basiliad, this was a large ministry complex that included a poorhouse and what we would today refer to as a hospital and a hospice.

From religious beginnings, a nursing tradition developed during the early years of Christianity as the benevolent outreach of the church broadened. A growing emphasis on charity continued with the proliferation of monastic orders in the 5th and 6th centuries and extended well into the Middle Ages. Religious orders of monks were the principal providers of nursing care; essentially, the first hospital nurses were the monks. A few such orders provided care for victims of the Black Plague in the 14th century, and about this time, communities began to establish institutions for contagious diseases such as leprosy.

The Seeds of the Voluntary Hospital Movement

So many early hospitals, however, were little more than places where the seriously ill were housed until overtaken by death, or places where victims of contagious diseases either recovered or died. The emphasis of the best of such institutions was on what we would today refer to palliative care, providing comfort as life faded away.

During the Middle Ages and the early Renaissance era, some European universities began to emphasize medical education, expanding upon the notion that with appropriate care, people could recover from disease; that is, that one who fell seriously ill was not automatically assumed to be terminal. During this period, hospitals were transitioning from religious-centered institutions to a central emphasis on medical care.

Also, during the Middle Ages, the hospital movement grew to accommodate the Crusades, which began in 1096. Military hospitals sprang up for the wounded and weary crusaders along all the traveled roads between the Holy Land and the West. However, the most rapid growth in the number of hospitals in Europe occurred during the 12th and 13th centuries. In the 12th century in particular, religiously based monastic hospitals flourished and some became important teaching institutions (Risse, 1999).

The Benedictines established the greatest number of monastic institutions, reportedly more than 2000 altogether. Hospitals were also established in Baghdad and Damascus during that period. The Arab hospitals were notable in that they admitted patients regardless of religious belief, race, or social order. Additionally, the Arab hospital system relied on resources from the community: all treatments were free of charge, and each member of society donated a portion of his or her wealth to support the institution (Risse, 1999).

The organization of hospital-like institutions began to change in the Middle Ages as secular authorities began to support some forms of institutional care. Hospitals served several functions during this period: they were **almshouses** for the poor, hostels for pilgrims, and institutions of learning for physicians in training. This gradual transfer of responsibility for institutional health care from the church to civil authorities continued in Europe after 1540 when Henry VIII dissolved the monasteries. Monastic hospitals had disappeared from England by the late 1600s, leading secular authorities to begin caring for the sick and injured in their communities. Toward the end of the 15th century, many towns and cities supported some type of institutionalized care. There were reportedly some 200 such establishments at this time, indicating a growing social need in Britain (Risse, 1999; Starr, 1982). This was the beginning of the voluntary hospital movement. In France, the first such institution was probably established by the Huguenots around 1718 (Risse, 1999).

By the turn of the 18th century, medical and surgical treatment had become a primary concern; no longer was simple comfort care the principal mission of the hospital. Hospitals had long been primarily religious institutions; they were now becoming true medical institutions. Yet throughout most of the 19th century, it was largely just the socially marginal, poor, or isolated who received care in hospitals; the upper and middle classes were treated at home or in private clinics owned and operated by physicians.

In 1859, at St. Thomas's Hospital in London, Florence Nightingale established her nursing school, essentially formalizing nursing as a healing occupation.

▶ Early American Hospitals

Hernando Cortes built the first North American hospital in Mexico City in 1524; it still stands today. Near the middle of the 1600s, the French established a hospital at Quebec City in Canada. Jeanne Mance, a French noblewoman, built a hospital of ax-hewn logs on the island of Montreal in 1644 (Starr, 1982). The order of the Sisters of St. Joseph, now considered to be the oldest nursing group organized in North America, grew out of this endeavor.

A hospital for soldiers established in 1663 on Manhattan Island was the first hospital in the United States. Almshouses served as early hospitals in the United States; one of the first of these was established by William Penn in Philadelphia in 1713 (Starr, 1982).

It is important to note that in the earlier hospitals, physicians were not a regular presence. Much of the population shunned hospitals, which were seen by many as little more than warehouses for the dying. Those who could afford medical care were often treated in their homes by physicians or in private clinics.

Pennsylvania Hospital and Incorporated Beginnings

The **Pennsylvania Hospital** in Philadelphia was the first incorporated hospital in America. This institution was organized by Dr. Thomas Boyd to provide a place for Philadelphia physicians to treat their private patients. Benjamin Franklin helped Boyd obtain a charter from the crown in 1751 (Starr, 1982). In contrast, in 1769, New York City, with 300,000 residents, still had no hospital; this was remedied when Dr. John Jones formed the Society of New York Hospital and obtained a grant to build a hospital. During the Revolution, however, the New York Hospital fell into the hands of the British who used it as part barracks and part military hospital. Other early hospitals of historic interest include two hospitals, one in Boston, Massachusetts, and one in Norfolk, Virginia, that were established in 1802 by the federal government to provide care for sick and injured servicemen (Starr, 1982).

The first psychiatric hospital was established in Williamsburg, Virginia, in 1773. Massachusetts General Hospital in Boston, one of the pioneer hospitals of modern medicine, admitted its first patient, a 30-year-old soldier, in 1821.

Phases of American Hospital Development

Early hospital systems in America developed in three distinct phases. The first, running roughly from 1751 to 1851, saw the formation of two kinds of institutions: voluntary hospitals operated by charitable boards and public hospitals descended from almshouses—unspecialized institutions that served general welfare functions and only incidentally cared for the sick—operated by municipalities. The second phase began in about 1850, when particularistic (primarily religious or ethnic) and specialized hospitals became established. The third phase saw the development of profit-making hospitals operated by physicians, singly or in partnership, or corporations (Starr, 1982).

Americans were not inclined to seek care from hospitals during most of the early 19th century, and for more than a century thereafter, most Americans gave birth and endured illness and even surgery at home. The reasons for this were multiple: First, the country remained a largely rural society at this time, and few people had ever even seen a hospital let alone had access to one. Second, the indirect cost of visiting a hospital could mean the loss of several days' work and perhaps the crops for that season. And, as noted earlier, hospitals also had a reputation, deservedly so, as death houses. Mortality rates in hospitals during this era were extremely high. Finally, during the Victorian era, when modesty and a desire for privacy prevailed, people preferred to be seen by their physicians at home (Starr, 1982).

Effects of Changing Social Structures

In the United States, the late 19th century was a period of economic expansion and rapid institutional development. Weber described the changing social structure as a general movement from communal to associative relations. After the industrial revolution, social structures changed and families were no longer able to provide care to family members as they had before. Families no longer lived primarily in large houses with many members; many had migrated to cities, had fewer children, and lived in smaller households. Households and communities gave up their functions to organizations, and these organizations also changed. Hospitals were first almshouses. Almshouses metamorphosed into modern hospitals by first becoming more specialized in their function and then becoming more universal in their use (Starr, 1982).

A Dark Period for Hospitals

Despite the fact that the number of institutions increased during the first half of the 19th century, this era nevertheless stands out as a dark period in the history of hospitals. More surgeries were performed during this time than in any previous period in the history of medicine. However, few of these surgeries were successful, and in contrast to earlier surgeons, who had at least attempted to keep wounds clean, physicians in this era considered the production and discharge of pus (suppuration) to be desirable and encouraged it. The mortality rates reflected the error of this belief (Starr, 1982). Surgeons wore the same operating gowns for months between washings, and the same bed linens served several patients. Gangrene, hemorrhage, and infections infested the wards of hospitals. Mortality rates from surgeries ran as high as 90%. To tolerate the stench of the wards, nurses used snuff and wore perfumed masks.

By the time of the Civil War, however, hospitals had largely managed to overcome much of their reputation for squalor. The Union had established a system of more than 130,000 beds by the last year of the war and treated more than 1 million soldiers. Germ theory was not yet fully formulated, but the influence of Florence Nightingale made the system work better (Starr, 1982).

The Rise of Professional Nursing and Antiseptic Surgery

The contributions of Florence Nightingale during the mid-19th century are unfathomable in today's clean and modern healthcare settings. In the 1830s, Florence Nightingale went to Kaiserswerth on the Rhine to train as a nurse. She wrote disparagingly of her training, especially regarding the hygiene practices, and gained a reputation for delivering effective and efficient nursing care. In 1854, she was sent by the English government to improve the deplorable conditions of the care given to the sick and wounded soldiers of the Crimean War. The appalling conditions she found, including wounded men vermin-infested and lying in dirt, were quickly remedied.

Florence Nightingale brought order and cleanliness to the practice of nursing. She organized kitchens, laundry services, and departments for supplies, often using her own resources to fund her projects. Florence Nightingale brought an organized approach to the operation of hospitals and is considered by many to be the first true healthcare administrator. One of her major contributions was her use of statistics to track infections and determine the real causes of mortality in the Crimean War. This was one of the earliest uses of the scientific method to determine the cause of disease and develop effective treatment plans. Before many of the lifesaving innovations of that time had even been discovered, Florence Nightingale had decreased the incidence of disease and the ensuing mortality with her hygienic approach to nursing care (Starr, 1982).

In 1859, Florence Nightingale established her innovative nursing school at St. Thomas's Hospital in London. Her approach to nursing education exerted considerable influence on future nurses' training in the United States and elsewhere.

Two additional developments brought about even more pronounced improvements. One was the professionalization of nursing. In 1873, nurse training schools were established in New York, New Haven, and Boston. The training of nurses and oversight of nursing in hospitals were taken up as a cause by upper-class women in New York. Some physicians opposed it, however, some saying that educated nurses probably would not do as they were told. But the women prevailed and nursing became a profession. The other development was the advent of antiseptic surgery in 1867, led by Joseph Lister (Rosen, 1993). Like nursing, surgery enjoyed a tremendous rise in acceptance and prestige in the late 1800s. The discovery of anesthesia made the practice of surgery much easier, and surgeries became slower, more careful, and safer endeavors. Surgery really began to take off in the 1890s and into the early 1900s, increasing in amount, scope, and daring. In 1883, the number of surgical patients exceeded that of medical patients for the first time in Boston hospitals. Hospitals also became more generally accepted and began to serve patients of different social classes. By the early 20th century, the occupational distribution of the adult patient population reflected that of the general population.

The introduction of the scientific method into medicine during this time was an important phase in the development of health care in this country and throughout the world. Louis Pasteur discovered bacteria while trying to help a friend determine why his beer was going bad before he could sell it. He further determined that it was also the cause of disease.

In Europe, early infection control was achieved through the efforts of Ignaz Semmelweis of Vienna, Austria. Appalled at the high rate of mortality among postpartum women in his hospital, Semmelweis used the statistical data he gathered from medical students on the maternity ward to determine the cause of the infections. He boldly informed his colleagues that the high mortality rate from puerperal fever in maternity patients was due to infection transmitted by students who came from the dissecting room to take care of the patients on the maternity ward. The mortality rate was much lower for poorer women who were cared for by midwives, who practiced better hygiene. Semmelweis required the medical students to scrub their hands before seeing patients, and although he made enemies, he also lowered the mortality rate in the Lying-in Hospital's maternity ward. This was the beginning of work on germ theory and, along with the findings of Pasteur and others, the origin of modern bacteriology and clinical laboratories.

Joseph Lister continued Pasteur's work. He noticed that broken bones over which the skin remained intact healed much faster and with fewer complications compared to fractures that were exposed. Lister theorized that some element that was introduced through the wound and then circulated within the body was responsible for the infections. By 1870, surgeons were following a protocol of spraying carbolic solution on both surgeons and patients and in the operating rooms, resulting in fewer surgery-related infections. Two other important developments were the introduction of steam sterilization by Bergmann in 1886 and rubber gloves by Halstead in 1890 (Rosen, 1993).

The end of the 19th century also brought the discovery of anesthesia and antiseptics, two of the most significant influences on the development of modern surgical procedures. One of the final major achievements of the century was the discovery of the X-ray in 1895. Additionally, hospitals began to care for patients with communicable diseases during this time. During the last decade of the century, the tubercle bacillus and malaria parasite were discovered, Pasteur vaccinated against anthrax, and Koch isolated the cholera and tetanus bacilli (Rosen, 1993).

Hospitals Proliferate

The discoveries and events of the 19th century resulted in a great many hospitals being established in a relatively brief period of time. In the United States, by the end of the century, there were 149 hospitals with a total capacity of more than 35,000 beds, and fewer than 10% of these hospitals and beds were under any form of government control (Starr, 1982). After 1900, the elite voluntary hospitals concentrated on acute care and had relatively closed medical staffs and the closest ties to universities. The municipal and county hospitals, usually the largest local institutions in terms of number of beds, cared for a full range of acute and chronic illnesses. The religious and ethnic hospitals were a mixed, intermediate group that rarely had significant endowments and consequently relied on patient fees. The profit-making hospitals were mainly surgical centers; they were usually small and had no ties to medical schools (Starr, 1982).

The **American Medical Association (AMA)** was founded in 1847 under the leadership of Dr. Nathan Smith. Also, during the latter half of the 19th century, women were finally being accepted as physicians following a considerable struggle. Also against considerable resistance, the AMA strove to raise the standards of medical education and professional competency during the early part of the 20th century. The Flexner Report, written by Abraham Flexner, a professional educator, was published in 1910 and proved to be a severe indictment of the system. Among the deficiencies Flexner wrote about were touted laboratories that did not exist, no disinfectant in dissecting rooms, libraries without books, alleged faculty members busily occupied in their private practices, and medical schools routinely waiving admission requirements for those who could pay. Flexner found a great discrepancy between medical science and medical education, and his report brought about great changes in medical education (Starr, 1982).

Overall, hospitals had stepped out on a path that would eventually lead to the healthcare system of today; the stage was now set for the widespread acceptance of the hospital as the apparent center of what would become loosely described as "the healthcare system."

Brief Chapter Summary

Hospitals began to care for the sick almost incidentally. The earliest hospitals were established for pilgrims, indigents, and plague victims. Later, they became institutions where people from all parts of society could come for diagnosis and recovery.

Early American hospitals were largely founded following the example of European hospitals. However, American hospitals developed rapidly and soon became quite different from their early foreign counterparts.

The hospital as an institution has become dynamic in nature; it exists to meet the needs of the people it serves. Today's hospitals continue to make history by reacting to the changing needs of society and providing better technologies, new services, and greater access.

Questions for Review and Discussion

1. According to medical anthropologists, where and when did hospitals begin?
2. Who is considered the father of medicine, and what was his approach to the practice of medicine?
3. Identify some of the functions of hospitals during the Middle Ages.
4. What is an almshouse?
5. When and where was the first hospital established in the United States, and what was its purpose?
6. What made the Pennsylvania Hospital different from previous hospitals?
7. Name the three phases in the development of hospital systems in America.
8. Why is Florence Nightingale important to the history of hospitals?
9. Discuss early infection-control efforts by Ignaz Semmelweis.
10. What is the AMA and why is it important?

References

Chilliers, L., & Retief, G. (2002). The evolution of the hospital from antiquity to the end of the middle ages. *Curationis, 25*(4), 60–66.

Chilliers, L., & Retief, G. (2005). The evolution of hospitals from antiquity to the Renaissance. *Acta Theologica Supplementum, 7,* 213–232

Risse, G. (1999). *Mending bodies, saving souls: A history of hospitals.* New York, NY: Oxford Press.

Rosen, G. (1993). *A history of public health.* Baltimore, MD: The Johns Hopkins University Press.

Starr, P. (1982). *The social transformation of American medicine.* New York, NY: Basic Books.

CHAPTER 2

Becoming the Center of the "Healthcare System": 1900–1945

Charles R. McConnell

CHAPTER OBJECTIVES

- To trace hospital development and to describe the increasing tendency for many hospitals to become clustered into groupings that would become identified as multihospital systems.
- To review efforts to establish health insurance programs and to highlight the development of the country's earliest health insurance programs.
- To overview the increasing importance of the hospital and the growing perception of the hospital as the perceived center of the nation's "healthcare system."

KEY TERMS

Diploma programs   "Healthcare system"

▶ Entering the 20th Century

This chapter briefly addresses the significant changes affecting hospitals in the United States from the start of the 20th century to about 1945. Also addressed are some of the societal issues that helped drive hospitals' proliferation and acceptance and that fostered the public perception of the acute-care hospital as the center of the country's **"healthcare system."**

In 1900, the start of the 20th century, the average life expectancy in the United States was approximately 47 years. Surely, this is a rather grim statistic when reckoned in terms of what is known today.

The early years of the 20th century saw a significant proliferation of hospitals established and operated under several different auspices. There were privately supported voluntary hospitals overseen by lay trustees and funded by public support, charitable donations, bequests, and patient fees. There were Catholic institutions in which Catholic sisters and brothers were essentially owners, administrators, and nurses; these relied largely on fundraising and patient fees.

There were public institutions supported largely by taxes and serving charity patients and the aged or infirm. There were proprietary hospitals established and owned and operated by physicians as profit-making enterprises, some developed as specialized institutions devoted to the owners' medical specialties, obstetrics becoming one of the earliest such specialties.

Specialized ventures aside, at the beginning of the 20th century, it was becoming apparent that the hospital established to serve the sick and injured in general was becoming increasingly more of a public responsibility. For example, it was reported that of all patients admitted to hospitals during 1910, 37% of adults were in publically operated institutions (U.S. Bureau of the Census, 1910). In terms of financial support, the 1910 Census reported that 45.6% of hospitals received public appropriations, yet most such institutions received the majority of their income from patients who paid for their care (U.S. Bureau of the Census, 1910).

In the United States, during the early years of the 20th century, there were voluntary hospitals, religious-based hospitals, and public and governmental hospitals. By about 1910, approximately half of all hospitals were receiving some form of public or governmental support; however, the majority of their income came from charge-paying patients. It was estimated that about one-third of total hospital income came from public funds.

By about 1925, hospitals were serving increasing numbers of paying patients and were beginning to feel increasing financial pressure and the rise of competition among hospitals. One can say with some justification that this period marked the true beginning of the modern American hospital. Also, during the 1920s and 1930s, the continuing development of nursing as a profession was a prominent force in shaping hospital utilization.

Between 1909 and approximately 1932, the total number of hospital beds in the country increased at a rate nearly six times as fast as the increase in the country's population. American hospitals at this time included:

- Institutions owned and operated by churches and religious orders
- Tax-supported municipal hospitals dedicated to serving charity patients—the aged, the orphaned, the debilitated, and such
- Voluntary not-for-profit institutions serving specific communities or collective of population
- Proprietary, for-profit institutions generally owned and operated by physicians and primarily serving patients who could pay

In addition, the early stages of the Great Depression brought a marked shift in usage from privately owned hospitals to public institutions.

▶ Interest in Health Coverage Emerges

In the first decade of the new century, one of the first applications of employee health coverage occurred when railroads began to provide medical programs for employees. In about 1902, the first state workmen's compensation law was enacted in Maryland; interestingly enough, it was declared unconstitutional barely 2 years later. But by 1908, the federal government had established workmen's compensation for civilian employees, and hence the issue of unconstitutionality vanished. In a landmark move in 1904, the American Medical Association (AMA) formed the Council on Medical Education to standardize the requirements for doctors of medicine. In 1910, organized medicine became a reality when the AMA brought together half of the country's physicians.

Also about 1910, President Theodore Roosevelt made national health insurance a major issue during his unsuccessful campaign for re-election. The health insurance idea went nowhere at the federal level, but in the decade of 1910–1920, parts of the country saw localized efforts by a number of employers to protect their employees from financial hardships by creating plans to compensate employees for worktime lost because of illness or injury. Some state legislatures offered model bills for health insurance but all were soundly defeated, opposed by insurance companies that wanted to preserve their accident and burial insurances, organized physicians who feared the possibility of limits on their fees, pharmacists who feared loss of control of their drugs, and organized labor fearing that government insurance would weaken the appeal of unions. Given the apparently unified opposition of these several disparate interests, the push for health insurance did not have much of a chance during this period.

▶ The "Modern" Hospital Takes Its Place

Between the late 19th century and the mid-1920s, throughout the United States, hospitals were transitioning into increasingly costly modern institutions. They were serving increasing numbers of paying patients, largely middle-class individuals who could afford to pay for their care. And throughout this period, hospitals were starting to experience increasing financial pressure and some degree of competition. There had long been something of a generalized feeling that "competition" in health care was at least marginally undesirable given the noble mission of health care, but as some institutions began to take steps to lure patients away from neighboring facilities, some degree of competition among hospitals could not be denied.

By about 1925, the American hospital had become the sort of human service that most people perceived during much of the 20th century: an institution offering up-to-date medical care by way of the latest in "modern" medicine practiced by specialized personnel.

As nursing became more important to hospital operations, many hospitals became sites for nursing education. Hospital-based schools of nursing were especially prevalent during the middle quarters of the 20th century. Nurses learned under what was essentially an apprenticeship arrangement under which students gained clinical experience while providing actual patient care. Much nursing education during this period occurred in 3-year hospital-based "**diploma programs**" that were generally known as sources of excellent clinical experience for students.

By the end of the decade of 1910–1920, healthcare spending was noticeably on the increase, and essentially, in parallel, the demand for workmen's compensation programs and other forms of assistance was increasing. Yet, one 1919 study reported that citizens were losing four times as much in wages as they spent treating their maladies, so many individuals purchased "sickness insurance" rather than health insurance to cover the costs of medical care.

During the same decade, 1910–1920, medicine began to be seen as more of a science than previously, and hospitals became more accepted as treatment centers. Inadequate medical schools closed and overall medical standards increased. The number of trained physicians decreased while fees and overall costs increased. Employer-provided insurance expanded as large companies such as General Motors contracted with insurance companies to cover their employees.

In the decade of the 1920s, the demand for medical care continued to grow and hospitals became more generally accepted. In the first known Presidential referral to American health care as in "crisis," President Coolidge convened a committee to address increasing concerns for access to and cost of health care. The end of the 1920s brought what was likely the first health maintenance organization (HMO) in the form of a clinic for employees of the Los Angeles Department of Water and Power. The same period saw the establishment of the first group hospital plan (by Baylor University Hospital in Dallas, Texas). Community hospitals organized with each other to offer hospital coverage and to reduce competition for patients, leading the way to the formation of Blue Cross Plans.

The end of the 1920s saw the onset of the Great Depression. During the worst of this period, there was a significant shift of patients from privately owned hospitals to public institutions. In 1932, there were about 6500 registered hospitals in the country, slightly down from the number reported in the previous census. Of 776 general hospitals operated by the government, 77% operated at or near capacity. However, just 56% of nongovernmental general hospitals were operating at or close to capacity (U.S. Bureau of the Census, 1910). Nevertheless, between 1909 and 1932, the number of available hospital beds increased six times faster than the general population. As a result, in 1933, the Council on Medical Education and Hospitals of the AMA asserted that the country was "over-hospitalized"; that is, there were too many hospitals in the United States (American Medical Association, 1933).

During the 1930s, the Depression essentially spurred interest in social programs such as unemployment insurance and senior benefits. Also, during the 1930s, methods of paying for hospital services were proliferating, specifically Blue Cross insurance plans that were becoming popular and accounting for an increasing percentage of hospital income.

In 1932, Blue Cross attained nonprofit status and became free of taxes and insurance regulations. Blue Cross then began to expand to numerous other states where existing laws allowed its presence. About this time, the coverage of some employer insurance plans was expanded to include families, although in most instances, this added coverage was provided at the employees' expense.

Over the period of 1932 through 1934, healthcare expenditures continued to increase to the point where hospital costs made up nearly 40% of a typical family's medical expenses.

In 1935, President Franklin Roosevelt deferred to the AMA, the insurance industry, and organized business groups and removed national health insurance from his proposed Social Security legislation before presenting it to Congress. To a considerable extent, the health insurance issue passed to the individual states some of which (California, for example) established compulsory health insurance based on income level, and numerous other states which did not address the health insurance issue.

In about 1939, the California Physicians' Service established the first pre-payment plan intended to cover physicians' services. Following this, the AMA encouraged the expansion of such plans to other states, marking the establishment of Blue Shield health insurance, a nonprofit entity free from taxes, insurance regulations, and restrictions on personal choice of physician.

The early 1940s saw the beginning of commercial, for-profit insurance plans as commercial insurance companies entered the healthcare market. Labor unions increasingly fought to have health plans included in their contracts with employers. Congress made employer-provided health insurance tax deductible for employers; enrollment in group hospital plans increased from about 7 million in 1940 to about 26 million by 1942.

In 1944, President Roosevelt again called for national health reform. In 1945, President Truman became the first president to publicly support national health insurance through his support of an unsuccessful bill calling for compulsory health insurance to be funded by payroll deductions.

▶ A Highly Informal "System"

At this time when one made reference to the healthcare "system," it was in fact actually reference to the widespread elements of what was essentially a cottage industry. In fact, there were instances in which some providers were organizationally interrelated, such as hospital chains operated by religious orders and those belonging to government, but most providers were individual, freestanding entities.

The acute-care hospital had essentially become the center of the healthcare "system." But in the mid-1940s, government involvement in the business of hospitals would trigger some serious and often irreversible changes in the "system."

Brief Chapter Summary

During the first half of the 20th century, American hospitals transitioned from what was essentially a cottage industry to a loosely perceived "system" of providers representing a mix of freestanding, government-operated, and sponsored groupings (mainly religious institutions) of providers. Also, during this period, interest in health insurance emerged significantly and health insurance programs began. At this time, the acute-care hospital was generally perceived as the center of the country's healthcare system.

Questions for Review and Discussion

1. In your own words, define "cottage industry" and state why this term was sometimes applied to health care.
2. How do you believe the acute-care hospital became seen as the "center of the healthcare system?"
3. Why was healthcare legislation not included in the Social Security Act as President Roosevelt intended?
4. What was it that likely boosted the adoption of health insurance program by some employers?
5. Why did the AMA assert in 1933 that the country was "over-hospitalized," that there were too many hospitals in the United States?

References

American Medical Association. (1933, March 25). Hospital service in the United States: Twelfth annual presentation of hospital data by the council on medical education and hospitals of the American Medical Association. *Journal of the American Medical Association (JAMA)*, *100*(12), 887.

U.S. Bureau of the Census. (1913). *Benevolent institutions. 1910* (p. 69). Washington, DC: Government Printing Office.

CHAPTER 3

The American Hospital from 1945 to the Present

Charles R. McConnell

▶ Era of Extensive Change

During the 20th century, two world wars ushered in major social, political, and technological changes in the United States. Among these changes was the dramatic increase of interest in the financing of health care, along with the growth of insurance plans such as Blue Cross and Blue Shield in the nonprofit sector and many for-profit insurance companies. The federal government also began to assume a larger role with regard to health care, as evidenced by the **Hill-Burton** Act and the establishment of research institutions such as the National Institutes of

Health. By 1965, the implementation of Medicare and Medicaid fostered the widespread belief that health care was a right, not a privilege. (Medicare and Medicaid are addressed but superficially in this chapter; Chapter 4 examines these in detail.)

During the 20th century, hospitals began to take on additional roles. Not only do modern hospitals provide care for the sick and ailing and clinical education for the entire continuum of healthcare professionals, many also serve as institutions of health education for the entire neighborhoods, communities, and regions. The hospital of today provides education for both professionals and laypersons and conducts research in medical sciences from medical records, patients, and the community.

▶ Post-World War II

So much for being "over-hospitalized" as the American Medical Association had claimed a decade earlier. A surge in demand for hospitals and their services occurred immediately following World War II. Although all levels of government—federal, state, and local—had been providing some measure of support to hospitals throughout the first decades of the 20th century, government became increasingly involved as apparent hospital shortages and shortcomings became evident: there were too few hospitals. Studies concluded that there were not enough hospitals to serve the population, that hospitals were unevenly distributed such that some geographic areas were underserved or not served at all, and that many existing hospitals, too small or technologically outmoded, were inadequate to serve their target populations. The country was now "*under*-hospitalized."

▶ Hill-Burton Arrives Upon the Scene

The expressed intent of the Hill-Burton Act, known formally as the Hospital Survey and Construction Act of 1946, was to provide federal financial assistance for the planning, construction, and improvement of healthcare facilities through financing guaranteed under Title VI and later Title XVI of the Public Health Service Act. It was sponsored by Senator Harold Burton of Ohio and Senator Lister Hill of Alabama and passed during the 79th Congress. It came about in response to a special message to Congress in which President Harry S. Truman outlined a multi-part program for improving the health and health care of Americans. The Act called for the construction of hospitals and related healthcare facilities and was structured to provide federal grants and guaranteed loans to improve the physical plant of the nation's hospitals. Money was designated for the states to achieve a bed-to-population ratio of 4.5 beds per 1000 people. The states were to allocate the available funds to their various municipalities.

Federal money always comes with conditions and requirements. Facilities that received Hill-Burton funding were forbidden to discriminate based on race, color, national origin, or creed. Separate-but-equal facilities in the same area were allowed (but the Supreme Court struck down this particular form of segregation in 1963).

Also, facilities receiving Hill-Burton funding were required to provide a *reasonable volume* of free care each year for those residents of the affected area who required care but were unable to pay. Hospitals were initially required to provide such uncompensated care for 20 years after receiving funding. Also, federal money was provided only in instances in which both the state and municipality were willing and able to match the federal loan or grant; thus, the federal portion accounted for just one-third of the total construction or renovation cost.

The states and municipalities were also required to prove the economic viability of whatever facility was in question. This requirement excluded the poorest munici-palities from the program, so most of the funding went to middle-class areas. It also served to artificially support hospitals that were nonviable financially; this served to hinder normal development that might otherwise occur in response to market forces.

The reality of the results fell short of meeting the written requirements of the law. For the initial 20 years of Hill-Burton, there was no workable definition of what constituted a "reasonable volume" of free care and no way to ensure that hospitals were providing any free care at all. This remained so until the early 1970s when attorneys representing people who were unable to pay began suing hospitals for not abiding the law's requirements.

Hill-Burton Act was scheduled to expire in June 1973 but was extended for 1 year in a last-minute move. In 1975, the law was amended and became Title XVI of the Public Health Service Act. Added were some regulatory mechanisms defining what constituted the inability to pay, and replacement of the 20-year commitment to a requirement to provide free care in perpetuity.

However, it was not until 1979 that specific compliance levels were defined.

▶ A Cornerstone of Society

Alongside important entities such as schools, police departments, firefighting ser-vices, and other public services, hospitals are a vital part of society's infrastructure. It is important to understand some macro information such as numbers of hospitals available, how hospitals are classified, typical hospital cost per day and per stay, and the average length of stay (ALOS) that might be expected.

Of equal importance are trends in hospital systems: Are hospitals increasing or decreasing in number, and are they becoming more or less profitable?

▶ Classification

Hospitals may be classified in a number of different ways, such as by location (e.g., rural or community hospitals) or specialty (e.g., women's hospitals, orthopedic hos-pitals, cardiac hospitals, surgical hospitals, or, as in the past, tuberculosis hospitals). Hospitals can also be classified by size, such as community-access hospitals (small, rural hospitals with fewer than 25 beds) or, at the other extreme, tertiary-care or academic medical centers that offer every specialty and subspecialty that is practiced in medicine (e.g., pediatric cardiology).

Hospitals may also be commonly classified as governmental or nongovernmen-tal. Examples of governmental entities are the Veterans Administration (approxi-mately 170 hospitals and 1245 healthcare entities overall, by far and away the largest healthcare system in the country), the Indian Health Service, and military hospitals.

When analyzing or comparing hospitals, for example, a physician-owned orthopedic hospital and a government-owned military hospital, it is important to bear in mind the institutional differences between them.

In 2008, the total of all U.S.-registered hospitals was 5815 (American Hospital Association [AHA], 2008). These included all federal, nonfederal, community state, not-for-profit, investor-owned, non-metropolitan, and metropolitan hospitals (AHA, 2008). By 2017, this number had fallen to 5564, a decrease of 4.3% (AHA, 2017). Not a staggering decrease in terms of actual numbers of hospitals, but significant when one considers that during the same period the country's population continued to increase while much of the Baby Boomer generation was aging out.

▶ Trends in General Acute-Care Community Hospitals

Trend 1: Downsizing, Mergers, and Closures

Since the late 1980s and early 1990s, the hospital industry in the United States has undergone a host of consolidations, mergers, and other affiliations in part reflecting the fact that the system was indeed "over-bedded," with too many providers overall. Many hospitals operated at less than 50% occupancy and struggled to maintain enough revenue to sustain efficient operations. It was commonplace to see several hospitals in large metropolitan areas close, downsize, or merge with competitors, although this was not always bad for the community. For example, in a metropolitan area with seven hospitals, three might battle to be the dominant purveyor of acute-care services. To avoid underutilization of the other hospitals, a common ownership could be established under which each hospital could specialize in a different field. For example, one might focus on cardiac care, the second on women's and obstetrics issues, and the third on general care (provided that this business arrangement would be allowed under antitrust statutes).

In addition to the issue of surplus acute-care beds, another factor that resulted in mergers and downsizing was physicians beginning to shift their focus from inpatient care to outpatient care, frequently in facilities in which they had partial ownership. Procedures that could be performed without an overnight stay in the hospital began to move to the forefront of many practices. These included procedures performed in outpatient surgery, outpatient imaging, and even outpatient cancer treatment. This reduction in hospitals was also driven by improvements in medicine, tighter reimbursement policies, and improved management. It is fair to say that those who were the lesser sick benefited from the greater availability of outpatient services and less hospitalization. Together, these factors led to both fewer hospital admissions and shorter stays in U.S. hospitals. ALOS presently stands at slightly less than 5.5 days, down from approximately 7.1 days per stay in 1992.

There has been some speculation that the trend in hospital closures, admissions, and diminishing ALOS could be reversed in the not-too-distant future. As the population continues to age, the need for additional health care is likely to increase and thus more facilities may be required to meet a growing demand. The country may now be at or nearing the bottom of a trough, and we may see the number of hospitals and hospital beds beginning to increase over the coming years.

Trend 2: Tighter Profit Margins

Many mergers and other affiliations involving hospitals went forward with their well-intentioned sponsors pursuing what they believed would be tangible cost savings and new economies of scale. For the most part, however, the merging or downsizing of hospitals has not resulted in significantly reduced hospital expenses. Causes include the skyrocketing costs of technology (physicians want the latest and greatest diagnostic equipment and other hardware), the significant number of uninsured persons seeking care, and the relatively low reimbursement rates paid by Medicare and Medicaid. Presently, the majority of acute-care hospitals receive 50%–55% or more of their income from Medicare and Medicaid, with most of the balance coming from commercial insurance and private pay. Overall, the trend is toward much tighter profit margins—if a profit (or "surplus," in the language of the not-for-profit entity) is realized at all. The future of many general acute-care facilities may be in jeopardy, while at the same time society will likely need more hospitals because of the aging baby boomers.

The payer mix for any hospital is of critical concern because of the relatively low Medicare and Medicaid payment rates. In its annual survey, the AHA estimated that the prevailing payment structure has resulted in a nearly $35 billion shortfall for all community hospitals in the United States. In conjunction with the so-called "normal" inflation, the existing negative payment structure is increasing operating costs while decreasing total profit (surplus) margins. Stated another way, when operating revenues and expenses are compared over time, we begin to see total costs exceeding revenues.

Trend 3: Increased Establishment of Specialty Hospitals

Specialty hospitals, which are frequently proprietary (for-profit) and physician-owned institutions, are sometimes controversial. Instead of offering care to the entire general population as traditionally done by acute-care hospitals, specialty hospitals appear to serve a favorable selection of patients and avoid charity care and emergency services. Critics also contend that physician ownership creates incentives that may inappropriately affect referrals and clinical behaviors.

Advocates contend, however, that specialty hospitals can provide better and more efficient treatment for greater numbers of patients who need the same specialization of care.

For most health services, the Stark Law (or physician self-referral law) prohibits the referral of Medicare or Medicaid patients to facilities in which the referring physician (or physician's family members) has a financial interest; however, the Stark Law included an important exception, termed the "whole-hospital exception," under which physicians would be permitted to refer patients if they have an ownership interest in the entire hospital and are also authorized to perform services there. This exception was limited by a section of the Patient Protection and Affordable Care Act (PPACA) of 2010 which restricts a proprietary hospital from increasing its aggregate physician ownership or investment interests after

March 23, 2010, and further forbid expanding its capacity beyond the number of beds, operating rooms, and procedure rooms for which it is licensed as of March 23, 2010, unless the Secretary of the Department of Health and Human Services (DHHS) were to grant an exception.

To address concerns about the negative effects of physician-owned hospitals on community hospitals, Congress established a moratorium from December 8, 2003, through June 7, 2005, to prohibit specialty hospitals from submitting claims for services as a result of physician-owner referrals. During this moratorium, the DHSS was charged with examining the overall impact of specialty hospitals. The result of the DHHS study was the recommendation that led to the limitation of the whole-hospital exception as described above. The PPACA of March 23, 2010, along with modifications specified by the Health Care and Education Reconciliation Act of March 30, 2010, banned physician ownership of hospitals beginning in 2011. Unless these laws are repealed or amended, they should dramatically slow the establishment of new specialty hospitals.

It is worth noting that physician-owned hospitals are exempt from Stark Law if they do not accept Medicare reimbursement. In fact, many such specialty hospitals tend to treat well-insured, lower-acuity patients while avoiding Medicare, Medicaid, and patients who are uninsured.

Trend 4: Increasing Shortage of Nursing Personnel

Because of the increasing number of aging baby boomers, hospitals and the entire healthcare industry in general will need an ever-increasing supply of nurses. Yet just the opposite could very well occur. The majority of nurses today are in their 40s, and presently for every eight who leave the field, only five enter. This is further exacerbated by the increasing number of opportunities for nurses outside of hospitals, for example, pharmaceutical companies, medical group practices, freestanding clinics, urgent care centers, and other health-related entities. The industry is likely to see an ever-increasing demand for nurses that severely outpaces the supply. As a result of supply-and-demand and staffing issues, hospitals can expect increasing interest in nursing unions and inevitable increases in nursing salaries.

▶ A New Era of Medicine

Beginning in the 1980s, restriction of growth and reorganization of the methods used to finance and deliver health care began to bring about a new era of medicine in the United States. Cost-containment policies and initiatives from Medicare and health insurance plans in general have resulted in diminishing reimbursements. Not only was there a decrease in the expansion of hospitals, there was also an increase in hospital failures and bed closings. The healthcare system began to emphasize outpatient rather than inpatient services, and to focus on expansion of ancillary medical facilities and freestanding outpatient centers.

Today, hospitals are just one among several components in the continuing evolution of organized delivery systems and the continuum of care. Some see the role of the hospital in the future continuing to change, with hospitals expected to serve only patients with complex problems. Many patients will probably be cared for at home or in other nonhospital settings. Many experts predict that hospitals will continue to downsize while still attempting to meet growing social needs and provide refuge for the poor and ailing.

▶ The Healthcare Landscape Forever Altered

The advent of Medicare and Medicaid brought about significant changes in the payment for hospital care and had a significant role in the nearly complete alteration of the healthcare "system." Beginning in the middle-to-late 1960s, a number of forces and circumstances came together to push healthcare costs upward, cost escalation that largely continues to this day as healthcare costs increase yearly at a rate exceeding the so-called "normal" inflation.

Although the passage of Medicare and Medicaid added to healthcare costs overall as increasing numbers of citizens became covered, these fairly comprehensive programs do not bear all of the blame for healthcare cost escalation. Consider just the more significant forces fueling healthcare cost inflation:

- *Increased cost of hospitalization.* Each year the cost of labor increases and the prices paid for materials and supplies go up as well; from 1966 to about 1976, the average hospital cost per patient-day doubled. Some elements of cost may increase no more than the country's rate of inflation, but certain others, such as the cost of pharmaceuticals, continue to increase at significantly more rapid rates.

- *Increased costs of prescription drugs.* This healthcare cost element has for quite some time been receiving a great deal of attention. Added costs here appear to be owing to a number of circumstances, foremost among them the steady and at times seemingly unjustified cost increases for many drugs, and the continually expanding use of prescription drugs overall. Some of the impact of increased drug prices is of course felt in the total cost of hospitalization, but most of the effect strikes elsewhere, specifically in the rates charged by insurance plans that cover prescription drugs in the co-pays that insurance plans charge their subscribers, and especially in the wallets and pocketbooks of those who do not have prescription drug coverage.

- *Increased use of related services.* Despite pressures to regulate their utilization, the aggregate use of laboratory tests and radiologic diagnostic procedures and other ancillary services continues to increase. Their costs continue to increase as well, some in keeping with inflationary pressures but many owing to technological improvements.

- *Advancing medical technology.* As increased sophistication in equipment and skilled labor are brought to bear on health problems and more resources are applied to specific emerging medical needs, associated costs cannot help but increase. Advances in medical technology lead to better health care, but they usually add cost as well—sometimes significant cost. Considering that the majority of diagnostic procedures ordered and conducted result in negative findings, for each person who benefits because of a positive finding, the healthcare system would have spent many times the cost of a single procedure.

- *Duplication of facilities and services.* Active overexpansion of hospital facilities no longer appears to be the significant problem it once was, but there still remains in some parts of the country unused and underused hospital capacity that contributes to cost. Chronically unoccupied beds still absorb fixed costs that contribute to the total healthcare bill. Also, in some parts of the country, competition has led to hospitals and health systems vying with each other to provide the same services for the same population.

- *Aging population.* We have known for some time that the average age of the population is increasing and that the numbers of elderly are at an all-time high. The privately insured population of 45- to 64-year-olds continues to grow. Average insurance claims for this age group tend to run higher than for persons younger than 45, and average claims run higher still for persons 65 and older. Generally, the older the average age of the population, the greater the healthcare bill will be.
- *Misuse and abuse.* Whenever a bureaucratic layer is inserted between providers and consumers, whether it be Medicare, Medicaid, Blue Cross/Blue Shield, commercial insurers, or otherwise, there are two factors that emerge: cost is added to the system without a corresponding increase in benefits, and the opportunity for fraud, abuse, and error is created. The more complex the arrangements, the more chance there is of waste in the system.

In addition to the foregoing, other factors make themselves felt in increased total healthcare system cost. Among these are malpractice awards and other legal settlements, increases in regulatory costs, and lifestyle issues, all of which conspire to add cost to the healthcare system. To date, the few well-intended cost-containment efforts that have been undertaken have done little to stem the seemingly runaway increase in the cost of health care.

Brief Chapter Summary

Although hospitals have declined in number, they presently do an improved job of holding down ALOS. Medicare and Medicaid expenses are exceeding revenues in a great many hospitals. Because of continuing changes in the country's relatively volatile economy and the continually shifting needs of business and industry, at any given time, there are significant numbers of Americans unemployed. Although recent years have seen some improvement in employment overall, many who remain jobless are without health insurance. The healthcare industry and hospitals in particular have steadily lost the support of employer-provided health insurance, which made up for much of the shortfall created by inadequate Medicare and Medicaid reimbursement.

The PPACA (Obamacare) was seen as a means of closing the insurance gap by mandating that most citizens purchase health insurance. However, with the haggling in the halls of government about the future of national health insurance, we cannot say at this time how this critical issue will be addressed.

Questions for Review and Discussion

1. What are the several ways in which a hospital can be classified?
2. Has the total number of U.S. hospitals increased or decreased in the most recent 30 years? Why?
3. Why has the ALOS decreased in hospitals?

4. Why was there an increase in the number of specialty hospitals, and what has occurred to limit this increase?
5. In addition to caring for the sick and ailing, what are some of the other roles attributed to the modern hospital?
6. What are some of the indications that a geographic area may by "over-bedded" in terms of hospital capacity?
7. What were the conditions imposed on hospitals that accepted federal funds provided under Hill-Burton?
8. What are the major forces that have resulted in diminished reimbursement for hospitals?
9. What appears to be the most significant personnel issue in providing hospital care to the expanding population?
10. What is the essence of the legislation known as the "Stark Law?"

References

American Hospital Association (AHA). (2008). Annual Survey Data, Fiscal Year 2008.
American Hospital Association (AHA). (2017). Fast Facts on US Hospitals, 2017.

CHAPTER 4

Medicare and Medicaid: Major Game-Changers

Danielle N. Atkins, Kendall Cortelyou-Ward, Reid M. Oetjen, and Timothy Rotarius

CHAPTER OBJECTIVES

- Describe historical perspective of the enactment and implementation of Medicare and Medicaid.
- Describe how Medicare and Medicaid financing has changed over time and how this affects delivery of and payment for care.
- Describe policies aimed at controlling costs and their impacts on delivery of and payment for care.
- Provide context for the need of governmental health programs.
- Explain the impact of enacting Medicare and Medicaid on the healthcare delivery system.
- Discuss the challenges of enacting governmental healthcare policies.

KEY TERMS

Cost-containment	Medicaid
Hospital closures	Medicare

▶ Introduction—Medicare and Medicaid

Medicare and **Medicaid** are cornerstones of the social safety net for elderly and impoverished Americans. Over 50 years ago, Congress passed the Social Security Act of 1965, which established Medicare and Medicaid and made hospitals central to the U.S. healthcare system (Martensen, 2011). Both programs provide publicly subsidized health insurance to vulnerable populations, which decreases financial risk and can provide health benefits; however, the programs differ in many respects. Perhaps, most notably, Medicare is an entitlement program for elderly and chronically ill Americans to safeguard them against bankruptcy due to illness and this program is financed and administered by the Federal Government. Unlike cash welfare and Medicaid, which require a person to meet certain income criteria, in Medicare, a person receives an entitlement program regardless of need. For example, persons with 65 years of age receive Medicare regardless of their income.

By contrast, Medicaid is a means-tested (or need-based) program that provides health insurance to low-income adults and children, and the financing and administration of Medicaid is shared between the Federal and State Governments. Since Medicaid is jointly administered by the States and Federal Government, the states have some leeway, within Federal guidelines, in setting the income eligibility limits for Medicaid. For example, in 2017, income thresholds to qualify for Medicaid for parents in a family of three vary from 18% of the Federal Poverty Line (FPL) in Alabama, which equates to an annual income of $3,675 for a family of three, to 221% in the District of Columbia, or $45,128 annually for a family of three (Centers for Medicare and Medicaid, 2018).

This chapter will cover the Medicare and Medicaid social insurance programs and their role within the American hospital system. It will provide a brief background of each program, and discuss the impacts of Medicare and Medicaid on patient care in the hospital setting, hospital financing, patient experiences, and patient outcomes. Efforts to contain costs and respective outcomes will also be explored. Finally, the early effects of the Affordable Care Act's (ACA) changes to Medicare and Medicaid in the hospital context will be discussed.

Medicare

During the Great Depression (1929–1939), unemployment peaked around 25%, and many people struggled to pay for medical care (Finkelstein & McKnight, 2008). Years later, in 1945, President Truman attempted to establish national health insurance as a response to the country's inability to pay for health care, but the proposal failed. In 1960, the Kerr Mills law was passed, providing states Federal money to provide health care for the elderly living in poverty; however, only 32 states participated, and many elderly adults remained without adequate coverage. In response, Medicare was passed in 1965 as an entitlement program for elderly Americans. At the time, enacting Medicare was the single largest change in health insurance coverage in U.S. history (Finkelstein & McKnight, 2008).

Prior to Medicare, older adults were often considered the most burdensome and least desirable type of patient as they were more likely to have multiple illnesses and were often unable to pay for their care. After Medicare was enacted, older adults became an attractive source of revenue for hospitals, representing a monumental shift in hospital financing (Martensen, 2011).

In the early years of the program, Medicare included Part A (Hospital Insurance) and Part B (Medical Insurance). Medicare Part A currently covers up to 90 days of inpatient expenses after a deductible and 25% coinsurance for days 61–90, paid for by a payroll tax. Medicare Part B covers physician costs after initial deductible and uncapped co-insurance, paid for by general revenues and individual premiums (Finkelstein & McKnight, 2008).

Medicare shapes how health care is delivered in the United States because it outlines how medical services will be reimbursed for the highest acuity (and most costly) patient populations (elderly and disabled). As the largest payer of healthcare services in the country, the Center for Medicare and Medicaid Services also has control over other hospital operations (Martensen, 2011).

Medicaid

Created in tandem with the Medicare program in 1965, Medicaid was enacted to extend healthcare services for low-income individuals. Medicaid covers children, adults, and pregnant women living below the poverty level. Additionally, the coverage includes elders and persons with disabilities receiving assistance through the Supplemental Security Income (SSI) program.

Unlike Medicare, which is administered solely at the Federal level, the Federal and State Governments jointly administer and share the costs of Medicaid, with the Federal Government subsidizing 50% of costs (Fichtner, 2014). The fixed percentage of costs paid by the Federal Government, or the Federal Medical Assistance Percentage (FMAP), reserves larger payments for impoverished states. This cost-sharing and matching payment not only insulates states from the rising costs of health care (Fichtner, 2014), but also means that Medicaid policy differs on a state-by-state basis within some broader, Federal requirements. Under these broad Federal guidelines, states are able to determine eligibility and benefits for individuals (Henry J. Kaiser Family Foundation, 2018).

In addition to covering acute services for low-income children and families, Medicaid also covers a significant portion of long-term care costs (Henry J. Kaiser Family Foundation, 2018), including assistance in activities of daily living, nursing home care, and home- and community-based services. Like Medicare, Medicaid plays an important role in hospitals by providing a substantial proportion of financing for the safety net. By law and through the Medicaid program, the Federal Government matches state funding for the Disproportionate Share Hospitals (DSH) program. The DSH program provides additional, subsidized payments to hospitals that supply a high proportion of uncompensated care to Medicaid enrollees and/or the uninsured.

Many have called for Medicaid reform in order to improve incentives for quality care at a lower cost, as the current design is incentivized to keep costs high because the Federal Government will match the funds (Fichtner, 2014). The constant increase in health costs is reflected in a 5.8% increase in Medicaid expenditures per year. The increase in Medicaid spending mirrors the increase in the projected share of aging and disabled program enrollees as previously mentioned (Centers for Medicare and Medicaid, 2009).

▶ By the Numbers

The Current State of Medicare

Enrollment

Enrollment in Medicare has increased 187% between 1966 and 2015 and is expected to continue to rise as Baby Boomers age into Medicare. The Baby Boomer generation represents those Americans born between 1946 and 1964 and represents nearly 20% of the

American public, and has had a significant impact on Medicare. It is anticipated that the number of Medicare enrollees will grow to 92.4 million in 2050 (see **FIGURE 4.1**).

Expenditures

Since the country's first Baby Boomer aged into Medicare on January 1, 2011, Medicare spending, like enrollment, has also greatly increased over time (Hur, 2011). **FIGURE 4.2** shows Medicare spending from 1960 to 2016 demonstrating the alarming rate, particularly over the past decade, with which spending has

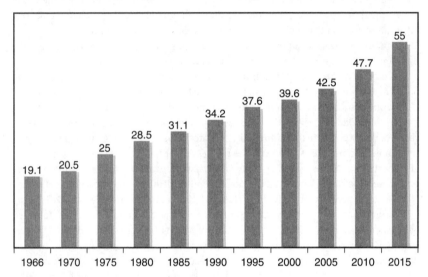

FIGURE 4.1 Medicare Enrollment in Millions 1995–2015

Data from the Kaiser Family Foundation.

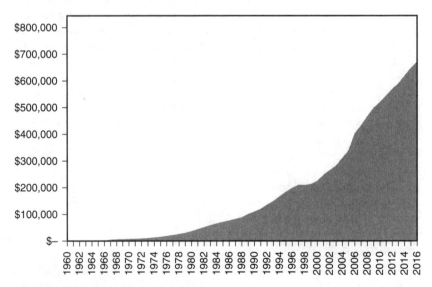

FIGURE 4.2 Medicare Spending 1960–2016

Data from the Centers for Medicare & Medicaid Services.

increased. Spending on Medicare accounted for 15% of total Federal spending in 2016. This amount is projected to increase to 17.5% by 2027 (Henry J. Kaiser Family Foundation, 2017).

Medicare Part A (hospital insurance) covers up to 90 days of inpatient expenses after a deductible and 25% coinsurance for days 61–90, paid for by a payroll tax. **FIGURE 4.3** shows Medicare Part A spending by benefit type in 2015. Inpatient hospital stays accounted for the majority of Part A spending in 2015, with skilled nursing facilities accounting for the second largest portion of Medicare Part A spending, while hospice and home health made up the smallest amounts of spending in Medicare Part A.

Medicare Part B covers physician costs after initial deductible and uncapped co-insurance, paid for by general revenues and individual premiums (Finkelstein & McKnight, 2008). **FIGURE 4.4** depicts Medicare Part B spending by type of service in 2015. Spending on managed care and physician services make up more than half of Part B spending, while outpatient hospital comes in third. The remainder is divided into other services such as laboratory and home health services.

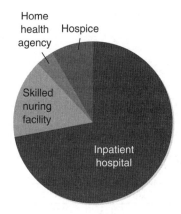

FIGURE 4.3 Medicare Part A Spending by Type of Service, 2015

Data from 2015 CMS Statistics, Table III.6, Washington, DC: U.S. Department of Health and Human Services.

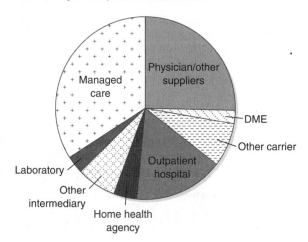

FIGURE 4.4 Medicare Part B Spending by Type of Service, 2015

Data from 2015 CMS Statistics, Table III.6, Washington, DC: U.S. Department of Health and Human Services.

The Current State of Medicaid

Enrollment

Unlike Medicare, Medicaid enrollment is made up of several disparate patient populations including adults, children, blind/disabled, and aged/elderly. **FIGURE 4.5** shows the growth of these populations since the 1975, and indicates not only an overall growth in Medicaid enrollment, but that the majority of that growth occurred in adults and children.

Expenditures

Growth in Medicaid spending (**FIGURE 4.6**) parallels the growth in enrollment. However, spending growth has increased at a higher rate than enrollments over time.

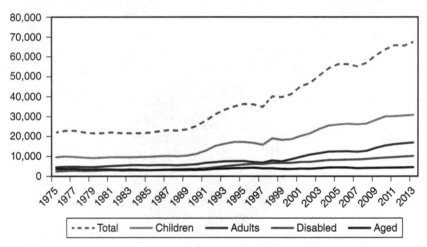

FIGURE 4.5 Medicaid Enrollment by Eligibility Group 1975–2013 (thousands)

Data from MACStats: Medicaid and CHIP Data Book, 2016, Exhibit 5, Washington, DC: MACPAC.

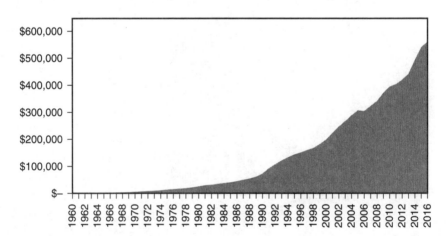

FIGURE 4.6 Medicaid Spending 1960–2016 (in millions)

Data from the Centers for Medicare & Medicaid Services.

In 2016, Medicaid spending accounted for 17% of National Health Expenditures (NHE), or $565.6 billion (Centers for Medicare and Medicaid, 2009).

As previously discussed, Medicaid is jointly administered and financed by the State and Federal Governments. The percentage share of Medicaid spending varies by state with the average split for the United States is 64% Federal dollars and 37% state dollars (see **FIGURE 4.7**). In 2016, Virginia paid the highest percentage of its Medicaid spending (49.8%) while New Mexico paid the least (20.6%).

Medicaid finances a variety of services (see **FIGURE 4.8**). The majority of Medicaid payments go to capitation payments that are non-Medicare, while the second

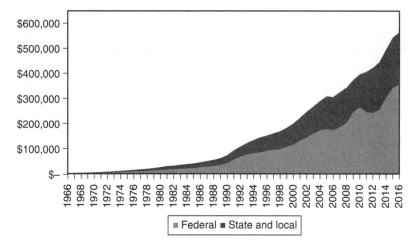

FIGURE 4.7 Medicaid Spending by Source

Data from the Centers for Medicare & Medicaid Services.

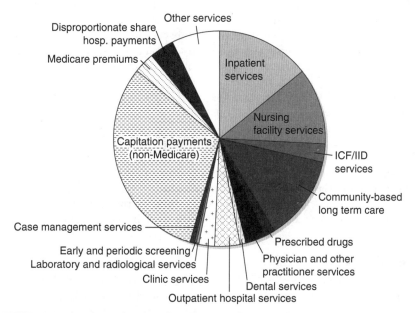

FIGURE 4.8 Medicaid Spending (in millions) by Type of Service, 2013

Data from 2015 CMS Statistics, Table III.8, Washington, DC: U.S. Department of Health and Human Services.

most common spending category for Medicaid in 2013 was for inpatient services. Community-based long-term care and nursing facilities are also commonly funded by Medicaid. The remainder of Medicaid spending in 2013 was split among a variety of sources such as DSH payments and outpatient hospital services.

▶ Initial Impacts

Medicare

While the original intent of the Medicare legislation was to improve health care for the elderly, the enactment of Medicare improved healthcare services across the board by requiring facilities to meet specific standards to be eligible to receive Medicare payments, and providing resources to health systems to improve their services by increasing the staff, and providing more care options (Stewart, 1967). For example, Medicare required standard incentivized nonaccredited hospital boards to improve services by updating the physical environment, influenced changes to the standards of the Joint Commission, contributed to changes for accreditation bodies for medical specialties, gave the pharmacist a more central role in the hospital setting, and increased nurses' activity in providing health care in hospitals.

Together, Medicare and the Civil Rights Act of 1964 significantly changed access to hospital care. These two pieces of legislation banned segregation in hospitals receiving Federal dollars. In addition to being able to receive care in a hospital that was previously only available for white patients, Medicare required that black physicians would have access to hospital privileges without discrimination (Stewart, 1967).

Medicare also changed the clinical workforce by covering training costs that were once the obligation of hospitals, allowing new specialties to emerge for which Medicare highly reimburses (Martensen, 2011). Rural hospitals were more easily able to recruit physicians after the adoption of Medicare (Stewart, 1967).

Much research has studied the initial impact of the Medicare program on a variety of outcomes for beneficiaries. One study found that, in the first decade of implementation, the program insured the elderly against out-of-pocket medical expenditure risk. Prior to Medicare, the elderly reported spending over 10% of income on medical care. Medicare was associated with a 40% reduction in out-of-pocket payments compared with pre-Medicare levels for the top quartile of spenders.

Not only did Medicare decrease the financial burden of health care for beneficiaries, it also affected health outcomes. Medicare coverage for individuals age 65 and over led to a reduction of health disparities related to differences in race and education (Card, Dobkin, & Maestas, 2008) and it is estimated that the insurance benefit alone (not accounting for savings from improved health) was enough to cover 45%–75% of the costs of Medicare (Finkelstein & McKnight, 2008).

Medicaid

Much research has been completed evaluating the effects of Medicaid on access to care, patient outcomes, and experience of care. Typically, individuals who are covered by Medicaid are poorer, and often sicker, when compared to adults with a lower socio-economic status on private health insurance (Henry J. Kaiser Family Foundation, 2017). However, the research continues to demonstrate that persons covered by Medicaid manage better than those who are uninsured. By providing coverage to more than 65 million Americans, Medicaid improved access to care, increased healthcare utilization, improved self-reported health outcomes, and reduced catastrophic medical expenses (DesHarnais, Kobrinski, & Chesney, 1987).

Medicaid also plays a large role in financing care for pregnant women, infants, and children. In 2016, Medicaid paid for 27% of births in New Hampshire and up to 72% of births in New Mexico, with 24 states covering at least half of births through Medicaid (DesHarnais et al., 1987). Research has shown that Medicaid was associated with large reductions in infant, child, and teen mortality. Birth outcomes for women on Medicaid are comparable to rates in private insurance when risk factors are known and controlled for (DesHarnais et al., 1987).

Additionally, research has found that Medicaid contributes to better educational outcomes as a result of access to health care, fewer inpatient stays, and less emergency department admissions in the long-run (Cohodes, Kleiner, Lovenheim, & Grossman, 2014; Wherry, Miller, Kaestner, & Meyer, 2015). Among adults, research on the effects of the Medicaid expansions under the ACA has found improved access to health care and lower mortality (Sommers, Baicker, & Epstein, 2012). Furthermore, this research consistently states that Medicaid reduces the economic barriers to health care for a large portion of the low-income population. Destruction of such barriers for Medicaid beneficiaries increases the prevalence and use of preventive and primary services; demonstrating that Medicaid can, and will continue to, increase access, improve utilization, and promote quality.

▶ Major Concerns About Cost Control

Generally, payment rates for Medicare and Medicaid are decided through legislation and not negotiation, like private insurers. Although Medicaid payments are often below cost, there are ways to increase hospital revenue (to the point of making more than cost) with supplemental payments and DSH payments (Kaiser, 2016; Smith et al., 2016). While private payer payments are above 100% of costs, topping out at around 150% of costs, Medicare payment-to-cost ratios dipped below 100% beginning around 2000. Medicaid payment-to-cost ratios were generally lower than Medicare's during this time period, except from about 2009 onward (American Hospital Association, 2015a). Payment shortfalls relative to costs have historically been highest for Medicare, ranging from about +$5 billion in 1997 to −$40 billion in 2012, whereas payment shortfalls for Medicaid ranged from about −$1 billion in 1997 to about −$15 billion in 2012 (American Hospital Association, 2015b).

Participation in Medicare and Medicaid by hospitals is voluntary, but to be eligible for tax-exempt treatment, non-profit hospitals must accept Medicare and Medicaid patients. Most private hospitals participate as well because Medicare and Medicaid patients account for over half of patient care provided in hospitals (White & Yee, 2013). Although Medicare and Medicaid pay less than the full costs of the hospital stay, resulting in underpayment, **cost-containment** has and continues to remain a major concern for the administration of Medicare and Medicaid since these programs, along with Social Security, are the top three domestic spending categories for the Federal Government, and Medicaid is the top spending category for states (Fichtner, 2014).

In addition to providing more resources for hospital-based care for the elderly, Medicare has evolved over time as the government attempts to balance quality with cost-containment measures. In the early years, Medicare essentially paid hospital bills. Over time, Medicare's involvement in shaping the healthcare system has expanded into improving quality of care and containing costs. Medicaid also plays a central role in hospital financing as well, particularly through emergency Medicaid spending and DSH.

In response to increased Medicare hospital spending, the Social Security Amendments of 1983 started the prospective payment system (PPS) for hospital inpatient care to replace cost-based payments with fixed, predetermined reimbursements, and bundled payments. Under the PPS, Medicare pays hospitals per beneficiary discharge, and the base rate for each discharge corresponds to one of about 750 Diagnosis-Related Groups (DRGs). The DRG determines the base rate for the payment, which is determined by the diagnoses and adjusted for severity. Generally, more treatment-intensive diagnoses or those that require more time in the hospital have higher payments.

In addition to patient care, Medicare reimbursements to hospitals also cover some of the hospital's operating expenses, and DSHs and teaching hospitals can receive additional compensation from Medicare for added costs associated with the care they provide. Conversely, hospitals that have higher Medicare readmission rates for certain conditions can receive reduced reimbursements. This means hospitals must provide care within that specified amount or lose compensation. These changes to the financing structure for hospitals were not limited to Medicare. Private insurance companies began to adopt similar payment structures. Thus, the PPS adopted by Medicare in the early 1980s changed the landscape of hospital financing throughout the healthcare system (Rudowitz & Garfield, 2015).

Within the first year of PPS, hospitals experienced surpluses due to higher-than-expected reimbursements. There were also large cost reductions due to decreases in hospital length-of-stay. Ultimately, the initial windfall from PPS declined as costs of providing care to Medicare beneficiaries increased at a faster rate than payments; however, hospitals still continued to profit under PPS, but rates of closures and mergers were on the rise after the introduction of PPS (Holmes, Pink, & Friedman, 2013; Kaufman, Thomas, Pink, et al., n.d.).

In fact, according to a report by the U.S. General Accounting Office, **hospital closures** doubled in the 4 years after the PPS, compared with the prior 4 years, and about one-half of closures post-PPS were rural hospitals, and 85% were small hospitals with less than 100 beds. To address the decreased hospital access in rural areas, the Centers for Medicare and Medicaid Services (CMS) created Critical Access Hospitals (CAHs) through the Medicare Rural Hospital Flexibility Program of 1997 (Flex Program). CAHs are rural hospitals with no greater than 25 beds and are reimbursed on a "reasonable cost basis" instead of fixed, predetermined rates (Centers for Medicare and Medicaid, 2017). This slowed rural hospital closures until the Great Recession in 2008. Between 2005 and 2009, there were 42 rural hospital closures, which increased to 72 between 2010 and 2016 (Wishner, Solleveld, Rudowitz, Paradise, & Antonisse, 2018).

Another cost-containment policy was the Medicare Catastrophic Coverage Acts of 1988, which defined a limit of out-of-pocket expenses for enrollees; however, these increases in coverage were required to be financed by Medicare beneficiaries, which led to a lack of support by voting elderly Americans, and the Medicare Catastrophic Coverage Acts of 1989 repealed the prescription benefit and the out-of-pocket maximum.

In 1995, Medicare officials projected that the program would not be able to pay all hospital costs by 2001, and in 1997, Congress passed the Balanced Budget Act to contain Medicare costs by creating a new formula to control increases in physician payments and established Medicare+Choice (later named Medicare Advantage in 2003), which are plans provided by private companies approved by Medicare that provide Parts A and B coverage. Increasing Medicare enrollment plays a critical role in the solvency concerns that the program continues to face, particularly as Baby Boomers continue to age into Medicare.

Many researchers have studied the effects of these cost-control strategies on outcomes. Research on the effects of the PPS found that it was indeed associated with decreased costs and did not compromise quality of care (DesHarnais et al., 1987). However, Sloan, Morrisey, and Valvona (1988) argue that these cost reductions were driven by reductions in inpatient stays. The authors suggest that this was a byproduct of the financial incentive to reduce admissions in the Utilization and Quality Control Peer Review Organizations (PROs) program, which was tasked with oversight to ensure that appropriate care continued to be provided under the PPS.

Some found no relationship between the Balanced Budget Act of 1997s Medicare reimbursement cuts and hospitals and mortality (Seshamani, Schwartz, & Volpp, 2006) or hospital-acquired infections (Zhang, n.d.). A few others found that in the long term, the cuts were associated with worse patient outcomes, such as higher adjusted 30-day postoperative mortality in hospitals most affected by the cut and acute myocardial infarction mortality in the long-run (Seshamani et al., 2006; Wu & Shen, n.d.). Another study examined the relationship between reimbursement cuts from 1995 to 2009 and found that cuts were associated with less use of inpatient care by Medicare beneficiaries. They note that the decrease in inpatient stays is a result of hospitals scaling down their number of beds (White & Yee, 2013).

Medicaid

As previously noted, since Medicaid's inception, costs increased rapidly. For example, between 1973 and 1989, payments to providers grew at more than 12% a year. This makes Medicaid an important factor in state budgets.

In 1965, when Medicaid was established, participating states were required to provide coverage for those on cash assistance and supplemental coverage to low-income Medicare beneficiaries, and states could cover additional populations if they elected to do so. In 1967, due to concerns about rising costs, Congress created legislation that limited eligibility for Medicaid to low-income, medically needy individuals in order to curb Federal costs for the program. Prior to 1972, states were prohibited from decreasing Medicaid expenditures year-to-year (known as "mainte-nance of effort"); however, this requirement was lifted in 1972. In 1981, The Omni-bus Budget Reconciliation Act (OBRA 81) lowered matching payments to states from the Federal Government and rescinded a mandate that states pay Medicare rates to hospitals, but also permitted states to reimburse hospitals providing care to a higher proportion of Medicaid and low-income individuals at higher rates, which ultimately became the DSH program.

In 1982, the Tax Equity and Fiscal Responsibility Act (TEFRA) allowed states to require minor cost-sharing for some beneficiaries and services. In 1986, OBRA 86 mandated that states provide emergency treatment for illegal immigrants otherwise eligible for Medicaid. The Medicaid Voluntary Contribution and Provider-Specific Tax Amendments of 1991 created a cap on Medicaid DSH payments after a 27% year-to-year increase in spending on the program. Welfare reform in 1996 replaced Aid to Families with Dependent Children (AFDC) with Temporary Assistance for Needy Families (TANF), which also decoupled Medicaid eligibility from cash wel-fare. The State Children's Health Insurance Program (SCHIP) extended coverage to uninsured children under 200% of the FPL, which was an annual income of $40,320 in 2017 for a family of three.

Cost-containment strategies in Medicaid commonly target drug expendi-tures; however, research has shown that few of the prescription medication cost-containment mechanisms can effectively reduce unnecessary prescriptions while preserving necessary prescription care (Cunningham, 2005; Moore & Newman, 1993; Soumerai, 2003; Soumerai, McLaughlin, Ross-Degnan, Casteris, & Bollini, 1994). One way states try to contain prescription medication costs is through drug formularies (Henry J. Kaiser Family Foundation, 2018). Prior authorization and mandatory generic substitutes have been shown to increase barriers to Medicaid enrollees obtaining prescription medications. In fact, some research suggests that the cost-savings from prescription drug cost-containment policies might be out-stripped by spending on unintended consequences associated with restricted access to pharmaceuticals.

▶ The Role of the Affordable Care Act

Although one of the main aims of the ACA was to increase health insurance cov-erage for the non-Medicare population, the Medicare program experienced signifi-cant changes under the ACA. First, like private sector insurance, the ACA requires zero-cost-sharing for preventive services for Medicare beneficiaries. The ACA also helps address the "doughnut hole" in the Part D program by covering more of the costs to seniors in the coverage gap. The ACA also provides reimbursement for hos-pitals to treat major chronic conditions. Although previous reimbursement changes to Medicare, like the PPS, have helped contain costs, they do not reward providers for better patient outcomes, and providers were not penalized for ineffective care or overconsumption of services (Davis, Guterman, & Bandeali, 2015). The ACA sought to change these incentives.

The Medicare Hospital Insurance Trust fund plays an important role in financ-ing Medicare Part A. The Hospital Insurance Trust Fund is financed by a 1.45% pay-roll tax, and is used to finance hospital services used by Medicare enrollees. Payments from the Hospital Trust Fund have generally been greater than the tax revenues used to finance it, and as Baby Boomers continue to age into retirement, this gap will widen. Before the ACA, the Trust Fund was predicted to be insolvent in 2017. After the ACA, this was extended to 2029 (Centers for Medicare and Medicaid, 2009).

The ACA created changes in the hospital payer mix, particularly in states that expanded Medicaid. Studies of the impact of the Medicaid expansion have found that it is associated with reductions in self-pay and increases in Medicaid payments, while states that did not expand Medicaid are not experiencing these changes in payer mix (Bachrach, Boozang, & Lipson, 2016; Nikpay, Buchmueller, & Levy, 2016; Rudowitz & Garfield, 2015). States that adopted the Medicaid expansion are also seeing reductions in uncompensated care, while states that did not participate in the expansion are not (Henry J. Kaiser Family Foundation, 2018). With the passage of the ACA, hospitals expected an increase in the number of insured patients; however, when state-level Medicaid expansions were made optional, this left many hospitals, particularly those in rural areas, in difficult financial situations. In Medicaid expansion states, hospital closures have been reduced in rural areas.

As state budgets have changed over time, hospitals have shifted to relying more heavily on supplemental Medicaid payments, like disproportionate share payments, than base payment rates. The American Health Association (AHA) estimated that in 2013, Medicaid payments covered 90% of patient costs and Medicare paid 88%; however, after adjusting for DSH supplemental payments, the Medicaid and CHIP Payment and Access Commission (MACPAC) reported hospitals made an average of 107% with a range of 81%–133% of patient costs (2016, May).

In addition to expanding Medicaid in participating states, the ACA also decreases DSH payments, which have important implications for hospital financing, particularly hospitals that serve a higher proportion of low-income patients. DSH payments were $11.7 billion in 2014. The ACA reduces these payments by $43 billion between 2018 and 2025. Hospitals that have heavily relied on these supplemental payments are particularly impacted by these changes (Henry J. Kaiser Family Foundation, 2016).

The ACA also created the Center for Medicare & Medicaid Innovation (CMMI), which is charged with creating, evaluating, and diffusing innovations to lower costs, provide better health outcomes, and improve patient experiences through the Medicare and Medicaid programs. Initial pilot programs include (1) a blended payment system (part fee for service, part managed care) for primary care with bonuses for better outcomes; (2) bundled payments that offer all-inclusive payments to hospitals, physicians, and aftercare services (care and support post-hospitalization) for a particular illness over a specified length of time for certain diagnoses and procedures treated in the hospital setting; (3) modification to the structure of Accountable Care Organizations (ACOs). An ACO is a group of providers receiving a set of payment to provide the majority of care to patients in the ACO. In this financing model, providers receive a portion of the savings they create conditional on providing quality patient experience and care.

In addition to payment reform, the ACA created incentives to increase quality and reduce cost. For example, hospitals are penalized for readmissions above the national average based on the National Quality Forum's benchmarks and hospital-acquired infections (Centers for Medicare and Medicaid, 2014; Davis et al., 2015). Initially, evaluations of the hospital readmission program suggest a reduction in readmissions from about 19% to 17.5% between 2010 and 2013. The Value-Based Purchasing program is a CMS initiative that awards hospitals with additional reimbursements if the hospital produces superior outcomes and patient experiences for Medicare beneficiaries.

The ACA had to meet a requirement that any costs incurred by the legislation would be covered by reductions in Federal expenditures elsewhere or an increase in revenues. One source of decreased outlays is a $43 billion reduction in payments to DSHs. The ACA also increased tax rates on higher income Medicare beneficiaries to increase revenue to support the Medicare Hospital Insurance Trust Fund (Davis et al., 2015).

▶ Looking Ahead

Between 2010 and 2016, Medicare annual spending increased 1.3% per year, compared with 7.4% annual growth between 2000 and 2010. Spending on Medicare accounted for 15% of total Federal spending in 2016. This amount is projected to increase to 17.5% by 2027, and the Part A trust fund is projected to be insolvent in 2029. Payments for Medicare programs have been shifting as well. For example, spending for Medicare Advantage plans doubled from 2006 to 2016, while spending on inpatient hospital stays decreased by 33%. Several policy proposals have been developed to help address the solvency issues approaching the Medicare program such as reforming cost-sharing and benefit structures, increasing the eligibility age, and additional increases on premiums for high-income beneficiaries (Henry J. Kaiser Family Foundation, 2013). The most recent Congressional Budget Office (CBO) projections predict that mandatory spending, which includes programs like Medicare and Social Security, will increase 2.4% points as a share of GDP, which is mostly attributed to the large aging population of Baby Boomers and rising healthcare costs (Congressional Budget Office, 2017).

During 2017, the Congress considered the Obamacare Repeal Reconciliation Act of 2017, which would repeal and replace the ACA. More specifically, it proposed to move Medicaid to a per-capita financing system. Although the proposal ultimately did not pass, it had important implications for Medicaid, such as eliminating statutory authority to cover childless adults and removing the higher Federal matching rate in states that expanded Medicaid under the ACA. Additionally, the current administration has indicated that it will allow states to use Section 1115 waivers to redesign Medicaid. Some of the waiver provisions that states are seeking include time limits on eligibility, drug screening, and work requirements (Henry J. Kaiser Family Foundation, 2018).

Brief Chapter Summary

Medicare and Medicaid, resulting from legislation passed in 1965, dramatically changed the delivery of health care in the United States by providing publicly subsidized health insurance to vulnerable populations, primarily the elderly and the economically disadvantaged. The costs involved in maintaining these programs quickly got out of hand by far exceeding all estimates of what the costs would be. Medicare, along with the Civil Rights Act of 1964, significantly changed access to hospital care for all population segments. Medicare alone was responsible for significantly reducing out-of-pocket healthcare costs for the elderly, but such gains by individuals were more than offset by growing expenditures of public funds.

Medicaid improved access to care, increased healthcare utilization, improved self-reported health outcomes, and reduced catastrophic medical expenses for more than 65 million Americans and has been instrumental in improving care for expectant mothers and children. Medicaid reduced the financial barriers to health care for much of the lower income population.

Medicare and Medicaid have, however, raised many concerns about continually increasing costs. Participation by hospitals is technically voluntary, but to remain eligible for tax-exempt treatment, not-for-profit hospitals must accept Medicare and Medicaid payments. Both Medicare and Medicaid continue to evolve in certain dimensions as financial problems continue to arise and as the landscape is periodically altered by federal legislation.

Questions for Review and Discussion

1. How are Medicare and Medicaid financed?
2. How are hospitals paid under Medicare and Medicaid?
3. What factors in the country led to the need for enactment of Medicare and Medicaid?
4. How did Medicare and Medicaid change healthcare delivery?
5. How did the enactment of the ACA impact Medicare and Medicaid?
6. What actions did the government take in response to hospital closures? Were they successful?

References

American Hospital Association. (2015a, February 9). *Trendwatch chartbook*. Chicago, IL: American Hospital Association. Retrieved from https://www.aha.org/system/files/research/reports/tw/chartbook/2016/2016chartbook.pdf

American Hospital Association. (2015b). *Underpayment by Medicare and Medicaid fact sheet*. Chicago, IL: American Hospital Association. Retrieved from http://www.aha.org/content/16/medicaremedicaidunderpmt.pdf

Bachrach, D., Boozang, P., & Lipson, M. (2016, June). *The impact of Medicaid expansion on uncompensated care costs: Early results and policy implications for states*. Princeton, NJ: The Robert Wood Johnson Foundation. Retrieved from http://www.rwjf.org/en/library/research/2015/06/the-impact-of-medicaid-expansion-on-uncompensated-care-costs.html

Card, D., Dobkin, C., & Maestas, N. (2008, December). The impact of nearly universal insurance coverage on health care utilization: Evidence from Medicare. *American Economic Review, 98*(5), 2242–2258.

Centers for Medicare and Medicaid. (2009, May 12). *The Boards of Trustees of the Federal Hospital insurance and federal supplementary medical insurance trust funds. Annual report*. Centers for Medicare and Medicaid. Retrieved from http://www.cms.gov/Research-Statistics-Data-and-Systems/StatisticsTrends-and-Reports/ReportsTrustFunds/Downloads/TR2009.pdf.24

Centers for Medicare and Medicaid. (2014, August 4). *Readmissions reduction program*. Centers for Medicare and Medicaid. Retrieved from http://www.cms.gov/Medicare/Medicare-Feefor-Service-Payment/AcuteInpatientPPS/Readmissions-Reduction-Program.html

Centers for Medicare and Medicaid. (2017). *Critical access hospital*. Centers for Medicare and Medicaid. Retrieved from https://www.cms.gov/Outreach-and-Education/Medicare-Learning-Network-MLN/MLNProducts/downloads/CritAccessHospfctsht.pdf

Centers for Medicare and Medicaid. (2018, February 14). *National expenditure fact sheet*. Centers for Medicare and Medicaid. Retrieved from https://www.cms.gov/research-statistics-data-and-systems/statistics-trends-and-reports/nationalhealthexpenddata/nhe-fact-sheet.html

Cohodes, S., Kleiner, S., Lovenheim, M., & Grossman, D. (2014). *The effect of child health insurance access on schooling. [Electronic Resource]: Evidence from public insurance expansions* [e-book]. Cambridge, MA: National Bureau of Economic Research.

Congressional Budget Office. (2017). *Budget and economic outlook.* Washington, DC: Congressional Budget Office.

Cunningham, P. (2005, May). Medicaid cost containment and access to prescription drugs. *Health Affairs* [serial online], *24*(3), 780–789.

Davis, K., Guterman, S., & Bandeali, F. (2015). *The affordable care act and Medicare: How the law is changing the program and the challenges that remain.* New York, NY: The Commonwealth Fund.

DesHarnais, S., Kobrinski, E., & Chesney, J. (1987, April 15). The early effects of the prospective payment system on inpatient utilization and the quality of care. *Inquiry (00469580)* [serial online], *24*, 7–16.

Fichtner, J. (2014). Medicaid's budgetary impact: The federal side of the budget equation. In J. Fichtner (Ed.), *The economics of Medicaid: Assessing the costs and consequences* (pp. 49–82). Arlington, VA: Mercatus Center at George Mason University.

Finkelstein, A., & McKnight, R. (2008, January 1). What did Medicare do? The initial impact of Medicare on mortality and out of pocket medical spending. *Journal of Public Economics* [serial online], *92*, 1644–1668.

Henry J. Kaiser Family Foundation. (2013, January 29). *Policy options to sustain Medicare for the future.* Henry J. Kaiser Family Foundation. Retrieved from https://www.kff.org/medicare /report/policy-options-to-sustain-medicare-for-the-future/

Henry J. Kaiser Family Foundation. (2016, June 9). *Uncompensated hospital care fell by $6 billion nationally in 2014, primarily in Medicaid expansion states; however many hospitals worry about future changes in Medicaid supplemental payments.* Henry J. Kaiser Family Foundation. Retrieved from https://www.kff.org/medicaid/press-release/uncompensated-hospital-care -fell-by-6-billion-nationally-in-2014-primarily-in-medicaid-expansion-states-however-many -hospitals-worry-about-future-changes-in-medicaid-supplemental-payments/

Henry J. Kaiser Family Foundation. (2017, September 13). *Where are states today? Medicaid and CHIP eligibility levels for children, pregnant women, and adults.* Henry J. Kaiser Family Foundation. Retrieved from https://www.kff.org/medicaid/fact-sheet/where-are-states-today -medicaid-and-chip/

Henry J. Kaiser Family Foundation. (2018, January 16). *Medicaid's future.* Henry J. Kaiser Family Foundation. Retrieved from https://www.kff.org/medicaid/fact-sheet/where-are-states-today -medicaid-and-chip/

Henry J. Kaiser Family Foundation. (2018, March 8). *Section 1115 Medicaid demonstration waivers: The current landscape of approved and pending waivers.* Henry J. Kaiser Family Foundation. Retrieved from https://www.kff.org/medicaid/fact-sheet/where-are-states-today-medicaid-and-chip/

Henry J. Kaiser Family Foundation. (2018, May 28). *The effects of Medicaid expansion under the ACA: Updated findings from a literature review.* Henry J. Kaiser Family Foundation. Retrieved from https://www.kff.org/medicaid/issue-brief/the-effects-of-medicaid-expansion-under-the -aca-updated-findings-from-a-literature-review-march-2018/

Holmes, G., Pink, G., & Friedman, S. (2013). The financial performance of rural hospitals and implications for elimination of the critical access hospital program. *Journal of Rural Health* [serial online], *29*(2), 140–149.

Hur, E. (2011, January 1). *Nation's first baby boomer turns 65 on new years day.* CBS. Retrieved from http://philadelphia.cbslocal.com/2011/01/01/nations-first-baby-boomer-turns-65-on-new -years-day/

Kaufman, B., Thomas, S. R., Randolph, R. K., Perry, J. R., Thompson, K. W., & Holmes, G. M., (n.d.). The rising rate of rural hospital closures. *Journal of Rural Health* [serial online], *32*(1), 35–43.

MACPAC. (2016, May). *Report to congress on Medicaid and CHIP.* MACPAC. Retrieved from http:// www.nasuad.org/sites/nasuad/files/March-2016-Report-to-Congress-on-Medicaid-and-CHIP.pdf

Martensen, R. (2011, November 1). How Medicare and hospitals have shaped American health care. *The Virtual Mentor: VM* [serial online], *13*(11), 808–812. MEDLINE, Ipswich, MA.

Moore, W., & Newman, R. (1993). Drug formulary restrictions as a cost-containment policy in medicaid programs. *The Journal of Law & Economics* [serial online], *36*(1), 71–97.

Nikpay, S., Buchmueller, T., & Levy, H. (2016, January). Affordable care act Medicaid expansion reduced uninsured hospital stays in 2014. *Health Affairs (Project Hope)* [serial online], *35*(1), 106–110.

Rudowitz, R., & Garfield, R. (2015, September). *New analysis shows states with Medicaid expansion experienced declines in uninsured hospital discharges.* Henry J. Kaiser Family Foundation. Retrieved from http://kff.org/health-reform/issue-brief/new-analysis-shows-states-with -medicaid-expansion-experienced-declines-in-uninsured-hospital-discharges

Seshamani, M., Schwartz, J. S., & Volpp, K. G. (2006). The effect of cuts in Medicare reimbursement on hospital mortality. *Health Services Research, 41*(3p1), 683–700.

Sloan, A., Morrisey, M., & Valvona, J. (1988). Effects of the Medicare prospective payment system on hospital cost containment: An early appraisal. *The Milbank Quarterly* [serial online], *66*(2), 191.

Smith, V., Gifford, K., Ellis, E., Rudowitz, R., Snyder, L., & Hinton, E. (2016, October 14). *Medicaid reforms to expand coverage, control costs and improve care. Results from a 50-state Medicaid budget survey for state fiscal years 2015 and 2016.* Kaiser Family Foundation and National Association of Medicaid Directors. Retrieved from http://kff.org/medicaid/report/medicaid-reforms-to -expand-coverage-control-costs-and-improve-care-results-from-a-50-state-medicaid-budget -survey-for-state-fiscal-years-2015-and-2016/

Sommers, B., Baicker, K., & Epstein, A. (2012, September 13). Mortality and access to care among adults after state Medicaid expansions. *New England Journal of Medicine* [serial online], *367*(11), 1025–1034.

Soumerai, S. (2003). Unintended outcomes of Medicaid drug cost-containment policies on the chronically mentally ill. *The Journal of Clinical Psychiatry, 64*, 19–22.

Soumerai, S. B., McLaughlin, T. J., Ross-Degnan, D., Casteris, C. S., & Bollini, P. (1994, September 8). Effects of limiting Medicaid drug-reimbursement benefits on the use of psychotropic agents and acute mental health services by patients with schizophrenia. *New England Journal of Medicine, 331*(10), 650–655.

Stewart, W. (1967, July). Positive impact of Medicare on the Nation's health care systems. *Social Security Bulletin* [serial online], *30*, 9. Applied Science & Business Periodicals Retrospective: 1913–1983. (H.W. Wilson), Ipswich, MA.

Wherry, L., Miller, S., Kaestner, R., & Meyer, B. (2015). *Childhood medicaid coverage and later life health care utilization* [e-book]. Cambridge, MA: National Bureau of Economic Research.

White, C., & Yee, T. (2013, October). When Medicare cuts hospital prices, seniors use less inpatient care. *Health Affairs* [serial online], *32*(10), 1789–1795.

Wishner, J., Solleveld, P., Rudowitz, R., Paradise, J., & Antonisse, L. (2018). *A look at rural hospital closures and implications for access to care: Three case studies.* Henry J. Kaiser Family Foundation. Retrieved from https://www.kff.org/report-section/a-look-at-rural-hospital-closures-and -implications-for-access-to-care-three-case-studies-issue-brief/

Wu, V., & Shen, Y. (n.d.). Long-term impact of Medicare payment reductions on patient outcomes. *Health Services Research* [serial online], *49*(5), 1596–1615.

Zhang, J. (n.d.). Bend the healthcare cost curve without pain? The health outcome after the Medicare reimbursement cut in 1997. *International Journal of Health Planning and Management* [serial online], *30*(2), 164–172.

CHAPTER 5

Enter Managed Care

Robert R. Kulesher

CHAPTER OBJECTIVES

- Review the development of managed care from the early 20th century to the present.
- Review the opposition to managed care from providers and patients.
- Examine the transition from traditional indemnity health plans to the many managed care options offered by private insurers and government programs.
- Review the influence of industry and government in shaping managed care.

KEY TERMS

Health maintenance organization (HMO)
Indemnity plan
Managed care plans

Preferred provider organization (PPO)
Point of service (POS)

▶ Beginnings of Managed Care: The Pre-Paid Health Plans

The concept of prepaid health care has been in U.S. healthcare systems since the early 20th century. Company-sponsored health delivery plans were established usually in remote areas where there were no regular providers. In 1910, one of the first known prepaid medical group practices was established in Tacoma, Washington. This was the Western Clinic which offered medical services to lumber mill employees for a payment of 50 cents per member per month (Mayer & Mayer, 1985). It was also an incentive to keep the medical clinic operating in the area by guaranteeing a predictable income. In the Midwest, a coop health plan was established in Elk City, Oklahoma. There, farmers purchased shares in the cooperative health plan for $50 per person to fund the building of a hospital in exchange for receiving personal medical care at a discount

(MacLeod, 1993). And in 1929, physicians Donald Ross and Clifford Loos created a comprehensive prepaid medical plan that may be the first example of a **health maintenance organization (HMO)** as it emphasized preventive care and routing health maintenance for the employees at the Los Angeles Department of Water and Power (Kongstvedt, 2016).

In the following decade, two **managed care plans** were created in 1937, one in California and the other in Washington, DC. In what eventually became the Kaiser Foundation Health Plan was a solution to provide health services to workers in remote areas such as the desert of southern California building the aqueduct to bring water to Los Angeles and in constructing the Grand Coulee Dam in Washington State (Kongstvedt, 2016). In the Nation's Capital, the Home Owners' Loan Corporation, worried about mortgage foreclosures caused by medical expenses, helped to establish the Group Health Association (Kongstvedt, 2016).

In the post-war years after World War II, other managed care plans became operational such as the Health Insurance Plan of Greater New York formed to provide health coverage for the employees of New York City, and Group Health Cooperative of Puget Sound in Washington State, which was started by Seattle citizens who paid the initial $100 per family tariff.

During this same time period of the early 20th century, the precursor to the Blue Cross/Blue Shield **indemnity plans** was developing, eventually becoming the "health insurance of choice" particularly during the Second World War. Due to a federal order to freeze wages in order to control inflation, large employers increased compensation to employees by instituting benefits such as life and health insurance. The common theme during the first half of the 20th century was that employers offered health benefits as a solution to the lack of providers in remote areas (prepaid health plans) or to keep employees on the job (traditional health insurance). What is noteworthy of these early prepaid health plans is that the managed care model, and in particular, the prepaid health plan model, was implemented for small specific populations, while the tradition health insurance model was used by most large corporation as part of employee benefit packages. Next, we will explore how federal legislation helped to accelerate the spread of managed healthcare plans across the nation.

Government Intervention in Managed Care Development

Up until the late 1940s, there had been no noticeable federal legislation affecting the operation of managed care plans. In 1945, the McCarran-Ferguson Act was passed, making insurance companies exempt from federal regulation and gave the authority to regulate the insurance industry to the states. By this change in authority, the aggregating of claims data for setting premiums and rates of charge was less likely to be considered violation of antitrust laws. Additionally, states varied in their rules and regulatory actions involving rate setting and determining what kind of commerce constitutes an insurance or risk product. Medicare and Medicaid were enacted in 1965 which brought additional federal and state dollars into the healthcare industry. No long after enactment of these reimbursement programs, large employers and legislatures with budgetary oversight of these programs became concerned about the rapid rise in healthcare spending. One answer to address the upward spiral of healthcare spending was the passing of the Health Maintenance Organization (HMO) Act of 1973 signed into law by President Richard Nixon (**FIGURE 5.1**).

FIGURE 5.1 President Richard Nixon signing Senate Bill

Linda Bartlett/National Cancer Institute.

TABLE 5.1 Provisions of the HMO Act of 1973

Services	■ Specific basic health services ■ Supplemental services if feasible
Membership	■ Annual enrollment period ■ Employers >25 employees must offer HMO option if available
Providers	■ Federally qualified ■ Exemption from state laws impeding HMO development ■ Federal funding for planning, developing, and expansion of HMOs

This legislation mandated that HMOs be part of the health plan offerings of employers. The major provisions of this act include:

■ Making federal grants and loans guarantees for planning and starting new health maintenance organizations and expanding existing HMOs.
■ Invalidating state laws that restricted HMO development.
■ Requiring companies employing 25 or more employees that already offer traditional health insurance as an employee benefit to offer at least one HMO option (Kongstvedt, 2016; U.S. Senate, 1974).

What is more, the Act specified a set of basic health services that must be provided in order to be a federally qualified HMO. These included (see **TABLE 5.1**):

■ Providing preventive services
■ Holding annual open enrollment periods during which anyone can enroll in the plan regardless of health status
■ Setting premiums that do not discriminate based on health status (Kongstvedt, 2016; U.S. Senate, 1974)

What had also developed by the 1950s was the independent practice association (IPA) model in which the HMO contracts with physicians either individually or collectively; many such associations were not deemed federally qualified. Being popular, they surpassed staff model HMOS in enrollment in the 1980s. However, another type of managed care plan began to take hold, which is the **preferred provider organization (PPO)**.

Preferred provider organizations made use of the cost savings mechanism developed by HMOs but allowed patients to choose their providers from within a network of independent providers. Precertification was required for routine hospital admissions and high-cost services such as CAT Scans and MRIs. Utilization review, requiring second opinions, and case management resembled processes of an HMO. Expansion of PPOs was fueled by employers and health insurers who were looking for ways to control premiums and provider costs to compete with more restrictive managed care options. See **FIGURE 5.2** for a comparison of HMO and PPO features. Additionally, most employees favored the wider range of provider choices and the ability to keep seeing the same practitioners as opposed to the clinic-like setting of the early HMOs.

In the closing decades of the 20th century, managed care plans grew rapidly at the expense of traditional indemnity health insurance. While HMO growth was rapid during this era, PPO growth had surpassed that of HMOs at the close of the century, leading to a 39% share of the health insurance market compared with 28% for HMOs (CMS, 2011). A new managed care plan called **point of service (POS)** was introduced at this time which allowed HMO members to choose a specialty provider outside of the HMO on an episode of care basis while maintaining a steady relationship with the HMOs primary care provider.

Employers now had a plethora of health plans to offer their employees. While small firms might offer a few plans, larger employers could offer everything from the traditional indemnity insurance plan to PPOs and HMOs, and offer several pricing options within each plan. Employers influenced employee choice of plans by adjusting levels of coinsurance and deductibles that employees paid.

The managed care industry showed signs of maturing as evidenced by the increase of mergers and consolidation of the industry. What were once regional HMOs serving specific populations now became national corporations. Many of the proprietary HMOs have been bought up by national insurance companies. The largest providers of HMO plans are the 36 insurance entities of the Blue Cross Blue Shield Association, with 106 million members. The largest for-profit provider is

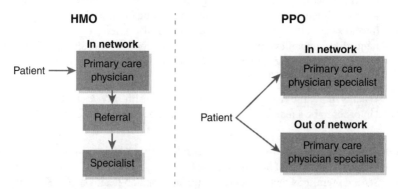

FIGURE 5.2 Difference between HMO and PPO

UnitedHealth Group with 70 million members in 2015 (Lists–News, 2017). **TABLE 5.2** lists the 10 largest providers of HMO plans in the United States.

As a result of consolidation, health plans could no longer selectively contract with providers; this diminished competition. Hospitals and their medical staffs formed integrated delivery systems (IDSs), corporate entities for contracting with a variety of payers especially HMOs. Hospitals accelerated their acquisition of physician practices to gain a favorable position in contact negations with HMOs.

TABLE 5.2 Ten Largest U.S. HMO Providers			
Provider	**Membership**	**Description**	**Organization**
Blue Cross Blue Shield Association	106 million	An alliance of 36 separate health insurance companies	Nonprofit
UnitedHealth Group	70 million	$155 billion market value trading as UnitedHealthcare and Optum	Proprietary
Anthem Inc.	39 million	Doing business as WellPoint Medicare, Anthem, and WellPoint Health Networks	Proprietary
Aetna Inc.	23 million	$60 billion in revenue	Proprietary
CIGNA Corporation	15 million	$38 billion in revenue d/b/a Cigna Medical Group	Proprietary
Humana Inc.	14 million	$54 billion in revenue d/b/a Humana Gold Plus	Proprietary
Kaiser Permanente	11 million	Largest nonprofit health plan. 60-year history	Nonprofit
Centene Corp	5 million	Managed care and specialty services	Proprietary
WellCare Health Plans, Inc.	4 million	Focus on Medicare and Medicaid managed care plans	Proprietary
Molina Healthcare, Inc.	4 million	$14 billion in revenue d/b/a Molina Medicaid Solution and other plans	Proprietary

Data from Insider Monkey. 10 Biggest HMOs in USA. News (2017) Sneha Shah in Lists, News.

As the managed care industry continued to mature, additional oversight by states' health departments, insurance commissioners, and the federal government increased. The National Committee for Quality Assurance (NCQA), established in 1990 with a grant from the Robert Wood Johnson Foundation, started to accredit HMOs. The NCQA established the Healthcare Effectiveness and Data Information Set (HEDIS) to measure the performance factors of care and service on the nation's health plans.

The managed care backlash of the 1990s—meaning the dissatisfaction with managed care's limits on consumer choice and denial of authorization for supposedly covered benefits—began to subside as we entered the new millennium and healthcare plans made adjustments to precertification and utilization review processes. Requirements such as obtaining authorization from a primary care provider to see a specialist and denial of payment for medically unnecessary care were relaxed. Claims that HMO policies were preventing members from obtaining care or discharging patients too early from acute hospital care were portrayed as alarming by the media. Network news broadcasts and major magazine article reported these "atrocities" with regularity in the 1990s. In response, states passed legislation implementing reasonable person standards and appeal rights. The Affordable Care Act, enacted in 2010, incorporated these practices (Kongstvedt, 2016). HMOs responded by expanding their networks and revised utilization review processes to a "reasonable" level. What follows in the early part of the 21st century is a decline in HMO market share and an increase in PPO plans.

The HMO market share declined in the new millennium from 29% in 2000 to 15% in 2016. POS plans also declined from 24% in 1999 to 9% by 2016. The PPO market share hit a high of 61% in 2005, then decreased to 48% in 2016 (Kaiser Family Foundation and Health Research & Educational Trust 2016 Annual Survey, 2016). During this period, managed Medicare enrollment declined from 6.4 million in 1999 to 4.6 million by 2003 (MedPAC Data Book, 2017). Part of this decline in managed Medicare enrollment was due to provisions in the Balanced Budget Act of 1997 which decreased payment levels from Medicare to the health plans that offered the managed care option of receiving Medicare benefits (Kongstvedt, 2016). However in 2003, the Medicare Modernization Act increased payment to health plans and enabled plans to promote managed care plans that had similar features like traditional Medicare. Medicare enrollment in managed health plans then grew to 18.5 million in 2017, covering 32% of all Medicare beneficiaries (MedPAC Data Book, 2017). The majority of state Medicaid programs became more dependent on private managed care plans, helping states to meet their budgets. In 2011, 74% of all Medicaid beneficiaries were on a managed care plan; however, that percentage fell to 61% in 2014 (CMS, 2016). As managed care continued to evolve as the primary health plan model, providers acted in ways to seemingly best position themselves for reimbursement. Next, we will look at how managed care changed the landscape of healthcare delivery.

▶ Managed Care as Agent of Change

In the last decades of the 20th century, hospital entities developed healthcare systems and began consolidation of the industry hoping to be in a more favorable bargaining position with managed care plans. Hospital acquisition of practices was thought to ensure inclusion by managed care of the hospital services along with physician services. Managed care was seen as a threat to hospital reimbursement as health plans; HMOs in particular actively diverted an increasing number of members toward outpatient services. This led to some experimentation to see what services could be safely delivered in surgical centers; cardiology practices and specialized radiology procedures heretofore thought too risky to be done on an outpatient basis. Physicians saw the threat of managed care as a reduction of practice income and increased surveillance by health plans on the practice of medicine. Physicians looked for ways to reduce overhead expenses or increase outpatients utilization, the latter in competition with hospitals if physicians set up their own surgery, imaging, and therapy centers.

Hospitals sought to acquire medical practices to (1) reduce the possibility of competing with physicians on the provision of outpatient services, and (2) demonstrate to managed care plans that the hospital and its medical staff is a health system that can efficiently take care of the health plan's members. As these new provider entities enter into risk contacts with managed care plans, such as accountable care organizations, and with enhanced health information technology support, healthcare systems are better able to manage the delivery of care and its costs (Kongstvedt, 2016).

Managed Care's Impact on Healthcare Delivery

The impact of managed care on the U.S. healthcare system has caused health care in general to be more cost conscience and to examine the efficacy of medical practice. HMO plans showed us that many procedures can be performed on an outpatient basis and that hospital stays can be reduced without ill effects (Kongstvedt, 2016). Health prevention and maintenance are concepts incorporated in nearly all health plans, managed or not. The early HMOs spent resources on examining the efficiency and efficacy of hospital and medical practice by disease. In the early days of managed care, public distrust of the perceived lack of service and restrictions on provider choice caused the creating of programs, like HEDIS and CAHPS, to examine managed care plans methods and provide an accreditation process to demonstrate what a quality healthcare plan should look like. What is more, managed care partnered with government to assist CMS to help reduce medically unnecessary costs in the Medicare and Medicaid programs.

Brief Chapter Summary

The three-legged stool of healthcare delivery policy is the relationship between costs of care, quality of care, and access to care. Adjustment to any one of these three elements will invariable impact one or both of the other. "An inherent problem in controlling healthcare costs is that one person's cost is another person's revenue" (Kongstvedt, 2016). As discussed in this chapter, managed care developed out of a specific need for healthcare delivery in places where there was none, such as remote construction sites and rural communities. As managed care demonstrated that keeping patient out of hospitals and delivering more on an outpatient basis, coupled with a focus on "health maintenance," costs can be reduced and quality of care can be improved. Regardless, managed care plans are the mainstay of employer-sponsored and individual health plans today.

Questions for Review and Discussion

1. Where and when did the first managed care plans emerge?
2. Who are the largest providers of managed care plans?
3. What were the provisions of the HMO Act of 1973 and how did it impact employer-sponsored health insurance plans?
4. Why did the traditional/indemnity health insurance plans lose market share in the last decades of the 20th century?
5. Who opposed health maintenance organizations and what were their reasons?
6. What impact did HMOs have on the delivery of hospital care?
7. Describe the incremental phases in the development of managed care in the United States.
8. What impact did NCQA and HEDIS have on the quality of healthcare delivery?
9. Describe the roles of government and the insurance industry in promoting managed care plans.
10. At present, what type of health plan is most offered by employers as a health insurance benefit?

References

CMS. (2011). Medicaid managed care enrollment report: Summary of statistics as of July 1, 2011.

CMS. (2016, Spring). *Medicaid managed care enrollment and program characteristics, 2014.* Princeton, NJ: Mathmatica Policy Research.

Kaiser Family Foundation and Health Research & Educational Trust 2016 Annual Survey. (2016). *Distribution of health plan enrollment for covered workers by plan type, 1988–2016* (p. 79). Chicago, IL: Health Research and Educational Trust.

Kongstvedt, P. (2016). *Health insurance and managed care: What they are and how they work* (4th ed., p. 34). Burlington, MA: Jones & Bartlett Publishers.

Lists–News. (2017). Published on February 21, 2017 at 4:30 pm by Sneha Shah in Lists, News. Retrieved from http://www.insidermonkey.com/blog/10-biggest-hmos-in-usa-531675/3/

MacLeod, G. K. (1993). An overview of managed health care. In P. R. Kongstvedt (Ed.), *The managed health care handbook* (2nd ed., pp. 3–11). Gaithersburg, MD: Aspen Publishers.

Mayer, T., & Mayer, G. (1985). HMOs: Origins and development. *New England Journal of Medicine, 312*(9), 590–594.

MedPAC Data Book. (2017, June). *Health care spending and the medicare program* (p. 133). Washington, DC: Medicare Payment Advisory Commission.

U.S. Senate. (1974, February). *Health Maintenance Organization Act of 1973.* Explanation of Act and Text of Public Law 93-222. Prepared for the Subcommittee on Health, Committee on Labor and Public Welfare.

Additional Resources

Knight, W. (1998). *Managed care: What it is and how it works.* Gaithersburg, MD: Aspen Publishers.

Kongstvedt, P. R. (2007). *Essentials of managed health care* (5th ed.). Sudbury, MA: Jones and Bartlett Publishers.

Kongstvedt, P. R. (2009). *Managed care: What it is and how it works.* Sudbury, MA: Jones and Bartlett Publishers.

Kongstvedt, P. R. (2013). *Essentials of managed health care* (6th ed.). Burlington, MA: Jones & Bartlett Learning.

Russell, J. A. (2000). *Managed care essentials: A book of readings.* Chicago, IL: Health Administration Press.

Smith, R. D. (2001). *The rise and fall of managed care: A comprehensive history of a mass medical movement.* Bristol, IN: Wyndham Hall Press.

CHAPTER 6

Health Benefits Coverage and Types of Health Plans

Peter R. Kongstvedt

CHAPTER OBJECTIVES

- Convey understanding of the core components of health benefits coverage.
- Describe the sources of health benefits coverage.
- Explain the differences in risk bearing.
- Develop understanding of the basic health insurer and managed care organization models.
- Describe the differences between models.
- Develop familiarization with the common challenges faced by hospitals and health systems that own or sponsor health plans.

KEY TERMS

Consumer-directed health plans (CDHPs)
Exclusive provider organizations (EPOs)
Health insurer
Health maintenance organizations (HMOs)
High-deductible health plans (HDHPs)
Independent physician (or practice) associations (IPAs)

Managed care organization (MCO)
Payer
Point-of-service (POS) plan
Preferred provider organizations (PPOs)
Third-party administrators (TPAs)

▶ Introduction

At its simplest, the U.S. healthcare system is made up of five types of people or organizations:

1. Individuals
   - *Patients*—individuals with benefits coverage who are receiving medical care
   - *Members*—individuals with benefits coverage who may or may not be patients
   - *Uninsured*—individuals lacking any type of health benefits coverage
2. *Providers*, including not only physicians and hospitals but also all licensed healthcare professionals and medical facilities
3. *Manufacturers*, such as drug and medical device manufacturers, as well as the vendors that sell those drugs and devices
4. *Payers*, referring to health insurers, **managed care organizations (MCOs)**, and **third-party administrators (TPAs)** of various services
5. *Regulators*, the federal, state, and local agencies that regulate the healthcare system under various state and federal laws and regulations

The fundamental obligation of any **payer** is to manage benefits for healthcare goods and services, meaning determining which goods and services will be paid for and under which circumstances, how much will be paid by the benefits plan when something is covered, and how much will be paid by the patient covered under that plan. This simple description, however, quickly becomes complex in the real world when determined by different types of payer organizations.

The generic terms "payer," "payer organization," and "health plan" apply to any type of organization that pays for healthcare services. A great many different types of payers exist, and it is sometimes difficult for consumers and even providers to differentiate. But each type is usually defined under various state and federal laws, and regulated accordingly. The most common types of payers include health insurers, **health maintenance organizations (HMOs)**, **preferred provider organizations (PPOs)**, and **point-of-service (POS) health plans**.

Two more additions to this stew of acronyms include the closely related **high-deductible health plans (HDHPs)** and the **consumer-directed health plans (CDHPs)** that are HDHPs with pre-tax savings options. However, both HDHPs and the related CDHPs are typically built on PPO platforms. To confuse things further, any of these types of plans, as well as other types of service companies, may also function as TPAs to self-funded employers (self-funding is discussed specifically later in the chapter); TPAs are described further at the end of the section on Types of Payers, as are all payer types.

As an aside, one result of the "managed care backlash" that occurred in the late 1980s through the 1990s was the appearance of the term MCO that came into common use for many different types of plans. MCO is a term that continues to be used today, albeit less frequently. But in all cases, an MCO is one of the other types of payer organizations.

The clear distinctions among types of payers have become progressively blurred over time, and organizational elements and features that had appeared previously in only one type of payer have found their way into other types of payers (one reason the term MCO remains in use). For all these reasons as well as in recognition of the widespread use of managed care techniques in all types of plans, this chapter will refer to these organizations as "payers," or sometimes "health plans," when addressing them broadly, but will identify the specific types of payers when it is important to distinguish between them.

▶ Health Benefits Coverage

Before describing the different types of payers, it is important to understand the core components of how benefits coverage is structured in almost any type of plan. Managing benefits, of course, is the fundamental obligation of any type of payer organization. Said another way, the plan manages benefits, but does not provide health care (with the exception of group and staff model HMOs to be described later). It can only manage what services it will and will not pay for, and under which circumstances. In other words, health plans cannot prevent someone from receiving a medical service, but it can determine whether that the service will or will not be paid for by the plan, and how much will be paid. This is not to say that health plan benefits coverage policies and decisions have no impact: It is hard to argue that a plan's denial of coverage for a $50,000 elective procedure would have no impact on a person's decision to have that procedure done. Nevertheless, it is useful to keep in mind that health plans manage benefits, meaning payments for medical goods and services, but do not provide the care and cannot prevent a physician from doing a procedure or a patient from receiving a treatment, drug, or device.

There are three interrelated core components of healthcare benefits:

- Defined benefits
- Cost sharing
- Coverage limitations

Defined Benefits

Defined benefits refer to what medical goods and services are covered, and under which circumstances coverage applies (subject to cost sharing and possible limitations described later). In other words, the type of medical good or service is defined as the benefit, regardless of what it ultimately costs to provide coverage for that benefit (although coverage may depend on meeting various requirements). This differs from defined contribution, which defines a fixed amount of money that may be put toward a benefit. For example, a defined benefit would be coverage of an inpatient stay regardless of cost. A defined contribution, in contrast, would be coverage of only $250 of the cost of that stay regardless of what it costs. All types of health plans discussed in this text, as well as in the Patient Protection and Affordable Care Act of 2010 (the ACA), are defined benefits plans.

Even in a defined benefits plan, the rules and requirements governing when coverage may apply vary by type of health plan. For example, HMOs typically cover nonemergency services only when they are authorized or when authorization is not required per the HMO's policies (e.g., seeing a primary care physician [PCP] or a gynecologist); they will not cover the cost of nonemergency care provided by noncontracting providers, unless authorized by the HMO; or unauthorized services that require authorization.

Other plan types may provide some level of coverage that HMOs do not, although the amounts and conditions vary by plan type. For example, PPOs or POS plans may provide less coverage for nonemergency out-of-network care than for in-network care, but that is more coverage than none at all.

Coverage may also depend on whether a treatment is considered reasonable based on a person's medical condition, particularly when there is more than one way to treat that condition. Said another way, a medical good or service may be covered in some circumstances but not in others; for example, certain types of plastic surgery may be covered to repair damage from disease or trauma, but not covered if done for cosmetic reasons.

To review a plan's defined benefits, existing members and individuals looking for coverage are required under the Patient Protection and Affordable Care Act (ACA) to be provided with a standardized document called the summary of benefits and coverage or summary of coverage. The document also summarizes how the plan defines "medical necessity," meaning how it determines whether coverage is appropriate based on a person's clinical condition and other factors. There is a far bulkier document that members have access to that is called an evidence of coverage that has greater detail about the plan, including greater specificity for coverage.

Benefits Defined in the ACA

The ACA further defines essential health benefits (EHBs), meaning services or goods that must be covered. EHBs apply to all types of plans, but the amount of cost sharing or levels of coverage may differ for various plans (with one exception—no cost sharing is allowed for preventive and wellness services). **TABLE 6.1** lists the EHBs as defined by the ACA. The ACA also limits plan participation in the insurance exchanges to qualified health plans (QHPs) covering the EHBs. The details of EHBs may differ slightly from state to state for reasons discussed shortly.

Under the ACA, health plans must also comply with the following benefits-related requirements (see Note 1)[1]:

- Health plans cannot exclude individuals because of a preexisting condition or discriminate based on health status for children younger than age 19.
- Plans cannot place lifetime limits on coverage.
- Plans cannot place annual limits on coverage.
- Plans must extend coverage to an employee's dependents until age 26.

The Impact of State-Mandated Benefits and Definitions of EHBs

The ACA requires insurers to cover EHBs, and for most benefits, there is little difference from state to state. But the ACA only listed the EHB categories seen in Table 6.1; it did not define them. Defining exactly what was included in each type of EHB was delegated to the states, who were instructed to base it on benefits provided by their largest insured plans in the individual and small group markets in 2014, and that included any state-mandated benefits in place at the time. The definition of a new EHB, habilitative care, was also delegated to states, which posed a challenge because it was not usually defined or included as a covered benefit at the time.

TABLE 6.1 Essential Health Benefits Under the ACA	
Benefit	**Cost Sharing Allowed**
Ambulatory patient services	Yes
Emergency services	Yes
Hospitalization	Yes
Maternity and newborn care	Yes
Pediatric services	Yes
Preventive and wellness services	No; first-dollar coverage required
Prescription drugs	Yes, but differ from cost sharing for medical benefits
Laboratory services	Yes
Mental health and substance-use disorder services	Yes, but may *not* differ from cost sharing for medical benefits
Chronic disease management	Yes
Rehabilitative and habilitative services and devices	Yes

Note: Any descriptions and discussion involving the ACA were current at the time of publication. However, the ACA has been and remains politically contentious, so what is described in this chapter may have changed by the time you read it.

The biggest impact of state-mandated benefits and state definitions of habilitative care is on coverage of ancillary services such as specialized testing and therapeutic interventions by nonphysician professionals. For example, most states mandate coverage of treatments for autism spectrum disorder, a condition for which treatment approaches can vary widely, and typically involves many different types of therapeutic ancillary services. However, exactly which of those different treatments must be covered is not uniform among various states.

There are even larger state-to-state differences for habilitative services. Some states adopted the definition created by the National Association of Insurance Commissioners (NAIC), but many other states crafted their own definitions. Examples of state-to-state differences of habilitative services definitions include one or more of the following:

- Confining it to a condition such as autism spectrum disorder
- Limiting it to those younger than 25
- Prohibiting limits on coverage
- Limiting coverage to a yearly set dollar amount or number of treatment sessions

State-mandated benefits may also include provisions that prohibit payers from using some of the usual approaches to manage utilization. For example, a type of treatment may not be required to meet the clinical evidence-based standards that might be applied to other medical/surgical interventions, prohibiting payers from classifying those as not medically necessary.

Cost Sharing

Cost sharing refers to the amount of money a member must pay out-of-pocket for each type of covered benefit. It applies only to benefits that are covered by the plan, not to services or goods for which no coverage is offered.

Basic Types of Cost Sharing

The three basic types of cost sharing are as follows:

- Copayment, meaning a fixed amount of money per type of service—for example, $30 each time a member goes to the doctor;
- Coinsurance, meaning a percentage of the total dollar amount that is covered—for example, 20% of the payment amount to a hospital for an inpatient stay;
- Deductible, meaning a fixed amount of money that a member must pay out-of-pocket before any coverage begins to apply—for example, a $1000 deductible for hospital stays.

All three types of cost sharing may be found in a typical health benefits plan. Deductibles and coinsurance may apply to the same benefit, whereas copayments typically apply only for services that are not subject to a deductible. For example, a visit to a PCP who is in the network of a PPO may require a $20 copayment, while a visit to a physician who is not in the network may be subject to a $500 deductible before the PPO makes any payment, at which point the member must pay 20% of the covered amount as well as any charges over what the plan covers; this is called balance billing and is discussed later in the chapter.

Cost sharing may also differ by type of service. For example, PCP visits may require a $20 copayment, whereas a hospital stay may be subject to a $1000 deductible and then 10% coinsurance after the deductible is met. Cost sharing may also differ, and be separately counted, for drug coverage than it is for all other benefits.

Cost Sharing Under the ACA

The ACA defines levels of allowable cost sharing for QHPs and insured coverage (self-funded plans may be somewhat different). For preventive services, the ACA does not allow cost sharing at all for any type of plan. For other covered benefits as listed in Table 5.1, the ACA defines four basic levels of cost-sharing percentages for EHBs in the individual, group, and insured markets:

- Platinum, defined as 10% or less total cost sharing
- Gold, defined as 20% total cost sharing
- Silver, defined as 30% total cost sharing
- Bronze, defined as 40% total cost sharing

The ACA also defines a special type of benefits plan that may be offered to individuals younger than the age of 30, which has a higher level of cost sharing but a very low premium.

Cost sharing is based on the average total amount of cost sharing for nonemergency services provided by network providers. In other words, it is the combination of copayments, coinsurance, and deductibles—not just one type of cost sharing. It is based on the average total amount of cost sharing for all members, rather than the amount of cost sharing by any particular member. The percentages also reflect how much a plan pays its network providers, such that members who receive nonemergency care from non-network providers are covered only up to the amount a plan would pay based on in-network services. These different tiers apply only to plans sold to individuals and small groups, but all plans must offer at least 60% coverage regardless of plan type, and as a practical matter, these concepts are used by nearly all health plans.

The ACA also limits the maximum out-of-pocket cost for individuals and for families, after which no further cost sharing may be applied. The dollar amounts are set by the U.S. Treasury Department each year. For example, in 2018, the maximum out-of-pocket costs could be no more than $7,350 for self-only coverage, and $14,700 for family coverage. Many health plans actually set their maximum out-of-pocket limits at a lower level, however.

Coverage Limitations

Several different types of coverage limitations exist. For example:

- A benefit may be covered only if it is provided through a contracted provider. For example, a plan that has different levels of coverage for nonemergency services provided by in-network versus out-of-network providers may cover long-term rehabilitative services only when they are provided by a contracted provider.
- The maximum dollar amount of coverage is usually based on what the plan pays providers in its network, not what a provider charges.
- Limits may be placed on the number of services or devices covered in a time period. For example, coverage may be limited to one pair of foot orthotics every 2 years.
- Coverage may be based on medical necessity. For example, the plan may not provide any coverage for care that is experimental or investigational (unless part of an authorized study as defined in the ACA), care that is for the convenience of the patient or provider, care for which a lower cost but equally effective alternative exists, and so forth.
- Some services may not be covered under any circumstances. For example, coverage is usually not provided for people who need custodial care because they cannot care for themselves.

In the past, many plans used to limit coverage to a total dollar amount paid in a year, in a person's lifetime, or both. The ACA, however, prohibits annual or lifetime limits on coverage.

▶ Sources of Benefits Coverage and Risk

The sources of benefits coverage refer to how groups or individuals obtain health benefits coverage, while risk refers to who or what is at risk for the cost of payment for those benefits. These two concepts are closely related but are not identical and are not the same for each group or individual. At its most fundamental, there are three basic types of coverage sources and three basic types of risk bearing.

Three basic sources of benefits coverage are as follows:

- Entitlement programs
- Individual coverage
- Group health benefits plans

Three broad forms of risk bearing are as follows:

- Government bears the risk
- Payer bears the risk
- Employer bears the risk

These sources of coverage and risk are not mutually exclusive, and health insurance or health benefits coverage for any individual can be some combination of them. **TABLE 6.2** summarizes the sources of coverage and risk.

TABLE 6.2 Sources of Coverage and Risk				
		Sources of Benefits Coverage		
		Entitlement Programs	**Individual Coverage**	**Group Health Benefits Plans**
Bears Risk for Costs of Covered Health Benefits	Government	Traditional Medicare, Medicaid, and other federal entitlement programs	N/A	Military health benefits plans*
	Health Insurer	Medicare Advantage, managed Medicaid	Individual Health Insurance	Employment-based group health insurance
	Employer	Retiree health benefits coverage when part of a defined benefit retirement plan	N/A	Employment-based group health benefits coverage*

*Health benefits for government employees are considered group health benefits, where the government is the employer.

Sources of Coverage

The sources of coverage refer to the organization or entity providing the coverage. This entity may be the company handling the claims, but this is not always the case. It is also not always clear what that source is depending on which type of payer is providing the coverage. Nevertheless, the easiest way to consider this issue is to look at the three sources:

- Government entitlement programs
- Individual health insurance
- Employer group health benefits plans, also referred to as group health benefits plans (dropping the word "employer")

Entitlement Programs

In the United States, approximately 40% of all national health expenditures were funded by federal and state entitlement programs. Coverage is provided to anyone who is eligible for it, meaning that person is entitled to that form of coverage. Government entitlement programs, which may or may not include all or some managed care features, include the following:

- Medicare
- Medicaid
- Military programs (both direct care by military providers and the Tricare program under the Civilian Health and Medical Program of the Uniformed Services [CHAMPUS])
- Veterans Administration
- U.S. Public Health Service
- Indian Health Service

The largest entitlement programs are Medicare and Medicaid. The Centers for Medicare & Medicaid Services (CMS), a branch of the U.S. Department of Health and Human Services (DHHS), administers Medicare. Medicare provides healthcare benefits for the elderly, for many individuals with end-stage renal disease, and for individuals with certain other conditions. The individual states manage their own Medicaid programs, which rely on state and federal funds and provide healthcare benefits to eligible individuals or families with low or no income; eligible individuals who are aged, blind, or disabled; and eligible institutionalized individuals. Managed care techniques have been applied to all types of government programs, with specific types of health plans being developed for Medicare and Medicaid.

In traditional Medicare and Medicaid programs, the federal or state government uses private payers, such as Blue Cross Blue Shield plans or other private companies, to administer the program. Those private entities, which are called intermediaries, provide only administrative services, so the government (i.e., taxpayers) remains at risk. In contrast, in private Medicare Advantage and managed Medicaid plans, the risk is transferred from the government to the private plan.

The Federal Employees Health Benefit Program (FEHBP) is an employee benefits program for federal employees. Likewise, state and local governments typically provide benefits to their full-time employees. These are not entitlement programs, however, but rather employer group health benefit plans.

Finally, the ACA provides federal assistance to certain low- or modest-income individuals or families, which is a form of entitlement but is not the same as being at risk for medical costs. Funding for such assistance remains a contentious issue at the time of publication.

Individual Health Insurance

Several different sources of coverage are available to individuals. For example, individuals may purchase health insurance policies directly from commercial insurance companies. In general, individual health insurance policies are more expensive or require more cost sharing than group health benefits plans.

Under the ACA, as of January 2014, individuals became able to purchase coverage either directly from a **health insurer** or through a health insurance exchange. Prior to 2014, individuals often needed to pass "medical underwriting," meaning their health status determined whether they could get coverage. That is no longer the case: Individuals cannot be refused coverage based on health status, at least during open enrollment. The ACA also required most individuals to have coverage or face a penalty, though enforcement was quite limited, but congress put that requirement aside in 2018.

Individuals can buy such coverage only during designated periods of the year, typically 1 month per year, although the ACA allows states to extend these open enrollment periods if they so choose (none have). Individuals' benefits and premiums are affected by provisions of the ACA but are supposed to be managed by the states. As noted earlier, subsidies are also available for qualifying low-income individuals and families.

Individuals may also be eligible for coverage following certain "life events," such as marriage or divorce, losing a job, or childbirth or adoption. They must apply for this coverage within 60 days of the life event or they lose eligibility. The coverage change may be to their existing benefits plan (e.g., adding a dependent), or to eligibility to obtain coverage through the health insurance exchange.

Coverage may also exist through the Consolidated Omnibus Reconciliation Act of 1986 (COBRA). This requires employers with 20 or more employees to offer certain former employees, retirees, spouses, former spouses, and dependent children the right to temporary continuation of health coverage at group rates. The individual must pay the full cost of that coverage, but it is usually less expensive than an individual policy unless the individual qualifies for subsidized coverage under the ACA. Coverage under COBRA is limited to 18 months in most cases, and the end of that period of coverage is considered a life event for purposes of obtaining coverage through the insurance exchange.

In the past, individuals could also obtain coverage under the terms of the Health Insurance Portability and Accountability Act of 1996 (HIPAA) once their COBRA coverage ran out. This was an important right for individuals who had medical conditions that made it difficult or impossible for them to buy coverage because insurers would not sell to people with preexisting conditions. HIPAA coverage was very costly and the benefits were poor, however. When the ACA made coverage available to all individuals during an open enrollment or following a life event, there was no longer a need for coverage under HIPPAA.

Group Health Benefits Plans

Employer-based group health benefits plans are the largest source of health benefits coverage in the United States, accounting for almost half of all coverage. While employers are not compelled to provide coverage, the ACA requires all employers with more than 50 full-time employees to offer qualified health benefits coverage plans or pay a penalty, and it provides tax incentives to encourage small employers to offer coverage. Large employers must automatically enroll new employees into their plan, but an employee can opt out. Even when an employer does offer health insurance, temporary or part-time employees are seldom eligible to participate in an employer's group health benefits plan.

*Group health benefits plans have several advantages:

- The cost of the coverage is paid on a pretax basis.
- Employers can either purchase group health insurance or self-fund the benefits plan.
- Employers, especially large employers, are usually able to obtain more favorable pricing and coverage than individuals can.
- Large employers often provide employees with different options for type of health plan or amount of cost sharing.
- Healthcare coverage benefits may be combined with other types of benefits (e.g., flexible spending accounts, health payment accounts, or life insurance).
- The employer—not the individual employee—manages administrative needs such as payroll deductions and payment of premiums.

If costs for a group health benefits plan increase, as they usually do each year, the employer generally absorbs much of that cost increase. Employees typically contribute part of their pretax earnings toward the cost of the coverage, usually around 25% of the total cost. As a consequence, as health plan costs increase, the dollar amount of the payroll deduction also rises even though it is the same on a percentage basis. In addition, employers have been steadily increasing the amount of required cost sharing in their benefits plans in order to keep premiums lower. Because healthcare costs usually rise faster than overall inflation, some of the money an employer might have used for pay raises ends up being used to pay for health benefits, so that higher employee payroll deductions also affect the amount of total take-home pay.

In all cases, however, the cost of the benefits plan paid by the employer as well as the payroll deduction are pretax expenses, meaning they are not considered taxable income to employees. That is not the case for individual health insurance: Individuals must pay their premiums with after-tax dollars, meaning they cannot deduct it from their income taxes (with some exceptions).

Bearing Risk for Medical Costs

Contrary to popular belief, a health insurance company does not always bear the financial risks associated with the medical costs of its customers or members. In fact, insurers bear the risk in fewer than half of all group benefits plans. Because many day-to-day payer operations are not tied to who is bearing the risk for medical costs, distinctions about who bears the financial risk will be made throughout this text only when this issue is important (as in this section).

---

*   The penalty applies only if any employees receive subsidized coverage through an insurance exchange. At the time of publication, it is not clear if congress will abolish this requirement.

Government Entitlement Programs

The government is at risk for the traditional entitlement programs. However, commercial Medicare Advantage plans and commercial managed Medicaid plans may contract with the government to provide and administer those benefits, in which case they assume the risk for medical costs.

Health Insurance

People purchase health insurance to protect themselves from unexpected medical costs. The insurer provides coverage of medical costs and charges premium rates that are calculated to cover those costs on average. A commercial payer can be a for-profit or nonprofit organization.

The central point of health insurance is that the risk for medical expenses belongs to the payer. In other words, in exchange for the payment of insurance premiums, the payer is responsible for paying some or most of the cost of medical care provided to individuals, subject to cost sharing and coverage limitations. Whether the actual costs for a group or an individual are higher or lower than average, the premium payment does not change during the period the insurance policy is in effect.

Federal laws and regulations under the ACA, HIPAA, and Employee Retirement Income Security Act of 1974 (ERISA) apply to health insurance, but generally speaking, regulation of insurance is the responsibility of the state governments. Because the regulatory system is highly complex, it is only described throughout this text when applicable.

Self-Funded Employer Health Benefits Plans

Most large corporations do not actually purchase health insurance to cover their employees. Instead, they fund the benefits plan themselves, a practice called "self-funding." Said another way, in a self-funded plan, the employer is the insurer and is also the entity at risk. Self-funding is mostly used in large groups, although some medium-sized employer groups have also moved to this practice. It is found in large groups because a risk pool (i.e., a group of covered people) must be large enough to be able to predict costs. In a small group, the impact of chance and luck—good and bad—is higher than in a large group, where chance and luck average out.

Assuming the risk of medical costs makes it possible for a large employer to avoid paying state premium taxes or offering state-mandated benefits. Costs in a self-funded group are based only on the actual costs incurred by the company's employees and their dependents (and in some cases the company's retirees) and are not affected by costs incurred by other groups or individuals. Self-funded plans also do not pay the charge that insurers build into their premiums for the cost of taking on risk and to ensure the insurer's profits or margin contributions. The cost of taking on risk is real, however, so self-funded employers also purchase reinsurance.

Self-funded benefits plans are not regulated by the states, but they are regulated by the U.S. Department of Labor and to some degree by the U.S. Department of the Treasury. Self-funded plans are also exempt from some, but not all, requirements under the ACA—although as a practical matter, they do comply with most of the important requirements. As long as an employer complies with the benefits plan requirements under ERISA and the ACA, there is very little regulation involved.

Self-funded plans may mimic any type of health plan. Employers with self-funded plans typically contract with TPAs (discussed later in the chapter) to perform the plan's administrative duties such as handling enrollment and eligibility, processing claims, and managing appeals. In most cases, the administrator is actually a large health insurance company or managed care plan that also offers and manages its own insured products, which may cause confusion among both members and providers as to who the insurer actually is.

Commercial payers acting as administrators not only provide administrative services but also pass along to the employers any discounts from the providers. In other cases, a TPA that is not also an insurer administers the plan but remains behind the scenes, and the self-funded plan contracts with different companies for different services such as accessing a discounted provider network, managing utilization, managing drug benefit claims, and so forth.

Provider Risk

In some forms of provider payment, a contracted provider may assume some portion of risk. The most common arrangement is HMO capitation, in which the provider receives a fixed payment for each member each month regardless of how many or what type of services those members receive from the provider. This type of provider risk is usually limited and does not apply to all medical costs, although some large health systems may take on substantial risk in the form of fixed payments. This is not the same as a provider-owned or sponsored health plan in which a health system also functions as an insurer, which is discussed later in this chapter.

Reinsurance

Reinsurance is a high-level form of insurance that applies only to very high-cost cases or in the instance of higher-than-predicted overall costs. Large payers are often able to manage risk themselves, but other payers purchase reinsurance that usually is uniform across all of its insured policies. Almost all self-funded employer groups purchase reinsurance, albeit specific to their group only.

Most states have rules regarding how much reinsurance a self-funded health benefits plan can have before it is considered a commercial group health insurance plan and, therefore, becomes subject to state regulation. For example, if an employer purchases reinsurance to cover expenses that are only 5% higher than what was budgeted for, the state may claim that the employer is insured and not self-funded, which means it must comply with all state laws and regulations for health insurance.

Reinsurance is not the same as health insurance. It comes in many different forms and is regulated differently from health insurance. A reinsurer can apply different rules for defining when something is covered and when it is not. Benefits plans must treat all of their beneficiaries equally and cannot deny ongoing coverage to an individual based on that person having high medical costs—but a reinsurer can do just that, resulting in the self-funded plan having to continue to pay the benefits costs but having no financial protection from the expenses incurred by the individual.

Prior to 2014, self-funded plans facing focused reinsurance coverage exclusions had no options because other reinsurers would include the same focused coverage exclusions, and health insurers would refuse to underwrite the group as a whole. However, the ACA now requires insurers and managed care plans to provide coverage to any individual or group that seeks it, at least during an open enrollment season, although large groups with high costs would also face high premiums.

▶ Types of Payer Organizations

Serious challenges are associated with attempting to describe the types of payer organizations in a field as dynamic as health insurance and managed care. The healthcare system has been continually evolving in the United States, and change is the only constant. Nevertheless, distinctions remain between different types of payers.

Originally, HMOs, PPOs, and traditional forms of indemnity health insurance were distinct, mutually exclusive products with different approaches to providing healthcare coverage. Today, an observer might be hardpressed to uncover the differences among these and many newer products without reading the fine print. Further confusing this issue is the existence of provider-based integrated delivery systems (IDSs).

Because of these continual changes, the descriptions of the different types of payer organizations that follow provide only a guideline to the various types of payer organization models or structures. In many cases, a company may offer multiple products based on many or nearly all types of payer models, and called by product names that provide little clue to what type each one is.

Nonprofit, For-Profit, and Member-Owned Payer Organizations

There are three different ways that most payer organizations are structured around ownership and governance. These arrangements are described only briefly here because the types of ownership and governance have no observable impact on general operations or marketplace behavior.

In a **nonprofit** plan, the payer is not owned by investors and cannot distribute profits. Such an organization is not really owned by anyone. In one sense, it owns itself, but that does not mean that any board member or employee can claim any ownership rights. Any profits or margins that a nonprofit organization earns belong only to the nonprofit plan. If a nonprofit organization is sold to a for-profit company, or if it converts from nonprofit to for-profit status, that is considered a type of sale. The nonprofit's assets and marketplace value must benefit the community overall, not any private person or group.

In a **for-profit plan**, the company is owned by investors and can distribute profits to its investors. Many of these organizations are publicly traded, meaning their stock is listed on the stock market. Others are owned by either a for-profit or a nonprofit company. Nonprofit companies typically establish for-profit subsidiaries so that the subsidiary's profits can be paid to its owners.

In a **member-owned plan,** the plan's members own the plan on a collective basis, albeit not in the same way as the shareholders own a publicly traded company.

Member-owned plans are technically neither nonprofit nor for-profit entities. Three types of member-owned plans exist:

■ Mutual insurers in which policyholders own the company on a mutual (shared) basis.

■ Cooperatives (CO-OPs), which are similar to CO-OPs found in agriculture or other industries, in which the members of the CO-OP receive the CO-OP's services.

■ Consumer-Owned and -Operated Plans (CO-OPs), a plan type that was created specifically under the ACA as a means of increasing competition in the health insurance exchanges. CO-OPs share some attributes of CO-OPs or mutual insurers but have specific requirements that CO-OPs and mutual insurers do not have. For example, the ACA is very specific about who may and may not be on a CO-OP's board of directors. The ACA also provided special funding for start-up CO-OPs, but that funding was cut by the Taxpayer Relief Act of 2012. Most CO-OPs that appeared right after the ACA went into effect failed and are now gone.

Nonprofit, for-profit, and member-owned plans are all generally subject to the same state and federal requirements, aside from certain specific financial and tax reporting requirements. As a practical matter, a payer can have any one of these structures and that choice will have no impact on the different types of health plans offered. In other words, all types of payer organizations compete in the same marketplace and are indistinguishable to most people.

The Continuum of Managed Care

Health insurance and managed care may be thought of as a continuum of models (**FIGURE 6.1**). These models are generally classified as follows:

■ Indemnity with precertification, mandatory second opinion, and case management
■ Service plan with precertification, mandatory second opinion, and case management
■ PPO
  • Traditional PPO
  • CDHP plan
■ POS plan
■ Exclusive provider organization (EPO)
■ HMO
  • "Open-access" HMO
  • Traditional HMO
    ○ Open-panel HMO
    ○ Independent practice association (IPA)
    ○ Direct contract HMO
  • Network model HMO
  • Closed-panel HMO
    ○ Group model
    ○ Staff model

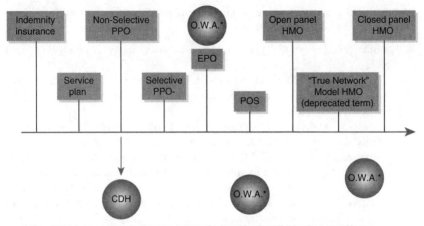

* Other Weird Arrangement; meaning some supposedly clever idea that will solve the cost problems forever but is difficult to administer or understand, and that typically has only a minor impact in the end.

FIGURE 6.1 Types of Benefits Plans and Managed Care Organizations

© P. R. Kongstvedt.

As models move toward the managed care end of the continuum, the following features begin to appear and continue:

- Provider contracts defining terms and requirements
- Tighter elements of control over healthcare benefits
- Addition of new elements of control
- More direct interaction with providers
- Increased overhead cost and complexity
- Greater management of utilization
- A net reduction in rate of rise of medical costs

Although it would be comforting to classify all payers using the models defined here, payers are anything but uniform and they often offer most or all of the various types of plans, though there are usually differences in how this is applied by type of plan.

The classification of health plans that follows has nothing to do with which party carries the actual risk for medical expense, or what the organization's ownership status is, both of which have been discussed already. The same may be said for how plans are licensed by states, with one common type of exception. The exception is an employer self-funded benefits plan that uses the same benefits design as one of the following payer types, but has that plan administered by multiple unrelated TPAs.

In the discussion here, various forms of provider payment and medical management approaches will be mentioned when they differ from one type of plan to another, but will not be fully described.

Traditional Health Insurance

Basically, two types of traditional health insurance exist: indemnity insurance and service plans. This type of plan is called traditional because it was the dominant form of coverage in the past—not because it still is. The costs of traditional health insurance rose rapidly beginning in the early to mid-1970s, such that it became very expensive compared with most types of managed care plans. Even with increases in the levels of cost sharing, traditional health insurance remained costlier than the newer types of plans and could not effectively compete in the U.S. marketplace.

The share accounted for by traditional insurance has now shrunk to less than 1% of the total market for healthcare coverage. Most of the traditional insurers remain robust, but either changed by adopting managed care, or by exited health insurance and focusing on other types of insurance.

Indemnity Insurance

Indemnity health insurance protects (indemnifies) the insured (i.e., the policy-holder) against financial losses from medical expenses. A person covered under an indemnity plan may receive coverage from any licensed provider. The insurance company may reimburse the subscriber directly for medical expenses, or it may pay the provider directly, although it has no actual obligation other than to pay the subscriber unless required under a state's laws. Payment to physicians and other professional providers is subject to usual, customary, or reasonable (UCR) fee screens, whereas payment to institutional providers is generally based on charges. There is no contract between the insurer and the providers.

Benefits are generally subject to a deductible and coinsurance. Any charges by the provider that the insurance company does not pay are strictly the responsibility of the subscriber. Most plans usually require precertification of elective hospital admissions and may apply a financial penalty to the subscriber who fails to obtain precertification. Case management may also be used to help control the very high costs of catastrophic cases (e.g., a severely premature infant, a trauma case). Second opinions may be mandatory for certain elective procedures (e.g., surgery for obesity).

Service Plans

Technically speaking, a service plan is not insurance, but rather a form of prepaid healthcare benefits, and it applies primarily, though not exclusively, to Blue Cross and Blue Shield (BCBS) plans. At the time service plans came into being, they were controlled by the hospitals or physicians providing the services, but that is no longer the case and service plans are now much more like traditional health insurers.

In service plans, relatively few restrictions are placed on licensed providers who sign a contract with the plan. This first appearance of a contract is an important milestone, and a feature of all types of plans except indemnity insurers. A service plan's provider contract typically contains certain key provisions:

- The plan agrees to pay the provider directly, eliminating collection problems with patients.
- The provider agrees to accept the plan's fee schedule as payment in full and not to bill the subscriber for any charges that exceed the amount the plan pays, other than the normal deductible and coinsurance.
- The provider agrees to allow the plan to audit the provider's records related to billed charges.
- Like indemnity insurance, service plans may require precertification, case management, and second opinions.

The principal advantage of a service plan over indemnity insurance lies in the provider contracts and the providers' agreement to accept the service plan's payment terms and not "balance bill" the plan's members for any charges above the amount allowed by the service plan. This, too, is a feature found in all of the other types of plans except indemnity insurance. It applies only to contracted providers, however; noncontracted providers can and do balance bill patients.

Professional fees allowed under the fee schedule represent a discount to the plan. More importantly, the plan usually obtains discounts at hospitals that indemnity plans do not receive. The hospitals grant these discounts for a variety of reasons, including large volume of business, and timely direct payment. Most service plans have evolved into PPOs, but even then the organization is technically a service plan for all but its HMO products.

Preferred Provider Organizations

Although PPOs are similar to service plans, there are some important differences between these types of payers. A service plan operating as a PPO remains licensed as a service plan. A PPO not operated by a service plan must be licensed as an insurer if it is a risk-bearing PPO described later in this section. Most PPOs have more terms and conditions for participation by providers compared with non-PPO service plans, such as a requirement that physicians be board certified. PPO provider discounts are generally below average billed charges.

A PPO network contracts with fewer than the total number of providers available in an area. It may be required by law to contract with "any willing provider" (AWP) or they may be selective about accepting providers into the network. In the former approach, any provider who wishes to participate in the organization and who meets the conditions and agrees to the terms of the PPO's contract is offered a contract. Selective PPOs, by comparison, apply some objective criteria (e.g., location-based network need, credentials, or practice pattern analysis) before contracting with a provider. AWPPPOs are more common, particularly given that numerous state laws require this arrangement, but the use of criteria-based selection still occurs, particularly with expensive or highly specialized services (e.g., for cardiac surgery). It is also being used by many insurers that offer "narrow network" products through the health insurance exchanges.

Precertification and case management are almost always components of PPOs, but mandatory second-opinion programs are relatively uncommon because they are no longer considered to be effective. Failure to comply with PPOs' rules results in a financial penalty to the provider, not the member. As with service plans, a contracting provider may not bill the member for any balance that the PPO does not pay, and that includes any payment penalties associated with the provider not complying with precertification.

A hallmark of a PPO is that benefits are reduced if a member seeks nonemergency care from a provider who is not in the PPO network. A common benefits differential is 20% based on allowed charges. For example, if a member sees a network provider, coverage is provided at 80% of allowed charges; if a member sees a provider who is not in the network, the coverage may be limited to 60% of allowed charges. If the nonparticipating provider charges more than the allowed charges, the member is responsible for all charges above what is allowed. Preventive services are not subject to any cost sharing, as required under the ACA.

Providers agree to discount their services to a PPO because the smaller networks combined with the benefits coverage differentials serve to channel patients toward participating providers. Of equal importance, this approach eliminates the risk of losing patients who switch to participating providers. PPOs are less expensive than traditional insurance, but usually more expensive than HMOs. Because they have fewer restrictions and typically contract with larger networks than do HMOs, PPOs have the largest share of the market.

Risk-Bearing PPOs

PPOs can be either risk bearing or non-risk bearing. A risk-bearing PPO combines the insurance, or payment, function with the management of the network of providers. As a risk-bearing entity, it must be licensed as a service plan or a health insurer itself, or be owned by one.

Non-Risk-Bearing or Rental PPOs or Rental Networks

Most payers have their own networks, but no payer—other than the federal Medicare program—has a network in place in all parts of the United States. Under the ACA, emergency care must be covered at the in-network level of benefits even for services provided by non-network providers. Mid-size to large employers, however, frequently have employees who live or work in locations where a payer may not have a contracted network. In those areas, this potentially means the PPO may have to pay for care delivered based on full charges, and members may not have the protections found in most provider contracts. Self-funded employer groups that use TPAs instead of a full-service payer face the same issue because TPAs typically do not have a network of their own.

BCBS plans address this risk through their BlueCard program, in which a member of one BCBS plan is able to access another BCBS plan's network providers when away from home. This mechanism is based on an agreement among the Blues plans because those plans are independent, but do provide for seamless access to any Blues network.

Non-BCBS plans must take a different approach for supplementing their own networks, as do self-funded employer groups that use TPAs. The solution in both cases is to contract with one or more rental networks. A rental network comprises a network created either by the providers themselves or by a company that is not affiliated with a single payer. Rental networks are almost always PPO networks, rather than HMO networks (which have more requirements than do PPOs). Any PPO created by providers must not violate antitrust requirements, meaning it cannot act as a means of suppressing competition.

Rental networks typically charge an access fee, and charge separate fees for other services they may provide. Usually, the rental network's providers send the claims to the rental network, which then reprices them and sends the claims on to the payer or TPA for payment. The rental network keeps a percentage of the difference between the full charges and the discount.

Some states require non-risk-bearing PPOs to be licensed, but not all. If the PPO performs any utilization management or even quality management functions, it may need to be licensed as a utilization review organization of some type. Likewise, if it performs any other administrative functions, including pre-pricing of claims, it may need to be licensed as a TPA.

In past decades, payers did not always make it clear that they had such contracts with rental PPOs, and there was no indicator on the member's identification (ID) card about any rental PPOs. Providers that contracted with the rental PPO but not directly with a payer would find themselves receiving the PPO payment and not the billed charges, requiring them to write down the difference. This could even happen in an area in which both a payer and a rental PPO had networks, but did not include all the same providers. At the time this was occurring, the arrangement was known as a "stealth" or "silent" PPO. Silent PPOs are now uncommon after several lawsuits were filed challenging this practice, and payers that contract with rental PPOs now typically put the logo(s) of the rental PPO(s) someplace on the member's ID card, usually on the back, though providers do not always look for it.

High-Deductible Health Plans and Consumer-Directed Health Plans

Each year, the Internal Revenue Service determines what the minimum and maximum deductibles need to be to qualify as a HDHP. For 2017, the minimum deductible was $1,300 for individuals and $2,600 for families; the maximum allowable for out-of-pocket costs (meaning deductible plus any other cost sharing) was $6,550 for individuals and $13,100 for families. In all cases, preventive services are not counted toward the deductible, and the amounts paid toward the deductible are based on in-network costs, not out-of-network costs, just as with any other type of PPO. The maximum deductible amounts for HDHPs are the same as the maximum amount of out-of-pocket spending allowed under the ACA for all insured health plans, and fall within the coverage requirements for a bronze-level plan.

A **CDHP** is an HDHP combined with a pretax savings account. A pretax account set up as part of an employer group health benefits plan is referred to as a health reimbursement account (HRA), and a pretax account applied to individual coverage is referred to as a health savings account (HSA). While they have differences, the overall concept is the same for both types of accounts.

In a CDHP, qualified healthcare costs (except preventive care) are typically paid first from the pretax account; when that is exhausted, any additional costs up to the deductible are paid out-of-pocket by the member (this gap is sometimes referred to as a bridge or a doughnuthole). The Internal Revenue Service (IRS) also defines what is considered a qualified medical cost, but it is similar to what would be considered a medical cost in any coverage plan. To be paid from an HRA or HSA, costs must have been incurred while the account existed. A simplistic schematic of a CDHP appears in **FIGURE 6.2**.

Point-of-Service Plans

POS plans combine features of HMOs and traditional insurance plans, but are similar to PPOs in some ways. In a POS plan, members may choose which system to use at the point at which they obtain the service. For example, if a member uses his/her PCP and otherwise complies with the HMO authorization system, minimal cost sharing is required. If the member chooses to self-refer or otherwise not to use the HMO system to receive services, the POS plan still provides benefits coverage but

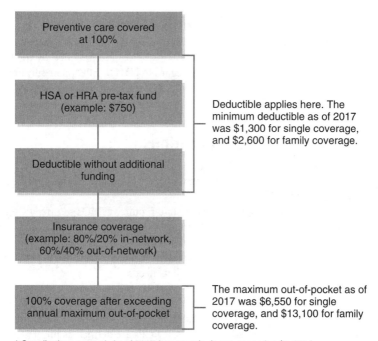

FIGURE 6.2 Example of Basic Construct of a CDHP
© P. R. Kongstvedt.

with higher levels of cost sharing, including a higher deductible and coinsurance instead of a copayment.

POS plans are typically based on HMOs, but even then there are two common forms they can take. The first is a POS plan with two options for cost sharing: (1) minimal cost sharing if the member chooses to stay within the HMO system and (2) significantly higher levels of cost sharing if the member chooses to go outside the HMO system. The difference between coverage for in-network services and out-of-network services is usually in the range of 30%–40%.

The second type of POS plan is a triple-option plan in which there is minimal cost sharing when the HMO system is used, but there is also an option to use a PPO that is part of the plan, so the amount of cost sharing will be higher than when the HMO is used, but more closely follows typical PPO benefits design. In other words, cost sharing in this middle tier is less than the amount of cost sharing required for using providers who are not in either the HMO or PPO network. The differences between coverage for HMO in-network services, PPO in-network services, and out-of-network services are usually approximately 20% between the HMO level and the PPO level, and from 40% to 50% between the HMO and out-of-network levels.

While they were initially popular, POS plans have become less common in recent years because their costs are often higher than either PPOs (with more cost sharing) or HMOs (with more controls).

Exclusive Provider Organizations

Exclusive Provider Organizations (EPOs) are similar to PPOs except benefits coverage is available only when nonemergency services are provided by the EPO's network providers, which is similar in that regard to HMOs. EPOs are really benefits design products offered by commercial payers that use their existing HMO or PPO networks, or based on rental networks in the case of some self-funded plans.

Health Maintenance Organizations

HMOs are unique in many ways. To begin with, HMOs are licensed differently than are health insurers. Insurers are licensed by states, while states issue a Certificate of Authority (COA) to HMOs.

Except for emergency care or when a state requires HMOs to offer POS benefits, benefits coverage in an HMO *only* applies when services are provided by the HMO's providers in compliance with the HMO's authorization policies and procedures. Exceptions may be made on occasion when the HMO authorizes benefits for non-network services based on specific medical needs.

The majority of HMOs also manage utilization and quality to a greater degree than do PPOs. In most HMOs, members must access nonemergency care by going through their PCPs. Members must go first to their PCP for medical care; any other services must then be authorized by their PCP. PCPs are defined as physicians specializing in family medicine, internal medicine, and pediatrics. Women can access their obstetrician/gynecologist (OB/Gyn) directly—direct access to OB/Gyns for women is required under the ACA but was allowed by HMOs even prior to the ACA's passage—but most HMOs still require them to choose a PCP. The exception to the use of the PCP as a "gatekeeper" is the so-called "open-access" HMO, which is really a type of EPO that uses an HMO license.

Benefits obtained through the HMO are almost always significantly more generous than those found in any other type of health plan. Payment for nonemergency services received from non-HMO providers is the responsibility of the subscriber, not the HMO, unless they have been preauthorized by the HMO. Financial penalties incurred by contracted providers who fail to obtain proper authorization are the responsibility of the provider, who may not bill the subscriber for any fees not paid by the HMO (this is also common with other types of payers such as PPOs).

Traditional HMOs are generally defined by how they contract with network physicians, and currently fall into two broad categories: open panel and closed panel. These terms are no longer as widely used as in the past, but are still helpful for understanding the different types of HMOs. A third category, the true network model, was once used for certain contracting situations involving very large medical groups, but is not a particularly specific term now. HMOs often combine or mix different model types in the same market, though usually not all types at the same time. With a few exceptions, HMOs contract directly with hospitals and other facilities on a direct basis.

Open-Panel HMOs

In an open-panel HMO, private physicians and other professional providers are independent contractors who see HMO members in their own offices or facilities. Physicians in the network typically contract with more than one competing health plan and see non-HMO patients as well. A variety of payment mechanisms may be used in an open-panel HMO. The total number of providers in an open-panel plan is larger than that in a closed-panel plan but usually smaller than that in a PPO. Members must choose a PCP, but may change PCPs at certain times, but only if the new PCP has the capacity to accept new patients.

Open-panel plans fall into two broad categories: **independent practice associations (IPAs)**, which are the most common type of HMO, and direct contract models, which are the second most common type. Although the terms IPA and direct contract model are often used synonymously, the two models are distinct.

In an IPA model, an IPA, which is a legal entity, contracts with private physicians (both PCPs and specialists) for purposes of then contracting with HMOs or other payers. The HMO in turn contracts with the IPA and pays it a negotiated capitation amount. The IPA may pay the physicians through capitation or use another payment mechanism, such as a fee-for-service scheme. The providers are at risk under this model in that if medical costs exceed the capitation amount, the IPA receives no additional funds from the HMO and must accordingly adjust its payments to the providers. Most IPAs purchase reinsurance to protect themselves financially, and some HMOs provide a similar type of protection from high costs as part of the overall contract. Finally, the scope of what IPAs do varies, with some IPAs focusing mostly on payment terms, and others taking on many routine HMO functions involving medical management and the like.

In a direct contract model, the HMO contracts directly with the providers; there is no intervening entity such as an IPA. The HMO pays the providers directly and performs all related management tasks.

Closed-Panel Plans

Unlike physicians in an open-panel plan, physicians in a closed-panel plan either are members of a single large medical group or are employed by the HMO. The total number of providers in a closed-panel plan is by far the smallest of any model type. Members usually do not have to choose a single PCP but may see any PCP in the HMO, though they may be asked to choose a primary facility to ensure continuity of care. When specialty care is appropriate, referrals are made to specialists who are also in the HMO to the extent the HMO has specialty physicians. Even closed-panel HMOs also contract with independent specialists to provide care to members who require services that the HMO does not itself provide.

Closed-panel plans fall into two broad categories: group model and staff model. In a group model plan, the HMO contracts with a single medical group to provide services to members. The HMO pays the group a negotiated capitation amount, and the group in turn pays the individual physicians through a combination of salary and risk/reward incentives. The group is responsible for its own governance, and the physicians are either partners in the group or employed by the group as associates. The group is at risk in that if the costs of the group exceed the capitation amount, physician compensation is less—although the HMO generally provides stop-loss reinsurance to the group to protect it from catastrophic cost overruns. Closed-panel HMOs also contract with private physicians to provide services that the HMO's physicians do not provide.

Several types of group model HMOs exist. In one type, the HMO and medical group are distinct entities that operate as if they were partners. The largest and best-known example of this type of group model HMO is Kaiser Permanente; the HMO is the Kaiser Foundation Health Plan, and the medical groups are the Permanente Medical Groups (there are different groups for each of Kaiser's regions). In another type of group model HMO, the medical group established the HMO. An example of this type of HMO is the Geisinger Health Plan, a large and successful HMO established by the Geisinger Clinic in Danville, Pennsylvania.

Some medical groups exist primarily on paper and operate strictly as cost pass-through vehicles for the HMO; that is, the costs are simply passed from the medical group to the HMO, and the group does not actually bear any risk for medical expenses. This arrangement resembles a staff model plan.

In a staff model plan, the HMO directly employs its physicians. In some cases, the physicians are employed by a medical group, but it functions like a staff-based organization. Physicians receive a salary, and there is an incentive plan of some sort. The HMO has full responsibility for the management of all activities. Staff model plans run by HMOs all but died out by the late 1990s, but have reappeared in products offered by large integrated healthcare delivery systems (IDS) with a large numbers of employed physicians.

True Network Model HMOs

The term "network model" is often used to refer to an open-panel plan, but it has also been used to refer to a model in which the HMO contracts with several large multispecialty medical groups for services. The groups receive payment under a capitation arrangement, and they in turn pay the physicians under a variety of mechanisms. The groups operate relatively independently and are best thought of as a variant of the IPA model. The phrase "true" network model is no longer commonly used.

Mixed-Model HMOs

Nothing in this world is pure and simple, and HMOs—like all types of payer organizations—are no exception. Many HMOs have adopted several model types, even in the same market, to attract as many members as possible and capture additional market share. And even large closed panel HMOs typically contract with independent physicians for some services. Mixed-model HMOs may offer the different models in the same products, or the models may operate independently of each other in different products.

Third-Party Administrators

TPAs refer to companies that administer benefits plans on behalf of a self-funded employer. Technically, they are not "insured," but are employee welfare benefits plans operated by an employer. They are not shown back in Figure 6.1 because self-funded plans typically mimic the benefits designs of the other types of payers described above. Many self-funded plans are administered by large payers such as BCBS plans, or large commercial insurance companies. But some are administered by multiple smaller TPAs that only do specific things such as process claims, handle utilization management, or rent access to PPO provider networks; even though all are TPAs, the term TPA is typically reserved for a company that processes claims.

Self-funded plans are not regulated by states and not subject to state benefits mandates or premium taxes. However, many states require TPAs to be licensed, but with limited and narrow requirements unrelated to those for licensed health insurers and HMOs.

▶ Provider-Owned or Sponsored Health Plans

The last major topic in this chapter is a brief discussion about health plans that are owned or sponsored providers, typically hospitals and health systems (which we will refer to from now on simply as hospital-owned). In a few notable cases, a plan is owned or sponsored by a large medical group, but this section focuses only on hospital-owned plans.

There are certainly many examples of successful hospital-owned health plans, but there are more examples of unsuccessful ones. Some of the reasons for this are related to challenges unique to a health plan being owned by a hospital, while others are common challenges in the payer industry.

What follows in the rest of this section are some of those reasons, beginning with some overall realities and challenges of the payer industry, followed by factors unique to hospital ownership.

All of the challenges and factors discussed in this section are much more likely to be found in new or growing hospital-owned health plans. To be sure, none of the challenges and factors that follow happen in all circumstances, and all may be overcome and successfully managed, but nevertheless exist at least in potential.

Challenges in the Payer Industry to Which Provider-Owned or Sponsored Plans May Be at Significant Risk

There are a few common financial and operational challenges that can affect health plans, particularly smaller non-national plans including provider-owned or sponsored health plans. Only four of them are briefly described here.

Undercapitalization

Health insurance is heavily leveraged, meaning the effects of profits and losses are magnified beyond those of a simple investment. A plan must have far more than the minimally required assets to operate safely, as discussed next, and it does not take a lot of financial losses for a small plan to deplete its capital to the level at which the state declares the plan impaired.

Capital must be used for many operational needs as well. Sales and marketing costs are high even well before any impact on enrollment, and even higher enrollment levels take quite a while to generate a positive return on that investment. Information technology (IT) in the payer industry is substantially different than that used in hospitals, and it represents a high cost in software licensing and equipment leasing, as well as training investments in IT personnel.

Statutory Reserves or Statutory Capital

A form of undercapitalization, statutory capital refers to the minimum level of capital that health plans must maintain in unused reserves on its insured (but not self-funded) business. Statutory capital cannot be used for operations. The dollar amount required depends on the number of insured members and the amount of financial risk. Each state has its own requirements, though most are similar to each other. Plans that fall below the required amount of statutory reserves are declared impaired by the Department of Insurance in the state in which it operates, and will soon be gone.

Statutory reserves are above any amount that the plan knows it will pay out in claims or use for operational purposes or used for routine investments. It is determined under special accounting standards that include only cash or cash-like assets, and cannot include (or are severely limited) assets that are normally included on a company's balance sheet; for example, property, IT systems, equipment, depreciating assets, deferred income, and the like.

⁰As a plan grows, so does its required statutory reserve level. Other than investments by parent companies (e.g., the hospital-owner) or a few other specific types of capital contributions, the primary source for this money comes from earning a positive financial margin. But making a profit is no easy matter. To make things even more difficult, the ACA places strict limits on how much profit or surplus an insurer can make or keep, through strict MLR limits, meaning the percentage of premium that must be used to pay medical claims. The ACA also prohibits an insurer from trying to subsidize losses from medical costs in future premiums.

Incorrect and Insufficient IBNR Calculations

A financial calculation of particular importance to health plans is called "Incurred But Not Reported," or IBNR. It is the amount of money that must be reserved for medical services that have been provided, but for which claims have not yet been received by the plan. Insufficient IBNR calculations are one of the most common problems incurred by new or growing health plans.

The simplest way to think about it is that medical care is provided all of the time but it takes time for any claims to be submitted. Claims may also be submitted by members, who tend to wait until they can send in a batch of them. Emergency care or covered out-of-network care also typically results in late claims.

If a plan's financial managers are not thoroughly familiar with how to compute an IBNR, it is nearly inevitable that it will be done dangerously wrong. One of the most common mistakes is to just add up the claims that came in for the month, and assume it represents the entire claims liability for that month. Another common mistake is related to rapid growth, as described next. Experienced financial managers know how properly to use lag tables (beyond the scope of this chapter) and when to be conservative with IBNR.

---

0 These accounting standards are known as Statutory Accounting Principles (SAP), which are not the same as the more familiar Generally Accepted Accounting Principles (GAAP).

Rapid Growth

All business must grow to thrive or even survive. But growth can be too rapid; think dandelions or cancer. Rapid growth in a small health plan quickly overwhelms everything: IT systems; accounting, IBNR, and statutory reserves calculations; member and provider services; provider payment. Everything. It creates claims processing backlogs that also result in duplicate payments, payment for care provided to members no longer covered by the plan, and so forth.

Challenges Unique to Hospital-Owned Health Plans

There are challenges unique to hospital-owned health plans, particularly new or growing ones. In many cases, these challenges amplify those facing health plans in general, meaning each is not exactly unique, but nevertheless arise because a hospital owns or sponsors the health plan. They are all interrelated and usually do not occur in isolation.

Misaligned Motives and Measures

Many hospitals decide to get into the health plan business to fill beds and increase utilization of their ambulatory and diagnostic facility services. These goals and motives may not be voiced, but if they exist, they will result in substantial challenges to running a successful health plan. While the hospital's goals may focus on increasing utilization, the health plan's goal is exactly the opposite.

At the most fundamental level, executives and managers will strive to meet their goals throughout the organization, not just at the top. But starting at the top, most hospital chief executive officers (CEOs) achieve compensation increases and bonuses for achieving volume and growth, as are many or most executives and managers throughout the hospital system. Managers rewarded for growing volume and profitable revenue for a clinical service will do just that, and the hospital's owned health plan is just another source of revenue; either that or a huge irritant threatening the manager's bonus. In most cases, cooperation will be less than enthusiastic, particularly when hospital executives and managers know that the plan must use only the hospital's services. This can bleed over into pricing concessions as well.

The existence of a large number of hospital-employed physicians can make this problem better or worse: Worse if physician compensation is based on productivity, meaning high utilization; and worse if physicians have no option for where they direct patients for services; Better if strong physician leadership is heavily involved with the health plan.

Underestimating the Value of Typical Health Plan Operations, Policies, and Procedures

The most common expression of this is a desire to "cut out the middleman." Even hearing that phrase should lead a health plan executive to sound Red Alert. It typically comes packaged with one or more of the other challenges identified in this section.

Common sense should clarify that if it were really that easy to successfully run a health plan, and at lower cost as well, then *somebody* would have done it; but pretty much every new venture that claims to have cracked this nut eventually flames out or else converts to more conventional views of health plan operations.

Health plans do things for reasons, even if that is not easy to understand from the outside. Existing plans are as reluctant as any industry to waste time and effort performing meaningless tasks that drive up their costs and irritate members and providers. But if those things do not get done, trouble follows and sometimes that trouble is fatal.

Said another way, a hospital cannot "cut out the middleman," but can only try to replace him. And if the hospital-owned plan is not a better middleman than those it is competing against, that is not a formula for success. Even if a hospital-owned plan does things right, it still faces a problem of economies of scale, particularly in IT. Standards continually change, and it takes a lot of investment to keep up. Automation can help to control costs, but it takes time to transition to that and have it work right; even then the savings will be less than those achieved by an automated competitor with 20 times the number of members.

Bringing in executives and managers with substantial successful experience in the payer industry can help deal with this, but only if they have proper system, IT, and managerial support.

Adverse Selection; and Thinking Patients, Not Members

This is a particular challenge for hospital-owned health plans. Adverse selection simply means that people who sign up for the hospital-owned health plan may be doing so because they are sick, and may have had services from the hospital already. People with medical conditions will be more concerned with the actual medical care than the coverage or the premium cost.

Hospital-owned health plans make this substantially worse when they think of plan enrollees as patients, not members. This is natural because those working in hospitals, and healthcare providers in particular, are in the business of caring for patients. But it undercuts the obvious need that any plan needs more members than patients in order to fund its medical costs. Focusing, even subconsciously on patients and on those individuals who they frequently see as patients, is a way to ensure that a hospital-owed health plan will experience adverse selection.

As noted in the introduction to this final section, all of these challenges can be overcome or avoided, as seen in the many examples of successful and long-standing hospital-owned health plans *and* successful overall hospital systems. But overcoming or avoiding these challenges does not happen by itself. It requires some fundamental reorienting of the system, skill, perseverance, and sufficient capital.

Brief Chapter Summary

Any understanding of health insurance and managed care requires a basic understanding of how coverage is accessed, what the basic components of coverage are, and the type of health plan structure providing and administering those benefits. But no matter which type of health plan or payer is involved, the sources and components change only in their specifics; they are always present regardless of any other features.

The means for providing and managing healthcare benefits coverage exist on an ever-evolving landscape of plan types with mutating definitions and operational structures. Even so, the traditional terms such as HMO and PPO retain considerable utility, including stability in the overall aspects of their operations. This characteristic should be looked on not as a hindrance toward understanding but as a mark of the exciting and dynamic nature of the industry.

Questions for Review and Discussion

1. Are health benefits plans and payers the same thing? Identify and discuss circumstances under which these two terms mean the same and when they do not.
2. Where does the money come from to pay for healthcare goods and services?
3. What are the key differences between and among the different types for payer organizations, and what makes these differences important?
4. Are there any real risks for health systems in "cutting out the middle-man" and becoming both the payer and provider of care?

Note

1. At the time this is being written, Republicans have controlled both houses of Congress as well as the Administration for the past 9 months. However, despite long-standing promises to "repeal and replace" the ACA, this has not happened, though certain elements of the ACA have not been funded. How this will continue to play out is unknown. But because the ACA is the law of the land at the time of writing, it is discussed here as appropriate.

CHAPTER 7

Reimbursement: Following the Money

James Gillespie, Kendall Cortelyou-Ward, Reid Oetjen, and Timothy Rotarius

CHAPTER OBJECTIVES

- To explain the ongoing evolution of healthcare reimbursement systems.
- To examine the shift in payment approaches from fee-for-volume to fee-for-value.
- To investigate the increasing role of the innovative bundled payments models.
- To review selective reimbursement effects arising out of the *Patient Protection and Affordable Care Act* (PPACA).

KEY TERMS

Activity-based costing (ABC)
Bundled payments
Center for Medicare and Medicaid Innovation (CMMI)

Patient Protection and Affordable Care Act (PPACA)
Third-party Payers

▶ Following the Money

In many industries, such as manufacturing, retail, hospitality, and real estate, gross sales are seen as a valid financial measure from which to assess the financial prospects of a specific firm. However, healthcare delivery organizations would be ill-advised to draw financial conclusions from gross sales (which are called gross charges in health care).

In non-healthcare industries, firms begin with gross sales and then subtract returns, cost of goods sold, and all other expenses to derive net income. In these non-healthcare industries, gross sales are calculated by multiplying each individual sale by the sales price. In fact, firms purposefully create a specific combination of "sales price per unique item multiplied by the sales volume of each unique item" and then use that pattern of "price × volume" to create competitive strategies.

Assuming a constant volume of sales, when a firm raises the sales price per item, the firm receives higher gross sales. Thus, using this oversimplified example, gross sales is a proxy measure of success as firms compare themselves with other firms in their industry. Since non-healthcare firms do not have to contend with **third-party payers** or with giving away products for which the customer does not have to pay, gross sales can be legitimately used as a proxy for financial success.

However, in the healthcare delivery industry, gross charges (i.e., gross sales) have very little to do with assessing the financial viability of a firm. Although gross charges in the healthcare industry are calculated similarly to gross sales in non-healthcare industries, healthcare firms end up giving away much of their gross sales in the form of contractual allowances, charity care, and bad debt (Note: these three accounts are collectively known as "deductions from gross charges").

Thus, a more appropriate method to measure financial success for healthcare delivery organizations is net charges, which represents gross charges minus deductions. In other words, net charges are the amount that a healthcare firm can reasonably expect to collect in the form of reimbursements from third-party payers and self-pay patients.

This chapter discusses the broad concept of reimbursements, including the evolution of payment practices from the early beginnings of fee-for-service to today's complicated reimbursement systems based on algorithms created to link payments to quality outcomes. Several key payment innovations (Gillespie & Privitera, 2018) will be examined, including hospital insurance, the "Blues", Kaiser Permanente, diagnosis-related groups (DRGs) classification, cost plus pricing, Medicare Cost Plus (MCP), resource-based relative value scale (RBRVS), and **activity-based costing (ABC)**.

The evolution of payment practices will be tracked from the beginning of inpatient fee-for-service to the current value-based care initiative. This covers the progression from simple fee-for-service through early "hospitalization" insurance, the expansion of insurance for both for-profits and non-for-profits to cover nonhospital care, and other approaches, including the development and refinement of DRGs.

Throughout the chapter, the bundled payment (BP) model is featured, both as a crucially important reimbursement approach on its own and also as a harbinger of the shift from fee-for-volume to fee-for-value reimbursement models.

▶ Introduction to a Changing Landscape: Volume to Value

Third-party reimbursement has traditionally been the linchpin in healthcare financing. The term "third-party" refers to the situation in which a payer entity (e.g., government, insurance company, or self-insured employer) becomes involved in paying for treatment received by a patient. In other words, rather than the patient being responsible for the treatment bill, a third-party payer assumes a large share of the treatment bill.

In a traditional episode of care, the patient is treated by multiple providers (i.e., primary care physicians, secondary care physicians, acute care hospital, rehabilitation hospital, nursing home, and so on). These separate treatment encounters resulted in a highly fragmented total care episode that had minimal coordination between providers. In addition, traditionally, each provider was paid on a separate fee-for-service basis by third-party payers. In other words, each provider was paid for the specific service they rendered to the patient, with more services resulting in higher payments to the providers. The fee-for-service model did not incentivize clinicians to focus on the patient's care beyond the point of discharge or to communicate and coordinate care with post-acute care providers.

Third-party payers often made the majority of payments to the individual providers of care. Traditionally, these third-party payers were focused on paying for an individual treatment event, with little or no examination into the relationship between treatment quality and payment amount. Separately reimbursing for services provided during an episode of care creates a financial incentive to increase the volume services, which not only increases costs, but has the potential to negatively impact outcomes.

A trend has begun in reimbursement to move away from fee-for-volume toward fee-for-value (Greeter, 2016). Providers are increasingly incentivized to deliver higher quality care at lower costs, thus resulting in higher value for each dollar of reimbursement (McClellan & Leavitt, 2016). Together, the BP and bundled payment network (BPN) represent a key innovation in this fundamental transition to a new method of healthcare reimbursement.

The **Center for Medicare and Medicaid Innovation (CMMI)** initiated the **Bundled Payments** for Care Improvement (BPCI) initiative in 2011 to encourage healthcare organizations and clinicians to improve quality and reduce cost both during the patient's hospital stay and post-discharge. See **TABLE 7.1** for a stylized total knee replacement example of how a BPCI approach can save payer's money because, rather than making disaggregated payments to multiple clinicians, there is one all-inclusive payment, which incentivizes providers to reduce costs.

TABLE 7.1 Total Knee Replacement with BPCI

Normal Multiple Payments System	Bundled Payments for Care Improvement	Savings to Payer
Consultation and Diagnosis ($750) Anesthesia ($1,300) Surgery ($13,750) Implants ($4,975) Operating Room and Recovering Room ($2,600) Physical Therapy ($4,800) Total of $28,175	Capitated (flat rate) payment of $25,000	$28,175 − $25,000 = $3,175

CMMI originated from the **Patient Protection and Affordable Care Act (PPACA)** of 2010 as a cost-cutting and quality-enhancement tool. CMMI was designed to support creativity and experimentation regarding alternative payment and delivery models that focus on decreasing costs, improving quality, and increasing efficiencies (Gillespie & Privitera, 2018). CMMI was the foundation for Medicare's episode-based bundled payment programs (Centers for Medicare & Medicaid Services, 2016a).

Leveraging alternative payment models, the Center for Medicare and Medicaid Services (CMS) accelerated the shift from fee-for-service to value-based care and payment to improve quality and care (Centers for Medicare and Medicaid Services, 2016b). CMS oversees approximately 56 million beneficiaries via Medicare and 73 million beneficiaries via Medicaid (Pizzo & Ryan, 2016). Medicare is a leading predictor of change for payment models. Generally, whenever Medicare makes changes to its payment schemes, all other third-party payers follow suit.

Many states have incorporated BP processes into their Medicaid programs. BPs are a potentially transformative change to the traditional fee-for-service incentives that, some say, encourage increased and often excessive utilization. BPCI shifts the first dollar risk of episodes to providers, whether they are health systems, hospitals, physician groups, home health agencies, or post-acute facilities such as nursing homes (Gillespie & Privitera, 2018).

▶ A History of Hospital Care Reimbursement Models

During the first 150 years of U.S. history, the home was the primary site of medical care for private citizens. Medical services were provided on a strictly out-of-pocket basis, which was a form of fee-for-service in which the patient paid the entire bill without any assistance from third parties (i.e., employers, government, or an insurance plan). The first hospitals in the United States primarily served these purposes: (a) sheltering the elderly, the dying, orphans, and vagrants, (b) isolating those with contagious diseases, and (c) imprisoning the mentally ill (who were assumed to present a danger to the public).

In 1887, there were only about 150 hospitals in the entire United States (Sade, 2008). However, by 1923, the number of hospitals in the United States had grown to approximately 6,850 (Sade, 2008). Along with this explosive growth in hospitals, the United States became more industrialized and urbanized. At the same time, the dawn of hospital insurance began to transform the hospital from the initial purposes stated earlier to a site of care ranging from primary care up through tertiary care.

From 1940 to 1986, the proportion of the U.S. population holding hospital insurance increased from 9% to 74% (Stevens, 1989). Hospital insurance fundamentally altered hospital utilization patterns, serving to substantially increase patient volume. The new payment process helped to: (a) finance investment in facilities, equipment, and personnel and (b) reduce bad debt; thus, providing greater confidence that bills incurred would be paid.

Blue Cross Blue Shield

The advent of the "Blues" was another pivotal development. Blue Cross began in the late 1920s as a prepaid insurance plan providing coverage for hospital services for various employee groups around the Dallas, Texas area and then expanded nationwide. The initial plan cost was $6 per year and guaranteed teachers coverage for 21 days of hospital care. Within a decade, the number of covered lives in the Blue Cross plan increased from 1,300 enrollees to more than 3 million subscribers (Blue Cross Blue Shield Association). In 1939, the American Hospital Association (2016) adopted the Blue Cross symbol as the emblem for health insurance plans complying with certain standards. This sharing of the Blue Cross emblem lasted until the early 1970s.

In the late 1930s in California, Blue Shield developed insurance plans for employers in order to provide coverage for medical services for their employees. The initiative grew rapidly and spread nationally. In 1982, Blue Cross merged with Blue Shield to create the *Blue Cross and Blue Shield Association*, an umbrella association composed of several large insurance companies (Blue Cross Blue Shield Association).

Kaiser Permanente

Another key juncture in the history of hospitals and insurance was initiated in the 1930s and 1940s by Henry J. Kaiser, a California-based general contractor (Silver, 1994). Kaiser developed arrangements to cover the medical expenses for his employees, principally construction, shipyard, and steel mill workers. The key innovation was Kaiser's development of a prepaid group medical practice for the workers that was led by Dr. Sidney Garfield. This new arrangement resulted in the embedding of healthcare delivery within the insurance company, itself. This created a vertically integrated provider–payer entity, which was referred to as the "California vertically integrated delivery model" (Slaughter, 2000).

From the beginning, Kaiser Permanente placed strong emphasis on preventive medicine and provided many educational opportunities for members to learn about their own health. In 1945, enrollment was expanded, making the general public eligible for what eventually became known as the Kaiser Permanente Health Plan. Kaiser Permanente remains a vertically integrated organization including the nonprofit Kaiser Foundation Health Plan and Hospitals and the Permanente Medical Groups. Kaiser is the health insurer, and it contracts exclusively with the Permanente medical group for the provision of healthcare services for its covered lives, achieving several vertical integration-related efficiencies (McHugh, Aiken, Eckenhoff, & Burns, 2016).

Fee-for-Service Payment Models

DRG is a classification system that was designed to cluster inpatient episodes of care into clinically related treatment occurrences. DRGs were developed in the 1970s by a group of Yale University researchers. The primary goal of the DRG system was to identify and organize the products and services hospitals provided (Bibbins, 2007). See **FIGURE 7.1** for a high-level view of the DRG trajectory from patient presenting problem to claim reimbursement. The process involves many complications and nuances not depicted here, but in order to maximize payments, the provider's basic goals are to correctly diagnose patients, accurately code per DRG, and then properly submit claims.

A grouping program assigns DRGs based on a variety of complex factors, including age, comorbidities, discharge status, ICD (International Classification of

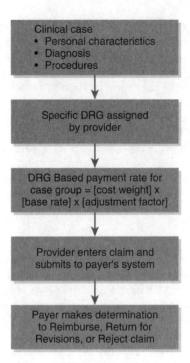

FIGURE 7.1 Diagnosis-Related Group (DRG) Flow Diagram

Diseases) diagnoses, modal complications, procedures, and gender. It was designed as a replacement for cost-based reimbursement. The DRG classification system has been in use by Medicare since 1983 to determine the reimbursement amounts paid to hospitals for these treatment categories. The fundamental logic is that patients within the same category are clinically similar and can be expected to consume approximately the same quantity of hospital resources (2017).

Cost-Plus Pricing

Cost plus pricing is another approach for determining the final price of a healthcare product or service by adding a specific dollar amount to the base unit cost (Wichmann & Clark, 2006). Cost-plus pricing functions as a "markup." In order to yield accurate cost estimates, the hospital must keep accurate track of cost breakdowns. There are three fundamental stages to arriving at the cost-plus price. First, the hospital has to determine the unit cost. The total cost is the addition of fixed costs (which do not vary with the number of units) and variable costs (which increase as the number of units increases). The total cost is then divided by the total number of units of the product or service to arrive at the "per unit cost."

Second, the hospital has to determine the acceptable rate of return to provide both reinvestment funds and profit (Ge & Anderson, 2016). This rate of return will drive the markup decision and the ultimate unit cost. Sometimes, the acceptable rate of return is determined purely internally by factoring in production costs and competitive dynamics. Other times, the acceptable rate of return is a product of negotiations between the provider and the third-party payer. Third, the markup is applied to the unit cost as a normative (i.e., flat) amount or as a set percentage basis to arrive to the final price to be billed the third-party payer and patient.

The primary advantage of cost-plus pricing is that it can provide stability in the marketplace. However, it is often criticized as adding inflationary pressures and not being attentive enough to quality of treatment provided. In many ways, cost-plus pricing is viewed as inconsistent with the general trend to shift away from fee-for-volume toward fee-for-value models. Indeed, in theory, paying hospitals and physicians based on customary and reasonable charges can incentivize increases in the normative baseline of expenses and serve as a disincentive to control costs.

Yet, there are examples when the application of cost-plus models can be disinflationary and, thus, help to control costs. For example, an increasingly popular reimbursement approach is MCP. With MCP, the payer does not utilize the PPO network to calculate charges covered, and the frequency of direct haggling over price with providers is minimized. Instead, the payer sets charges at a multiple of what Medicare allows for a specific procedure in that particular market.

Insurance plans utilizing MCP often set this charge level at 120% of what Medicare allows, but the percentage multiple can be higher or lower depending on market dynamics. In addition, the percentage multiple can change based on factors such as inpatient, hospital outpatient, and ambulatory care. Medicare often achieves large volume discounts given its significant market power, so pegging prices to Medicare exerts a downward pressure on prices.

In these cases, it is the payer rather than the provider that is driving the use of cost-plus pricing. In addition to stability, another potential benefit of cost plus pricing is transparency. If the input costs are clearly and comprehensively delineated, with full visibility for patients, payers, and providers, there can be high confidence in and transparency of both the unit cost and the selected markup.

Resource-Based Relative Value Scale (RBRVS)

The RBRVS was developed in the 1980s by a multidisciplinary research team from Harvard University (Gao, 2018). The RBRVS payment system assigns various "relative values" to the services performed by a physician or other clinician. These "relative" portion of these values derive from different geographic regions of the United States (because a medical procedure performed in an urban area is costlier than the same procedure performed in a rural setting). The resulting assigned value is then multiplied by a fixed conversion factor to determine the final amount of payment. The conversion factor is reviewed annually to determine if adjustments are warranted.

RBRVS calculates prices based on three separate variables: physician work (54%), practice expense (41%), and professional liability insurance (5%). Physician work is a function of judgment, mental effort, physical effort, stress, technical skill, and time to perform the procedure (Latimer, Douwe, Yntema, & Causino, 1992). The exact mix and the weights of the three separate variables are updated annually to take into account changes in best medical practices. Practice expense relates to the general overhead expense of the practice and represents the cost to operate the medical practice. This specific category is then further delineated into facility (hospital) and non-facility (office) expenses. The professional liability insurance portion, which includes estimates of the relative medical malpractice risk of each

Current Procedural Terminology (CPT) code, focuses on the cost of malpractice insurance for both the individual physician and the overall practice.

In the early 1990s, Medicare began using RBRVS, as did many other public and private payers. Providers submit their reimbursement bills using approximately 10,000 different CPT codes. The codes and the new values are developed by the CPT Editorial Panel and by the AMA/Specialty Society Relative Value Scale Update Committee (RUC), respectively.

CMS, via the RUC, reviews and updates the entire scale at least once every 5 years. Over time, the scale has moved away from historical costs and payment rates toward resource-based methodology. The two primary data sources utilized for review and updating are the Clinical Practice Expert Panel (CPEP) survey and the Socioeconomic Monitoring System (SMS). The core principle of RBRVS is that reimbursement for provider services should vary according to the costs expended in providing those services, and the goal is to make the payment system more efficient and stable.

Activity-Based Costing (ABC)

ABC grew out of the U.S. manufacturing sector in the 1970s and 1980s (Fito, Llobet, & Cuguero, 2018). ABC was a reaction to the perceived deficiencies of traditional cost management systems, which sometimes struggled to accurately determine the precise costs of production and related services. This struggle was exacerbated as automation led to increased relative proportion of indirect costs (e.g., depreciation of the new automated assembly line machine) to direct costs (e.g., labor by assembly line workers). Relative to traditional accounting, ABC allocated more indirect and overhead costs into direct costs.

One goal of ABC is to avoid the issue of inaccuracy when indirect costs are allocated equally across products and services that do not actually contribute equally to those indirect or overhead costs. It is critical for organization to eliminate inaccuracy so that they do not base decisions on inaccurate data in cases of multiple products. ABC focuses on finding "cause and effect" relationships, which then allows objective allocation of the specific costs of each activity to the extent that the products or services actually use or receive that activity.

When performed properly, ABC can help identify high overhead costs per unit, allowing for subsequent management action to reduce those costs and/or to increase the price on those products and services. ABC also has the advantage of being able to account for the cost of not doing a particular activity (e.g., the opportunity cost of project delays attributable to waiting on a needed piece of equipment).

Although ABC originated in the manufacturing sector, ABC quickly spread to other sectors, including healthcare organizations. For example, hospitals quickly embraced the benefits of ABC because the nature of hospital care delivery inherently involves complex cost-accounting issues. For ABC, the cost driver is the variable that serves as the catalyst for the expenses of a particular activity. For example, the cost of intensive care nurses can be allocated to each patient based upon the length of the patient stay. In this case, nursing is the cost, and duration of stay is the driver. In the hospital context, if behavioral incentives are attached to cost reduction activities, ABC can help foster cost consciousness among executives and clinicians, particularly in terms of lowering overhead costs.

Some healthcare organizations utilize a modification to the ABC model called time-driven activity-based costing (TDABC) (Keel, Savage, Rafiq, & Mazzocato, 2017). TDABC measures (a) the cost of each resource used in a specific episode of care and (b) the amount of time a patient spends with each resource. TDABC involves the following steps: (1) select the episode of care, medical condition, or patient population to be costed, (2) define the chain of delivery of the selected episode of care, (3) create process maps of each activity (i.e., step) in this delivery chain, (4) estimate the time consumed by each step in the process, (5) estimate the cost of supplying the needed patient care resources to ensure quality outcomes, (6) determine the capacity of each resource and estimate its capacity cost rate, and (7) calculate the final total cost of patient care.

Bundled Payments as a Reimbursement Paradigm

BPs include (a) packaging a full set of services related to a single episode of care into one predetermined payment and (b) contracting with participants to take on financial risk and liability for patient care (Gillespie & Privitera, 2018). Bundling aims to fundamentally alter financial incentives (Press, Rajkumar, & Conway, 2016). The use of BPs has proliferated in the United States. The first hospitals to bear risk under BPCI occurred in October 2013, and the program has already grown to more than $10 billion in Medicare spending.

Over 1,300 hospitals in the United States participate in the voluntary BPCI program, and several other BP initiatives are developed by providers and commercial health plans or employers. New BP programs are expected to cover heart attack, cardiac bypass surgery services, and cardiac rehabilitation. There is an increasing use of mandatory BP systems. CMS now has a mandatory BP program for comprehensive care for joint replacement called Comprehensive Care for Joint Replacement (CJR), which covers one-third of all hip and knee replacements.

The concept of BPs is not new. The model was originally introduced in the early 1980s with the introduction of DRGs covering acute inpatient episodes (Mehrotra & Hussey, 2015). The BP is a previously established set payment for a specific episode of care. It provides incentives for greater care coordination, with the ultimate goal being decreased costs, with an expectation that enhanced quality will follow.

Health systems, hospitals, and physicians assume the downside financial risk for delivering care for a set price for a set time period for a single care episode. The healthcare organization bears the burden of developing the component elements needed to be effective across the care continuum. These component elements include data analytics, evidence-based diagnosis and treatment, patient-centered care delivery models, and risk stratification. The BPCI aims to shift the reimbursement model from fee-for-service to a value-based one (Gillespie & Privitera, 2018).

Regarding BP models, a single episode of care is defined as all the healthcare services related to treating a specific condition or conducting a particular procedure. The timeframe for a BP extends from patient admission to the point of hospital discharge. Substantial variation exists across bundles in terms of length of coverage and services covered. The duration of the bundle after hospitalization can be either 30, 60, or 90 days.

Some BPs even cover the "prehabilitation" period designed to improve the patient's health and strength prior to surgery (Pizzo & Ryan, 2016). There are 48 different medical and surgical conditions, incorporating 179 DRGs, covered by BPCI (Hardin, Kilian, & Murphy, 2017). BPCI provides a multitude of options based on factors such as which baseline to utilize, which indexing scheme to use, and whether payments are prospective or retrospective. However, all of the options are based fundamentally on the ideas of risk sharing and shifting from volume to value.

BP programs can include potentially complex episodes such as coronary artery bypass grafting, hip and femur fractures, major bowel procedures, stroke, and total joint arthroplasty. A new BP model involving complex episodes is the Oncology Care Model (OCM) initiated by CMMI.

BP models work best if there are established, definitive criteria for intervention and treatment, as well as restricted patient and physician discretion. BPs are most applicable when the episode of care has a clear starting and ending points. Surgeries are the typical category in the BP model because they consist of distinct, definable steps in the care process and contain clear pathways across the continuum (Gillespie & Privitera, 2018).

Of the 48 episodes of care in the BPCI program, the most popular are asthma, bronchitis, chronic obstructive pulmonary disease, congestive heart failure, major joint replacement, and simple pneumonia and respiratory infections. The most relevant conditions for the elderly include acute myocardial infarction, cardiac valve replacement, chronic obstructive pulmonary disease, congestive heart failure, major joint replacement of the lower extremity, pneumonia, sepsis, and stroke (Kivlahan, Orlowski, Pearce, Walradt, Baker, & Kirch, 2016). Although a few providers decided to assume risk for all 48 conditions, most participants assume risk for three or less clinical episodes.

There are certain medical conditions that are not amenable to distinctive care intervention pathways. Episodes are excluded if they involve exceptionally high-cost procedures such as transplantation surgeries. Also, certain medical conditions are particularly complex and severe, with comorbid conditions that increase the probability for adverse events and readmissions. The inclusion of complex comorbidities in an episode of care can generate unexpected and unmanageable costs (Gillespie & Privitera, 2018).

Healthcare organizations participating in BPs have accountability for the full spectrum of care, including acute and post-acute periods. If the BP delivers final total expenditures less than CMS's target price, CMS awards that positive amount to the provider. However, if final expenditures exceed CMS's target price, the provider must rebate that amount to CMS. Thus, BPs provide both an upside and downside risk to healthcare organizations.

▶ Federal Legislation Affecting Reimbursements

Reimbursements for healthcare services come from both third-party payers and self-pay patients. Since the 1960s, the Federal government has been a particularly large third-party payer, primarily through the entitlement programs of Medicare and Medicaid. These programs periodically revamp the entire reimbursement landscape by introducing new payer schemes and mechanisms. And, as has been shown throughout history, when the Federal government makes changes to reimbursement mechanism, the entire private third-party industry soon follows suit.

While the most recent Federal legislation to affect health care is the PPACA of 2010, there is a strong history of Federal laws and acts that have, in their time, completely shifted the reimbursement processes of the Federal government. A commonality between all Federal healthcare reimbursement legislation is that each new law or act was created and implemented in response to the following societal beliefs (Liberman & Rotarius, 1999):

- Everyone is entitled to unlimited access to health care.
- Everyone is entitled to the highest quality of care.
- Individual patients expect this access and quality to be delivered without regard for cost.

A short list of selected Federal legislation that has most impacted healthcare reimbursement includes (Liberman & Rotarius, 1999):

- *Title XVIII of the Social Security Act* (1965), which created the Medicare program.
- *Title XIX of the Social Security Act* (1965), which created the Medicaid program.
- The *Tax Equity and Fiscal Responsibility Act of 1982*, which created DRGs.
- The *Omnibus Budget Reconciliation Act of 1989*, which created the RBRVS.
- The *Federal Balanced Budget Act of 1997*, which required the creation of Ambulatory Payment Classifications (APCs). APCs were implemented in 2000.
- The *Medicare Prescription Drug, Improvement, and Modernization Act of 2003*, which authorized Medicare to cover outpatient prescription drugs beginning in 2006.

As seen by this list, the PPACA is only the latest in a long line of reimbursement-changing federal legislation. Some see the PPACA as the best hope and last opportunity to bring increasing healthcare costs under control.

▶ The Patient Protection and Affordable Care Act (PPACA)

This particular Federal legislation includes a multitude of initiatives, from creating insurance exchanges to raising a myriad of taxes to fund a national healthcare program. Specifically, the PPACA created a template for a coordinated focus on specific and, some suggest, ideologically driven sets of health services changes that, heretofore, have been addressed in (or ignored by) fragmented and relatively unregulated and localized healthcare delivery systems that vary across the expanse of America (Rotarius, Liberman, & Perez, 2011).

The PPACA was signed into law in March 2010. As a whole, PPACA consists of 10 titles. As explained by Rotarius et al. (2011), these titles include:

Title I: Quality, Affordable Health Care for All Americans

This section establishes health insurance exchanges, prohibits insurance companies from denying coverage, creates tax credits, and provides individual and employer penalties for not purchasing health insurance.

Title II: The Role of Public Programs

This section improves Medicaid access, enhances the quality of Medicaid services, offers protections to Alaska Natives and American Indians, and strengthens maternal and child health services through educative and home support programs.

Title III: Improving the Quality and Efficiency of Health Care

This section remodels the payment system by linking payment for Medicare services to healthcare quality, creates pilot programs to encourage the development of new patient care models, while offering rural protections to low-volume hospitals.

Title IV: Prevention of Chronic Disease and Improving Public Health

This section outlines innovations in disease prevention and public health strategies, while delineating efforts to create healthier communities through the use of grants and various wellness and prevention programs.

Title V: Health Care Workforce

The purpose of this section is to improve the quality of the healthcare workforce to lead to an improvement in both access and quality of care, particularly for low-income, minority, underserved, and uninsured groups.

Title VI: Transparency and Program Integrity

This section increases transparency regarding (a) physician ownership of medical practices and (b) nursing home quality. Significant efforts are to be expended increasing the integrity of various programs including Medicaid, Medicare, and the Children's Health Insurance Program.

Title VII: Improving Access to Innovative Medical Therapies

This section focuses on the price competition of biologics and seeks to ensure more affordable medicines for children and underserved groups.

Title VIII: Community Living Assistance Services and Supports Act (CLASS)

This section focuses exclusively on establishing a national voluntary insurance program for purchasing community living assistance services and support.

Title IX: Revenue Provisions

This section delineates (a) the various taxes that will be levied in health care, including the excise tax on high-cost plans, and (b) the imposition of annual taxes on pharmaceutical and insurance companies.

Title X: Strengthening Quality, Affordable Health Care for All Americans

This section makes retroactive amendments to Title I through Title IX. These amendments include efforts to improve the earlier titles and also to appease members of the legislative body so that their votes can be assured.

These 10 titles cover a broad range of Federal- and state-level action items. While reimbursement issues are present in each of the various titles, for illustration purposes, the following 10 examples of specific PPACA provisions that affect reimbursements are presented (Rotarius et al., 2011).

1. Physicians treating newly eligible Medicaid patients shall be paid 100% of their Medicare rates (HealthCare.gov., Section 1202). *Explanation*: This provision represents an increase in reimbursements because Medicare payments are typically higher than Medicaid payments.

2. Hospitals are granted a "presumptive eligibility period" when they are permitted to make presumptive eligibility determinations for all Medicaid-eligible persons. Hospitals do not have to be concerned with being paid for a presumed Medicaid-eligible patient even if the patient ultimately is determined not to be covered by Medicaid (HealthCare. gov., Section 2202). *Explanation*: This provision represents an increase in reimbursements since hospitals will not have to pay back amounts billed to patients who are subsequently deemed not to have a Medicaid coverage.

3. Medicaid payments will be prohibited for certain healthcare-acquired conditions (HealthCare.gov., Section 2702). *Explanation*: This provision represents a decrease in reimbursements for patients who acquire a disease pursuant to receiving treatment.

4. Differential Medicare payments will be made depending on the quality of care that is offered (HealthCare.gov., Section 3007). *Explanation*: This provision generally represents a decrease in reimbursements until the specific quality goals are attained.

5. Medicare payments will be reduced by 1% for certain hospital-acquired infections (HealthCare.gov., Section 3008). *Explanation*: This provision represents a decrease in reimbursements.

6. Medicare reimbursements will be reduced where preventable readmissions occur (HealthCare.gov., Section 3025). *Explanation*: This provision represents a decrease in reimbursements.

7. Expenses (such as rent and employee wages) for medical groups in different geographic regions are analyzed to account for the difference in expenses in different parts of the country (HealthCare.gov., Section

3012). *Explanation*: The effect of this provision is dependent on geographic location. Some providers will receive less reimbursements, while other providers will see an increase in reimbursements.

8. Medicare will continue to offer bonus payments and increased payments for ground ambulance services (HealthCare.gov., Section 3105). *Explanation*: This provision represents an increase in reimbursements.

9. Certified nurse midwives will be paid 100% of the fee schedule for physicians for the same services offered by physicians (HealthCare.gov., Section 3114). *Explanation*: This provision represents an increase in reimbursements.

10. A 10% bonus will be paid out by Medicare to primary care physicians and general surgeons practicing in shortage areas (HealthCare.gov., Section 5405). *Explanation*: This provision represents an increase in reimbursements.

Overall, these 10 selective examples illustrate the magnitude and importance of the PPACA as a vehicle to effect changes to the reimbursement process utilized by the Federal government.

▶ The Future of the PPACA

While Federal legislation is always subject to the idealism of the constituents of whomever is voted into the current congressional delegation, the PPACA, from its inception in 2010 through most of 2017, remained virtually undisturbed. However, in late 2017, a key provision of the PPACA, the individual mandate, was repealed by the *Tax Cuts and Jobs Act of 2017*.

This repeal of the individual mandate effectively removes the tax penalty for those individuals who choose to not buy health insurance. According to the Congressional Budget Office (Repealing the Individual Health Insurance Mandate, 2017), this repeal will result in 4 million U.S. residents choosing to voluntarily forego their health insurance coverage in 2019. According to the Joint Commission on Taxation (Repealing the Individual Health Insurance Mandate, 2017), this repeal will save the Federal government (acting as a third-party payer) $338 billion over 10 years. Other long-term effects of this repeal will not be known for years to come.

From a "future reimbursement" perspective, the PPACA is likely to negatively affect reimbursements. The following two examples illustrate how the PPACA has the potential to harmfully affect healthcare providers' reimbursements:

- *Medicare Margins are Sinking*: There is a widening gap between Medicare reimbursements and the actual costs to treat Medicare patients, with Medicare payments expected to cover only 90% of the actual cost of treatment (Dickson, 2017). This widening gap is caused by a number of factors, including: PPACA requirements vis-a-vis expensive information technology systems; a 2% overall reduction in Medicare reimbursements under the Budget Control Act of 2011; and decreases in Medicare disproportionate-share hospital payments.

- *Strict Enforcement of the 60-Day Overpayment Rule*: This PPACA provision requires a provider to return Medicare and Medicaid overpayments within 60 days from which the overpayment is identified. There is considerable interpretive room, however, as to when the 60-day time period begins. To date, enforcement of this provision has been ramping up and there have been several multi-million settlements paid by providers because of violating the 60-day overpayment rule (Wood, 2018). Due to this PPACA enforcement provision, providers should expect Federal audits as a matter of operations, rather than as an exception (Castellucci, 2017).

▶ Conclusion

Financing and reimbursement are crucial components of what hospitals are and how they work. Just as a hospital cannot function without patients, it cannot sustain itself without reimbursements from patients and third-party payers. This chapter began by tracing the history of financing for hospital services. The key innovation in reimbursement was the proliferation of hospital insurance, including the rise of "the Blues" (i.e., Blue Cross and Blue Shield) and the "California vertically integrated delivery model" as exemplified by Kaiser Permanente. Also discussed was the development of important frameworks and models for reimbursement, including ABC, cost-plus pricing, the classification into DRGs, MCP, and RBRVS.

This chapter then shift edits focus to discuss the BP model as a harbinger of reimbursement direction. Episodic-based payments are here to stay as a fundamental element of alternative payment models being advanced by CMS and private payers. Particularly, with regard to episodes of care characterized by high cost, high variance, and high volume, the BP model will continue to be one of the primary mechanisms for CMS to share treatment risk with providers. CMS continues to advance both voluntary and mandatory alternative payment models, with the goal of prioritizing value over utilization. As such, the outpatient environment will continue to experience growth, while the inpatient situation experiences stagnation as public and private payers continue seeking to push care into lower acuity, lower cost settings (Gillespie & Privitera, 2018).

Following the money will increasingly mean staying on the "value" pathway, of which the BP model is and should continue to be an essential element. Providers will continue to evolve in response to increasing expectations for data-driven outcomes, greater efficiency, improved quality, and lower costs. During this exciting era in hospital financing, these expectations will be impacted by and have an impact on reimbursement policies and systems, including the BP model, as "following the money" will provide more challenges and opportunities than ever.

Brief Chapter Summary

Hospitals are paid—that is, reimbursed for providing services —through third-party payers and to a very limited extent by self-pay patients. The simple fee-for-service practices of earlier years long ago gave way to complicated reimbursement systems such that third-party reimbursement is now central in healthcare financing.

The advent of hospital insurance fundamentally altered hospital utilization patterns and served to substantially increase patient volume. Not-for-profit insurers, such as Blue Cross/Blue Shield, evolved alongside insurance programs offered by commercial insurance companies. Through Medicare and Medicaid, the government essentially became the largest third-party payer. These programs regularly alter the reimbursement landscape by introducing new payer schemes and mechanisms.

New laws and rules reflect the social beliefs that everyone is entitled to health care of the highest quality. Through its various titles and provisions, the PPACA has had a significant impact on reimbursement for healthcare services.

A hospital cannot function without patients, and a hospital cannot sustain itself without reimbursement from patients but largely from third-party payers. "Following the money" in health care promises to be a continuing challenge of perhaps increasing complexity.

Questions for Review and Discussion

1. What are bundled payments and why are they increasingly important in healthcare finance?
2. Identify how the fee-for-volume model differs from the fee-for-value model.
3. Describe the Center for Medicare and Medicaid Services (CMS) and the role it plays in hospital financing.
4. What is the diagnosis-related groups (DRGs) classification and why is it so important in reimbursement?
5. Explain activity-based costing (ABC) and provide an example.
6. Explain how the resource-based relative value scale (RBRVS) works.
7. From a reimbursement perspective, how important is the Patient Protection and Affordable Care Act (PPACA)?

References

AHIMA. (2017). The evolution of DRGs. *Journal of AHIMA, 88*(6), 48–51.

American Hospital Association. (2016, January 19). Medicare's bundled payment initiatives: Considerations for providers. *AHA Issue Brief.*

Bibbins, B. (2007). Medicare severity diagnosis related groups (MS-DRGs) set stage for documentation and coding paradigm shifts. *Journal of Health Care Compliance, 9*(6), 11–61.

Blue Cross Blue Shield Association. Health insurance from invention to innovation: A history of the Blue Cross and Blue Shield companies. Retrieved from https://www.bcbs.com/learn/bcbs-blog /health-insurance-invention-innovation-history-blue-cross-and-blue-shield-companies

Castellucci, M. (2017). Unintended outcomes: Readmission program might be harming patients. *Modern Healthcare, 47,* 16.

Centers for Medicare & Medicaid Services. (2016a, October 20). About the CMS Innovation Center. Retrieved from https://innovation.cms.gov/About/index.html

Centers for Medicare and Medicaid Services. (2016b, July 25). Notice of proposed rulemaking for bundled payment models for high-quality, coordinated cardiac and hip fracture care.

Congressional Budget Office. (2017, November). Repealing the individual health insurance mandate: An updated estimate from the Congressional Budget Office and the Joint Commission on taxation. Retrieved from https://www.cbo.gov/publication/53300

Dickson, V. (2017). Slumping Medicare margins put hospitals on precarious cliff. *Modern Healthcare, 47,* 18.

Fito, M., Llobet, J., & Cuguero, N. (2018). The activity-based costing model trajectory: A path of lights and shadows. *Intangible Capital, 14*(1), 146–161.

Gao, Y. (2018, January 1). Committee representation and Medicare reimbursements—an examination of the resource-based relative value scale. *Health Services Research.* doi:10.1111/1475-6773.12857.

Ge, B., & Anderson, G. (2016). U.S. hospitals are still using chargemaster markups to maximize revenues. *Health Affairs, 35*(9), 1658–1664.

Gillespie, J., & Privitera, G. (2018). Bringing patient incentives into the bundled payments model: Making reimbursement more patient-centric financially. *International Journal of Healthcare Management*. doi: 10.1080/20479700.2018.1425276.

Greeter, A. (2016). Navigating the shift to value-based reimbursement: How fast is too fast, and how slow is too slow? *Journal of Medical Practice Management, 31*(6), 340–343.

Hardin, L., Kilian, A., & Murphy, E. (2017). Bundled payments for care improvement: Preparing for the medical diagnosis-related groups. *Journal of Nursing Administration, 47*(6), 313–319.

HealthCare.gov. The Affordable Care Act, Section 1202. Retrieved from https://www.healthcare.gov/

HealthCare.gov. The Affordable Care Act, Section 2202. Retrieved from https://www.healthcare.gov/

HealthCare.gov. The Affordable Care Act, Section 2702. Retrieved from https://www.healthcare.gov/

HealthCare.gov. The Affordable Care Act, Section 3007. Retrieved from https://www.healthcare.gov/

HealthCare.gov. The Affordable Care Act, Section 3008. Retrieved from https://www.healthcare.gov/

HealthCare.gov. The Affordable Care Act, Section 3025. Retrieved from https://www.healthcare.gov/

HealthCare.gov. The Affordable Care Act, Section 3012. Retrieved from https://www.healthcare.gov/

HealthCare.gov. The Affordable Care Act, Section 3105. Retrieved from https://www.healthcare.gov/

HealthCare.gov. The Affordable Care Act, Section 3114. Retrieved from https://www.healthcare.gov/

HealthCare.gov. The Affordable Care Act, Section 5405. Retrieved from https://www.healthcare.gov/

Keel, G., Savage, C., Rafiq, M., & Mazzocato, P. (2017). Review: Time-driven activity-based costing in health care: A systematic review of the literature. *Health Policy, 121*, 755–763.

Kivlahan, C., Orlowski, J., Pearce, J., Walradt, J., Baker, M., & Kirch, D. (2016). Taking risk: Early results from teaching hospitals participation in the Center for Medicare and Medicaid innovation bundled payments for care improvement initiative. *Academic Medicine, 91*(7), 936–942.

Latimer, E., Douwe, B., Yntema, D., & Causino, N. (1992). Physician and practice characteristics, frequency of performance, and the resource-based relative value scale. *Medical Care, 11*, NS40.

Liberman, A., & Rotarius, T. (1999). Managed care evolution—Where did it come from and where is it going? *The Health Care Manager, 18*(2), 50–57.

McClellan, M., & Leavitt, M. (2016). Competencies and tools to shift payments from volume to value. *JAMA, 316*(16), 1655–1656.

McHugh, M., Aiken, L., Eckenhoff, M., & Burns, L. (2016). Achieving Kaiser Permanente quality. *Health Care Management Review, 41*(3), 178–188.

Mehrotra, A., & Hussey, P. (2015). Including physicians in bundled hospital care payments: Time to revisit an old idea? *JAMA, 313*, 1907–1908.

Pizzo, J., & Ryan, D. (2016). Four strategies for succeeding with bundled payments. *Journal of Healthcare Management, 61*(5), 314–318.

Press, M., Rajkumar, R., & Conway, P. (2016). Medicare's new bundled payments: Design, strategy, and evolution. *JAMA, 315*(2), 131–132.

Rotarius, T., Liberman, A., & Perez, B. (2011). The effects of national health care reform on local businesses—Part I: The law and its applicability. *The Health Care Manager, 31*(1), 3–24.

Sade, R. (2008). Foundational ethics of the health care system: The moral and practical superiority of free market reforms. *The Journal of Medicine Philosophy, 3*(5), 461–497.

Silver, G. (1994). A model for national health care: The history of Kaiser Permanente. *Bulletin of the History of Medicine, 68*(1), 180–181.

Slaughter, J. (2000). Kaiser Permanente: Integrating around a care delivery model. *Journal of Ambulatory Care Management, 23*(3), 39.

Stevens, R. (1989). *In sickness and in wealth: American hospitals in the twentieth century*. New York, NY: Basic Books.

Wichmann, R., & Clark, R. (2006). Developing a defensible pricing strategy. *Healthcare Financial Management, 60*(10), 72–80.

Wood, I. (2018, January). 60-Day overpayment rule update. *Reimbursement Advisor, 33*(5), 11–13.

CHAPTER 8

Is Bigger Better? Hospitals and "Merger Mania"

Cristian H. Lieneck

CHAPTER OBJECTIVES

- Examine mergers and other healthcare organizational combinations from two perspectives: the macro outlook of organizational executives and boards of trustees, and the micro outlook in terms of effects on organizational managers and staff.
- Discuss and differentiate among multiple partnership levels of healthcare organizations.
- Review internal and external organizational market characteristics that may influence strategic management decisions involving healthcare partnerships.
- List advantages and disadvantages related to each partnership level for the healthcare organization.
- Discuss examples of present-day partnerships and the resulting advantages/disadvantages of such decisions.
- Address the effects of organizational combinations on the people in the lower organizational levels, specifically the first- and second-line managers and the rank-and-file employees.

KEY TERMS

Acquisition
Agreement
Completed staff work
Joint operating agreement
Joint venture

Merger
Partnership
Span of control
Unity of command

▶ Introduction

O nce very much a cottage industry consisting of many scattered providers, health care has become an industry essentially dominated by large organizations and multi-institutional systems. Various organizational combinations continue to occur, especially in the form of mergers, affiliations, and the creation and expansion of healthcare systems.

This chapter examines healthcare organizational combinations as viewed from two perspectives: first, from the overall perspective, that of top management (boards of trustees and the community) and second, from the position of the management at the point of care and their all-important employees—the people who are responsible for the actual delivery of healthcare services. Everyone at every organizational level in health care and everyone who utilizes healthcare services in any way maybe affected in some way when organizations combine to form new and usually bigger organizations.

▶ The Macro View: Mergers, Affiliations, and Other Organizational Combinations

Healthcare partnerships, including the strategic decisions involving both mergers and acquisitions are often newsworthy topics. As healthcare policy (and related reimbursement models) drives organizational practice, the collaboration within and between healthcare business entities continues to result in an increase of both informal and formal **partnership** agreements. Such collaborative partnerships may take on a variety of levels and involve a multitude of healthcare organizational types consisting of multiple characteristics intended to provide quality care for the patient while also meeting the requirements of a highly regulated industry.

The provision of health services is a team effort. Such collaboration is necessary both within a healthcare organization (among medical providers and their associated team members), and between organizations. Often, two heads are better than one, while economies of scale arise and benefit such collaboration or partnership among healthcare entities. A significant influencer of such partnerships in the industry continues to be that of the external environment—which consists of many known, and especially unknown, variables for the healthcare leader to continuously prepare, analyze, and manage to ensure current and future organizational success.

Hospitals and their '**merger** mania' activities of recent years are typically one of the most transparent and newsworthy organizational partnerships, most likely owing to their vast size, organizational benefits to multiple stakeholders, and other related socio-economic contributions to the local community. Announcements, Internet news articles, and especially healthcare management listservs and related blogs have well-documented such collaborations between and among such organizations, especially within the most recent 2–5 years. For instance, Kaufman Hall cites hospital system partnerships continuing an upward climb, up 8% compared with the first quarter in 2016 (Kaufman Hall, 2017). Specific examples of large systems conducting these activities include (Healthcare Finance, 2017):

- McLaren Health Care in Michigan working to acquire the Indiana health plan MDWise
- Anthem acquiring Florida's Medicare Advantage plan HealthSun

- A merger of ZirMed and Navicure revenue cycle organizations
- New Jersey's Cooper University Healthcare, Lourdes Health, and St. Francis Medical Center merger
- Presence Health merger with Ascension's **joint venture** system
- HCA Gulf Cost Division acquiring four Tenant hospitals in the Houston market

It is important to note that these partnership examples, as with many others, are not simply hospital-to-hospital mergers, acquisitions, etc. They are among a variety of healthcare delivery organizations, as well as healthcare service support entities (Saunders, 2017). Organizations conducting partnership activities in the healthcare field are also of a variety of organizational size, for-profit/not-for-profit status, as well as primary mission in the healthcare field.

Types of Healthcare Partnerships

Healthcare organizations may engage in various forms and levels of partnerships with other external organizations. These relationships can range from a loose affiliation category of basic partnerships, to that of total affiliation with another organizational entity (Saunders, 2017). Finnerty (2016) summarizes the various models of partnerships on a continuum, increasing in affiliation level and related control of organizational equity. This continuum is demonstrated in Appendix A, adapted with practical healthcare partnership examples for further explanation.

As presented by Finnerty (2016), the affiliation level among organizations in the healthcare field is easily delineated by loose, medium, and strong ordinal categories (Finnerty, 2016). Therefore, affiliation levels A, B, and C (from Appendix A) are primarily a measure of partnership as pertained to the transfer of organizational net worth (or net assets, equity) on the balance sheet, as well as overall strategic board control of the organization. Moving from a loose **agreement** between two organizations (which could simply be a de facto patient referral protocol) to a true merger or **acquisition** that involves the procurement of another organization's assets and total management control takeover, the level of partnership among healthcare organizations is all a result of a multitude of variables—with an intent that the end result of the partnership will leave both organizations in a better market position than prior to their collaboration efforts (Neprash, Chernew, & McWilliams, 2017; Schmitt, 2017).

Level 'A' Partnerships

Clinical agreements (both written and unwritten) to full or partial clinical service line integration are often conducted in regular, everyday organizational workflow activities. A physician's referral patterns may fall into this category, based upon the needs of the patient and the specialty provider or other ancillary medical services required to treat the patient, beyond that offered at the current treating organization. While anti-kickback laws ensure no remuneration among entities occurs, there are benefits to standard protocols and best practice referral patterns between physician practice organizations and other healthcare entities. A group purchasing organization (GPO) works to integrate several administrative practices (offering of healthcare and other insurance products for employees, supply purchase, and ordering discount opportunities, etc.) and even allows for this level of partnership to benefit administrative practices, in addition to clinical opportunities.

Level 'B' Partnerships

The joint venture has been a common partnership practice in healthcare, in the past as well as most recently. In this arrangement, two organizations retain their organizational identity yet create a new organization that is designed to accomplish a specific task. It would be local, regional, or even broader in scope and mission. The key to identifying what type of joint venture is present primarily focuses on the retention of each organization's primary management rights and control over their section of the joint agreement. While a contribution of net wealth (equity) is required to fund the joint venture by each organization, this value may not be a 50/50 perfect split. As a result, the level of management control over the newly created organization (established by the joint venture) often (but not always) follows that of the net equity distribution. Such partnership is most beneficial when two parties need something to further their organizational mission, the other is able to offer what is valued, and specific capital funding is required to ensure the future success of the joint initiative.

Level 'C' Partnerships

The final level of partnerships concerns that of majority control over another organization. While initially this may sound aggressive or similar to a potential "hostile takeover" of another organization, often times this practice is agreed upon by both organizations involved, with one organization's leadership bowing out to allow for another's to step-in and take majority control. Such majority does not have to be a full 100% control agreement, but as long as at least 50.1% of the management and board control is conveyed to a single entity, a majority control does exist.

While the joint venture from 50.1% to 99% and a full merger or acquisition-type partnership under the Level C category do possess similar characteristics regarding management control, the **joint operating agreement** remains unique in that an effort to prevent any type of monopolistic effect works to ensure (but not promise) organizational characteristics and individual entity agreed-upon contributions to the partnership from the beginning of the agreement. For instance, the Accountable Care Organization (ACO) could easily fall within this partnership category, as it simply is a contract among a variety of medical providers and other healthcare organizations (both large and small), across the continuum of care for a Medicare patient receiving care from an ACO. Each specialty provider, hospital, service-support entity, etc. is treating that patient as if they were a single entity, accountable for that patient's outcome collectively. Because of this characteristic—and the follow-on pay-for-performance (P4P) reimbursement methodology for the various ACO models, the joint operating agreement allows for multiple organizations to participate as one, contributing only their specialized services for the ACO patient. In the end, this partnership agreement should allow for the P4P Medicare reimbursement payment to be distributed equitably among those partners' organizations that cared for the patient and ensured an optimal care outcome.

Strategic Management of Healthcare Partnerships

Change happens; this is important to remember as healthcare leaders work to ensure the ongoing and future success of their organizations. Organizational directives (mission, vision, values, and goals), as well as the internal and external environment, continuously drive leadership decisions, practices, and expectations of organizational performance. These activities involve organizational partnerships, often multiple partnerships at a variety of levels, to effectively treat patients.

Internal environmental analysis (strengths and weaknesses) are often the driving force for partnerships of self-identified organizational needs, wants, and sometimes even "wish-we-had" leadership requests. If a physician pain management practice is experiencing a significant increase in patient referrals related to addiction management (versus simply pain management or control), then it may be decided to create a partnership agreement to ensure this increased volume of patients being referred are treated for their addictions accordingly. Likewise, a rural hospital may be experiencing an ongoing shortage of board-certified emergency room physicians and may therefore partner with a physician staffing firm or organization to contractually staff their emergency room, controlling for the potential liability otherwise to occur without that provider ready to receive emergency room patients.

External environmental analyses (opportunities and threats) are often a primary driving force to create healthcare organizational partnerships at a variety of levels. Probably one of the most contributing variables, healthcare policy, remains the primary reason why organizations are collaborating and both formally and informally partnering to navigate their healthcare policies and procedures at the local, state, and especially federal echelons. The Patient Protection and Affordable Care Act, or ACA (2010) and now the Medicare Access and CHIP Reauthorization Act (2015) remain the federal legislation driving healthcare reimbursement and P4P initiatives for Medicare beneficiaries, as well as health insurance product access for many Americans. As a result, healthcare organizations are constantly planning, reacting, and often times partnering to accomplish initiatives set by these laws and the patient populations they serve (Schmitt, 2017). While the specific strategic management of any type of healthcare organization in the current-day policy environment is beyond the scope of this chapter, the strategy decisions of healthcare leaders in today's healthcare management and related legislative environment should most likely involve partnerships at a variety of levels among a multitude of healthcare organizations. The policies were created to enhance accountable care among a multitude of providers, interoperability of electronic health records (EHRs), and especially patient outcome responsibility—so naturally the management of any organization should now involve collaboration within and beyond its four walls of operation, requiring effective partnerships with other organizations to meet the ACA's objectives.

Partnership Example Case #1—Whole-Hospital Joint Venture

St. David's HealthCare System is now one of the largest health systems in Texas, currently operating more than 100 facilities (hospitals and physician practices, among other facilities) in the Central Texas area, and beyond. It is one of the two main health systems in Austin, Texas, and has even been bestowed the prestigious Malcolm Baldrige National Quality Award in 2014—a stellar achievement (Alpert, Hsi, & Jacobson, 2017). The hospital system operates under a management service contract (agreement) with two not-for-profit foundations at the local level, and the system continues to provide a significant amount of charitable community benefit to the Central Texas region. However, current organizational structure was not always as secure for this large, award-winning health system.

Initially, a church-affiliated hospital housed in a Victorian residence in downtown Austin more than 100 years ago, the facility provided care to the community and maintained its not-for-profit status as a sole organization since 1938. However, due to industry dynamics and financial stressors, the hospital leaders decided to enter into a joint venture with Hospital Corporation of America (HCA) in 1996. HCA is a for-profit hospital network based out of Nashville, TN. In 1998, St. David's Health Care System was audited by the Internal Revenue Service (IRS) and it was determined that the hospital system had ceded a majority of its net worth to HCA in the joint venture transaction, and it was determined by the IRS that the organization no longer participated in the original charitable purposes, now being majority controlled by the for-profit entity (National Institute for Standards and Technology (NIST)).

Questioned in the decision by the IRS were St. David's ongoing charitable activities and benefits to the local and regional communities. While the umbrella of a for-profit hospital network organization offered significant financial securities desperately needed by St. David's prior to the joint venture decision, the ability to secure the organization's not-for-profit status was continuously questioned and tied-up in legal battles. The IRS contended that the for-profit hospital network now possessed majority control over St. David's, while the hospital continued to appeal case findings, stating that its primary charity care purpose continued to remain, as well as other important management and control details entered as restricted covenants in the joint venture agreement with HCA; for example, St. David's retained the right to terminate their hospital CEO, the right to appoint a chairman of the board, and to even dissolve the joint venture relationship with HCA if the tax exemption status were over in question or threatened by the hospital's relationship with HCA (Clark-Madison, 2003).

In *St. David's Health Care System v. The United States*, the United States Court of Appeals, Fifth Circuit, vacated the district court's summary judgment in favor of St. David's and related rulings that granted it tax-exempt status previously. As a result, the three-judge panel made the decision that St. David's would be considered a for-profit entity in the end, even with a 50/50 equity split with the HCA organization, because (Clark-Madison, 2003; Woods, 2004):

1. A 50% governing control will only allow St. David's to veto decisions regarding charity care with its parent corporation, HCA.
2. A long-term management contract existed with HCA, which involved remuneration to the parent company based upon revenues resulting from the joint venture.
3. The limited restricted covenants in the joint venture agreement (previously mentioned) were discussed as extreme steps that St. David's would have to take to dissolve the entire partnership—which was perceived by the court as highly unlikely to occur by the hospital.

St. David's sought a joint venture partnership with a larger hospital network firm in order to continue to provide the same level of care to the Austin community, while also remaining solvent as a not-for-profit healthcare organization in a highly competitive (and growing) Central Texas healthcare industry. Such advantages of the joint venture may have seemed beneficial to the hospital's leadership team at the time while also working to ensure other management and control criteria were included in the agreement in order to preserve the hospital's ability to maintain its primary charity care purpose to the community and exit the agreement if necessary. The Fifth Circuit court's findings provide valuable insight into joint ventures regarding not-for-profit organizations entering into 50%/50% equity agreements with for-profit corporations while also stressing the importance of governing control over the organization and the ability to enforce such actions in a plausible manner. St. David's HealthCare Network continues to provide exceptional healthcare to the Central Texas region and pursue extensive charity care initiatives, and is still managed by HCA and maintains a for-profit tax status.

Partnership Case #2—Joint Operating Agreement

It is normal for the execution of many strategic plans to require a significant amount of time. This may be because of the ongoing scrutiny and formative evaluation of the implementation steps as they progress, or just simply because of the extent of the size of the organizations involved. The University of North Carolina (UNC) Health Care system is an extensive not-for-profit health system based in Chapel Hill and includes all of UNC Hospitals, related provider networks, the UNC School of Medicine, as well as nine affiliate hospitals and hospital systems across North Carolina. Additionally, the Charlotte-based not-for-profit Carolinas HealthCare system is a highly integrated health system with more than 900 locations across the southeast United States. Both organizations initially announced in 2017 that they were working on entering into a joint operation agreement for the near future, specifically deemed as a "marriage" by UNC Health Care CEO Bill Roper (Martin, 2017). Such partnership agreement, if pursued to maturation and approved by the Federal Trade Commission, would have represented one of the largest not-for-profit partnerships to occur in the entire United States.

Characteristic of a joint operating agreement, both organizations planned on continued operations in a similar manner, while under the umbrella of a new organization, to be named. Assets for both organizations would not be pooled, as with a typical merger or acquisition. Instead, all finance and operation-related decisions were to be centralized for both organizations and they will continue to operate as separate facilities. By pursuing a joint operating agreement, many of the legal challenges and obstacles would be avoided, while also ensuring that the new, rebranded not-for-profit entity prohibited any one organization from establishing a monopoly of the region's healthcare market.

Many mergers and acquisitions have been occurring with each of the two large healthcare systems for some time. However, at this much larger level, the two were simply proposing a joint operating agreement in the end, with the intent of capitalizing on massive economics of scale benefits (group purchasing agreements, quantity and bulk supply discounts, expanded provider access networks, etc.). A strategic initiative for both not-for-profits was to establish a single, large, homegrown healthcare system that is self-sustainable, therefore not having to rely on any out-of-state hospital corporation. While this partnership plan was significantly larger than usual, ongoing collaboration and teamwork among healthcare entities are certainly needed to increase the value of care delivered across the United States healthcare system. Caution must be heeded to ensure future growing pains and questions of organizational control are not experienced as a result of any joint operating agreement. In the end, some concerns arose from the public and other healthcare shareholders, questioning whether this decision has been made with the ultimate stakeholder in mind—the patient. Such decisions are never easy—and as a result—the two organizations eventually decided to suspend partnership negotiations during the first quarter of 2018 (Roberts & Murawski, 2018).

▶ The Micro View: Adjusting to the Blended Organization*

The Changing Organizational Environment

The more the practice of management changes, the more the essential mission of management remains the same. Management in health care has been experiencing much pressure for change, but the central task of management—*getting things done through people*—remains unchanged. Yet, *how* the central task of management is accomplished is changing at a sometimes-bewildering pace. A considerable amount of change in the fulfillment of the management role is being forced by change in the healthcare organizational environment.

Much of the change that has affected the day-to-day fulfillment of the healthcare management role has come about as healthcare organizations have combined and grown through merger and acquisition. In some instances, hospital mergers have been resisted for years at a time out of community pride. Often logic and common sense dictated that two communities could best respond to the pressures mounting on the hospital system by combining their resources into a merged entity more efficient than either alone. However, their competitive postures regarding each other, a condition not uncommon between hospitals in the same town or in adjoining communities, has precluded agreement to come together and become one as one or both refuse to surrender any part of their individual identity. Some organizations that should logically have been merged with others have held out independently for so long that they failed financially or were forced to close for other reasons. Occasionally some boards of directors have resisted a merger for so long that, when they finally agreed to do so, there was hardly anything to acquire other than debt.

The healthcare environment of recent years has grown increasingly unpredictable and hospitals and other providers have had to adjust, often rapidly, to stay current. As a result, hospitals have become much more than just providers of acute care. They have taken steps to shape themselves to the changing needs of the population and in response to limitations on financial resources. To that extent, a great deal of merger and acquisition activity can be described as owing to the need for organizational adaptation and survival.

Seeing Doom on the Horizon?

Much of the time, reduced staffing is one of the results of mergers involving organizations of all kinds. Often the desire for savings in payroll costs is one of the drivers of a merger. Also, even if reduced staff is not a merger goal, some amount of

---

* Portions of this section were adapted from McConnell, C. R. (2015, April–June). The manager and the merger: Adjusting to functioning in a blended organization. *The Health Care Manager, 34*(2), 166–174.

reduction ordinarily results from the establishment of economies of scale. There-fore, it should come as no surprise that talk of a potential merger immediately gives rise to fears of potential job loss, and the event gets closer to actuality the more intense this fear becomes.

Since an overwhelming number of mergers do indeed result in layoffs of both managers and rank-and-file staff, many employees have good reason to feel uneasy when merger is in the works. To many employees at most organizational levels, impending merger will appear as doom on the horizon—even if the merger will not do away with their positions, at the very least it will most likely change the way they perform their jobs. Additionally, few organizations can realistically extend a "no-layoff" guarantee in advance of a merger. In one specific merger situation, the merging organizations did exactly that—guaranteed no layoffs, pledging there would be no job cuts because of the merger. Management's reasoning was based in part on the knowledge of their normal attrition rate and on the assumption that the merger itself would prompt at least a slight increase in voluntary turnover. The intention was to allow attrition to vacate positions which would then not be filled, and rearrange remaining staff internally to cover areas of need. However, two factors intruded on this plan. First, a long-considered decision to outsource a certain function resulted in the elimination of two positions, and because of timing, the immediate and unalter-able perception was that the two jobs were lost because of the merger. Second, some employees who sought other work during the weeks leading up to the merger were perceived as having been "forced out" by the merger. Thus, management's best inten-tions left employees feeling betrayed and unintended consequences resulted. Better perhaps to avoid the subject of potential layoffs entirely or issue a simple pledge to accomplish the merger with as little impact on employment as possible.

Culture Shock, Corporate Variety

Economic factors invariably loom large in considering mergers or affiliations, but often the issues of whether cultures may assimilate or not are overlooked. Finan-cial and operational issues are usually prominent in considering merger or affil-iation, but frequently there is insufficient consideration given to people issues. Decision-makers are ordinarily utilizing the so-called "hard" data in assessing the worth of a merger situation, and whether consciously or unconsciously, they do not want to risk clouding the situation with people issues that are invariably seen as "soft" and thus arguable.

Corporate cultures must be examined in advance of a merger or affiliation because they can sometimes indicate whether a particular deal will or will not work. However, most mergers are usually undertaken with little or no consideration of corporate culture. It then becomes necessary to attempt to structure a hybrid cul-ture incorporating the elements of the cultures of both parties even though some employees may perceive one culture or the other as dominant. It is more frequently being suggested that healthcare collectives are so focused on increased size that they are no longer appropriately serving people concerns. Cultural change is always dif-ficult, sometimes painful, and invariably much more involved and time-consuming than anyone may expect. Following a merger, it is necessary to create a blended culture, and doing so requires plenty of time and leadership. Even when one organi-zation is so small as to be perceived as totally absorbed by the other, it nevertheless takes time for the remnants of the old culture of the smaller to assimilate.

Merger's Effects on the Manager's Role

Most people experience the need to be in control of their circumstances or to at least feel as though they have some measure of control, but they are aware—often painfully so—that a corporate merger is totally beyond their control. A merger is perceived as bringing a major change that is likely to affect everyone and is especially upsetting because it all lies well beyond their influence. So, people resist; they resist that which they fear and that which they cannot control, often with all the determination they can command. It may well be that such resistance is no more or no less than a person's need to protect themselves from harm.

Management Role Changes

Mergers and affiliations usually result in layoffs, and layoffs often affect managers as much if not more than rank-and-file staff. In many merger situations, management salaries are often a target for considerable savings. Cost savings are often owing to the elimination of supposedly duplicate management. Consider, for example, the merger of Hospital A with Hospital B. Both were small-to-medium acute-care facilities serving a semi-rural population. Not long after the merger was finalized, where once there were two human resource managers, then there was one; where once there were two health information management (medical record) managers, then there was one. Two each of rehabilitation service managers, plant operations managers, general accounting managers, payroll managers, finance directors, and various other managers, in all instances became one. Within a few weeks essentially, half of the two hospitals' combined management team was eliminated. The few related costs that had to be reckoned with as additions, primarily travel between facilities and a few other considerations, were inconsequential compared with the cost of the duplicate management positions that were eliminated.

Except at the highest organizational levels—think chief executive officer, chief operating officer, and very few others—the manager is both a worker and a supervisor of other workers. In other words, except at the highest organizational levels, the manager is both management generalist and functional specialist. However, when a manager's territory is expanded, perhaps essentially doubled (as in the aforementioned Hospital A and Hospital B merger), the manager will find it necessary to become *more* manager and *less* worker. Among the first things to give are often some long-held management concepts, beliefs upon which many of today's managers were educated. Three primary examples are found in sanctioned violations of **unity of command**, dramatic changes in **span of control**, and drastic reductions in *visibility and availability*.

Unity of command is an age-old organizational concept that calls for a straight line of authority down through the organization. That is, for each task to be done or each responsibility to be fulfilled, there is one person responsible; for each group of workers, there is one supervisor; each supervisor or manager reports to one higher manager; and so on. Split-reporting relationships were felt to violate unity of command, as was having multiple individuals responsible for portions of a task, group, or area. In the merged organization, however, unity of command is no longer inviolate; it has given way to expediency and necessity. It is now common, for example, to find a manager with responsibility for a function that serves multiple locations who is partially answerable to managers at the different locations, as though a halfway organizing effort had resulted in a matrix or project-management organization partially overlaying a traditional functional organization.

Span of control refers to the breadth of responsibility that a manager can effectively fulfill and specifically to the number of employees one manager can oversee effectively. An individual manager can effectively supervise only a certain number of workers, with this number rather unscientifically determined by a number of factors. These factors include the manager's knowledge and experience, the amount and nature of the manager's nonsupervisory work, the amount of supervision required by the employees, the variability of the employees' tasks, the overall complexity of the activity, and the physical area over which the employees are distributed. Modern healthcare mergers frequently have the effect of dramatically expanding the "territory" over which a manager must exercise control. About the only flexibility, the manager is able to apply in adjusting is the aforementioned necessity to become less of a worker and more of a manager. However, other things must often give way. For example, some staff problems that might otherwise be noticed and corrected will instead remain unseen until they have grown into bigger problems. Also, the quality with which some important tasks are accomplished can suffer. For example, it is nearly a given that the quality of performance evaluations will suffer, at least in the short-to-intermediate run, when a manager finds that he/she must now do double or triple the previous number of evaluations in the same span of time.

It has long been held important for the manager of a group to maintain a significant level of *visibility and availability* to the group. To a considerable extent, many employees take some level of comfort from the fact of the manager's regular presence; that person is seen as reachable when needed and usable as a resource. Following a merger and reorganization, the surviving manager will have found his/her visibility and availability drastically reduced. Consider the manager who must now supervise staff in two locations several miles apart. Visibility and availability have been cut in half, and more likely reduced even further by travel time and increased meetings away from the department. A myriad of employee relation issues may result by the managers reduced by visibility and availability; such issues become all the more important as the manager experiences reduced exposure in any specific area.

Another common feature of reorganizing as it occurs in today's environment, whether happening relative to merger or affiliation or within the context of "reengineering," is *flattening* of the management structure. Flattening refers to the effects on an organizational chart when layers of management, most particularly those referred to as "middle management," are eliminated; therefore, the chart is literally "flattened." When flattening accompanies the reorganizing that is part of the fallout of a merger, there is some vertical integration of responsibilities occurring as well as the horizontal integration of duties that happens when two comparable management positions become one. The newly constituted management position may acquire additional vertical reporting responsibilities as well as a considerably broader range of departmental responsibilities.

In a split-reporting relationship, it becomes all the more important to practice the concept of **completed staff work** in relating to one's superior. This means that when a problem occurs, one does not simply request assistance and then expect the boss to provide an answer. Rather, it is necessary to research the problem and propose a solution. In other words, it is necessary to make it as easy as possible for the boss to respond by framing the issue in such a way that your manager can either say "yes" or "no" or provide additional direction. The manager of the merged department needs to keep in mind that his/her immediate superior may also be coping with greatly expanded responsibilities.

Overall, the increased scope of the manager in the merger situation brings a number of changes in how the manager functions. The manager's expanded scope necessitates:

- More time spent managing, thus less time spent doing nonmanagerial work;
- More planning and organizing on an ongoing basis;
- Greatly increased need to practice proper delegation, truly empowering employees;
- Increased attention to the priorities among a greater number of responsibilities;
- Improvements in one's ability to use time effectively;
- Constant attention to personal organizing for effectiveness;
- More people to oversee, and this leads to the following issues: more performance appraisals, more disciplinary actions, and more people problems in general.

The Manager Adapts

Generally, the easier parts of organizational change involve processes, methods, procedures, tools, structures, and such. The more difficult parts of change involve human reactions: attitude, commitment or lack thereof, and resistance. It is relatively easy for the manager in the merger to become spread too thin and easily led into trying to do too many things at once. When this occurs, it is frequently the manager's newly expanded staff that suffers from lack of attention. It is necessary to remember that for a significant proportion of the staff, specifically those people who used to report to the other manager, you may be one of the most significant of all causes of resistance: the unknown quantity. A change in department management is guaranteed to be accompanied by uneasiness that becomes reflected in resistance, especially if the incoming manager is a stranger to the surviving staff.

As one's staff increases, so do the potential people problems and so do the number of staff-related duties. With more people to manage comes the need to establish and maintain the all-important one-to-one relationship with more employees. This relationship with each employee is a critical aspect of maintaining one's employees as effective producers, yet the manager in the merger situation is likely to be affected by an increase in non-people concerns as well. In short, in this new situation, the manager will likely have more people to be concerned about with and less time available per employee.

From an individual manager's perspective, three major challenges to productivity are personal disorganization, inadequate planning, and procrastination. Productivity depends on attention to *priorities*. No matter how much work the manager is faced with at any given time, one can do no better than focusing on the single most important task of the day. Since the job will appear as an endless series of demands, it becomes necessary to realize that some demands may never be addressed. One can only ensure that the demands that are never addressed are indeed of low priority.

In many instances, the manager of a merged function will be split between two teams in two locations. This alone makes proper delegation—that is, true empowerment—absolutely essential. With more and more to do, it becomes increasingly obvious that the manager cannot do everything by him/herself, so it is necessary to take the time to educate and properly delegate to get the most effective performance from employees who are capable of expanding their scope. Employee development and managerial delegation take on a new importance, and may include the development of some capability for backing up the manager at each site.

The key to the effective management of people may well lie in the manager's conscientious use of *deadlines and follow-up*. This is in fact a practice which, if faithfully employed until it becomes habit, will improve a manager's effectiveness dramatically. There are two simple parts to this: first, *any task worth assigning is worth a specific deadline*, and second, *never let a deadline pass unanswered without following up*. This practice should be adopted only with a determination to make one's deadlines sufficiently reasonable that staff can respond without reacting to undue pressure that the manager may have created through procrastination or delay. Now, more than ever the manager in the merger situation needs to be proactive, to and exercise control of the job. The manager who assumes a reactive posture in these expanded circumstances will quickly become spread too thin. In the merged organization, it is necessary for the manager to get organized and stay that way.

▶ Conclusion: When the Dust Settles

It was stated earlier that mergers are driven largely by financial issues and other "hard" data, and that all too often the human issues—the "soft" side of the merger—are rather consistently overlooked or afforded too little attention. Too often the focus on organizational growth is accompanied by the failure to encourage the development of the needed culture of operational excellence. There is, however, a strong need for a culture of continuous clinical quality improvement. Without such, as organizations grow and their activities expand, quality problems also expand as a function of size.

Too often a great many of the problems and issues to be faced in truly making one organization out of two or more are never evident to the executives and trustees who decide to merge. Since the executives and trustees operate at a macro level, their view is ordinarily one of being outside looking in, but to the line managers and front-line employees who must do the organization's work, the view is entirely different. Consider again, for example, the merger of Hospital A with Hospital B, two small-to-medium acute-care facilities serving a semi-rural population. These were two provider organizations just a few miles apart, both in the same business providing the same services to the people in overlapping services areas. Several physicians were on staff at both, and a few employees of A worked part-time or per diem at B and vice versa. Externally it looked like a simple merger of two similar organizations. Internally, however, there appeared to be vast differences of two kinds. First were the differences encountered in the *details of task performance*, necessitating the application of extreme unanticipated effort in merging methods, procedures, policies, and practices. This entailed many employee challenges based on "our way" versus "their way." Then, there are the *cultural differences* to be encountered. Hospital B, the larger of the two, had experienced several years of severe financial difficulty and had undergone three significant staff reductions for several years. The culture of B reflected pessimism, insecurity, and defeat. Hospital A (which was smaller) had been fiscally sound right up to the point of the merger and had never experienced a staff reduction in its history. The culture of A, having long reflected optimism, suddenly gave rise to resentment at being "absorbed by the larger" or being "used to save B from bankruptcy."

Whether it is the merger of two small provider organizations into one or the creation of a major healthcare system from a dozen formerly separate organizations, human values must rank high among the governing concerns. If human values are not prominent in forging the merged organization or system, it follows that these values are not likely to be prominent in either the regard for employees or the delivery of service to patients. It is the manager's responsibility to be ever mindful of human values in the provision to people (patients) and through people (employees), during merger/acquisition activities.

Brief Chapter Summary—"Is Bigger Better?"

In today's dynamic healthcare environment, collaborative efforts among healthcare and even non-healthcare organizations are a must. New initiatives, payment models, treatment expectations, and patient outcomes comprise a new normal, involving partnership agreement at a variety of levels, among a variety of organizations. Gone are the days of conducting an internal analysis of your organization's productivity and working to improve only that which lies within the organization's control. Industry-level initiatives, to include P4P, population health, patient outcomes, and effective healthcare delivery models will require collaboration and an increasing integration of healthcare provider efforts. Partnerships, to include mergers and acquisitions, will continue to be common as our industry works to achieve effective integrated delivery of care.

The human side of any merger situation cannot be ignored. Mergers and affiliations and other combinations upset peoples' equilibrium, and it is the people who must be depended upon to make the blended organization function as intended. In most merger situations, there will always be a perceived inequality of participants, with people from one former entity resentful of being "absorbed" by the other entity. It becomes important to be highly mindful of the need to pay serious attention to the time-consuming and sometimes painful process of blending two organizational cultures into one. First-line managers and supervisors, middle managers, and the majority of rank-and-file employees are often far from the minds of those who are planning a merger or affiliation, yet these vital individuals at or near the base of the organizational pyramid can make all the difference in how well the organizational combination does or does not succeed.

Questions for Review and Discussion

1. Identify the three partnership levels of affiliation and describe what differentiates each level with regard to organizational assets and associated risk.
2. Discuss the differences among an agreement, joint venture, and a merger or acquisition.
3. Using the Internet, locate a healthcare organization that fits into each partnership model level of affiliation in Appendix A and discuss why it falls into this category. What specific partnership type is it?

4. What industry and market characteristics make partnership models common in today's healthcare industry? Which partnership type do you believe will become more common as the industry continues to move toward increasing the health of the overall population?

5. You are the group practice administrator of a specialty practice that is considering entering into an ACO with surrounding entities. What specific information would you like to know prior to entering into this type of partnership?

6. Describe the concept of "completed staff work."

7. What is "organizational flattening"? What are its likely effects on both first-line supervisors and middle managers?

8. What are four important factors that figure in the determination of an individual manager's span of control?

9. How do mergers, affiliations, and other organizational combinations contribute to violation of unity of command?

Why is it important to carefully study the individual organizational cultures of two corporate entities that are under consideration for merger into a single entity?

References

Alpert, A., Hsi, H., & Jacobson, M. (2017). Evaluating the role of payment policy in driving vertical integration in the oncology market. *Health Affairs, 36*(4), 680–688.

Clark-Madison, M. (2003). *St David's loses tax case.* Retrieved from https://www.austinchronicle.com/news/2003-11-21/187307/

Finnerty, M. (2016, November 6). *Models for partnership.* Kaufman, Hall & Associates presentation to Navicent Health's strategic committee.

Hall, K. (2017). *Hospital merger and acquisition activity expands in first half of 2016, according to Kaufman Hall analysis.* Retrieved from https://www.kaufmanhall.com/news/hospital-merger-and-acquisition-activity-expands-first-half-2016-according-kaufman-hall

Healthcare Finance. (2017). *Healthcare mergers, acquisitions, and joint ventures in 2017: Running list.* Retrieved from http://www.healthcarefinancenews.com/slideshow/healthcare-mergers-and-acquisitions-2017-running-list?p=16

Martin, M. (2017). *St. David's Health Care System vs. United States: How should a joint venture protect its tax exempt status?* Retrieved from https://www.law.uh.edu/healthlaw/perspectives/HealthPolicy/040409StDavids.html

National Institute for Standards and Technology (NIST). (2017). *Baldrige performance excellence program.* Retrieved from https://www.nist.gov/baldridge/st-davids-healthcare

Neprash, H., Chernew, M., & McWilliams, J. (2017). Little evidence exists to support the expectation that providers would consolidate to enter new payment models. *Health Affairs, 36*(2), 346–354.

Roberts, D., & Murawski, J. (2018). *Questions about control kill merger between Atrium Health and UNC Health Care.* Retrieved from http://www.charlotteobserver.com/news/business/article203125129.html

Saunders, N. (2017). The strategic value of affiliation partnerships in securing future relevance. *Frontiers of Health Services Management, 34*(1), 3–17.

Schmitt, M. (2017). Do hospital mergers reduce costs? *Journal of Health Economics, 52,* 74–94.

Woods, L. (2004). *The Fifth Circuit's decision on St. David's Health Care System: Control is key in whole-entity joint ventures with for-profits.* Retrieved from https://www.dwt.com/advisories/The_Fifth_Circuits_Decision_in_St_Davids_Health_Care_System_Control_Is_Key_in_WholeEntity_Joint_Ventures_With_ForProfits_01_01_2004/

▶ Appendix A: Healthcare Partnership Continuum

Partnership Type	Level of Affiliation[1]	Description	Practical Healthcare Industry Example
Nonequity collaborative agreements	A	Written and/or nonwritten collaboration and affiliation among organizations sharing a similar goal or outcome	A medical group practice consistently refers a specific type of patient to a specific specialty provider organization for further treatment/care
Management agreement	A	Contractual accord among organizational management teams to pursue a mutual initiative for a coordinated effort	A group purchasing company (GPC) formed to allow smaller medical practices to be considered one large entity for purposes of health insurance/employee benefit plans
Clinical integration	A	Independent organizations working together to provide an increasing integration of services	A service line network to assist in the continuity of care (a level I trauma center accepting patient transfers from surrounding urgent care centers)
Joint venture (less than 50% equity with no management rights)	B	Specific organizational entity created for a specific initiative that entails minority ownership and provision of service delivery responsibilities only	Integrated Delivery System (IDS) of physicians and hospitals, of which each has limited ownership and provides their specific services to support the system
Joint venture (less than 50% equity with management rights)	B	Specific organizational entity created for a specific initiative that entails minority ownership; the provision of service delivery responsibilities, and administrative control	IDS of physicians and hospitals, of which each has limited ownership and provides their specific services to support the system. Each entity is involved in day-to-day operational decision-making

Partnership type	Level	Description	Example
Joint venture (50%/50% with management rights)	B	Specific organizational entity created for a specific initiative that entails equal ownership, the provision of service delivery responsibilities, and administrative control	IDS of physicians and hospitals, of which each has equal ownership and provides their specific services to support the system. Each entity is involved in day-to-day operational decision-making
Joint venture (50.1–99% equity)	C	Specific organizational entity created for a specific initiative that entails majority ownership, the provision of service delivery responsibilities, and administrative control	IDS of physicians and hospitals, of which one entity retains majority ownership and provides their specific services to support the system
Joint operating agreement	C	A contractual agreement among entities that creates a new organization in order to accomplish a preestablished initiative, yet allows for each organization in the agreement to provide a specific operation or contribution to prevent a future monopolistic effect	CMS/Medicare ACO formation by either entire organizations or individual medical providers
Merger/acquisition	C	A centralized authority (or parent company) retains control of another organization's assets and management control	A medical practice is purchased by a larger hospital system in order to secure future hospital referral streams

[1]Level affiliation: (A) Loose affiliation, and/or nonbinding; (B) Medium affiliation with increasing risk and investment involved; (C) Strong affiliation with significant risk and ultimately conveyance of board control.
Data from Finnerty, M. (2016). "Models for partnership." Kaufman, Hall & Associates presentation to Navicent Health's strategic committee, November 6, 2016.

CHAPTER 9

The Health System Emerges

Meghan Gabriel, Kendall Cortelyou-Ward, Timothy Rotarius, and Reid M. Oetjen

CHAPTER OBJECTIVES

- Describe how the healthcare system in the United States emerged from a historical perspective.
- Explain the complex rationale for and the implications of hospital mergers in the United States.
- Highlight the different classifications of hospitals including: religious, academic, government, and critical access.
- Differentiate between not-for-profit (NFP) and for-profit run hospitals based on ownership.

KEY TERMS

Certificate of Need (CON)	Merger
For-profit	Not-for-profit

▶ Introduction

A hospital system is composed of two or more hospitals that are owned, sponsored, or contract-managed by a central organization. This chapter addresses the how and why of health system formation in the United States and the advantages and disadvantages of bundling providers together in a geographic area. In addition, the rationale behind long-existing systems consisting of affiliations such as religious and government will be explored. This chapter continues by examining the effects of system competition and the extent to which it may or may not benefit patients, and addressing the apparent reasons for system membership.

119

▶ History of Health Systems in the United States

Hospitals in the modern sense have only existed for roughly 100 years and were originally designed to treat the poor (Fillmore, 2009). As the healthcare industry matured, these small-scale charitable organizations transformed into health systems that are large, influential, effective, and profitable (World Health Organization [WHO], 2000). Health systems have continued to take over independent facilities with the proportion of acute care hospitals controlled by the largest 25 health systems growing from 23% to 33% in a 15-year time period (Khaikin, Uttley, & Winkler, 2016). Currently, there are approximately 5,500 hospitals in the United States (American Hospital Association, 2017).

▶ Rationale for Hospital Mergers

Hospital **mergers** have accelerated over the last 30 years for a number of reasons, including an inability for independent facilities to remain competitive with larger systems, a need for increased market share to successfully negotiate with insurance companies, a capability to coordinate care across multiple sites, a desire to consolidate resources such as technology and staffing, and most recently, to meet the value-based stipulations of the Affordable Care Act (ACA) (American Hospital Association, 2017; Calem, Dor, & Rizzo, 1999; Cutler & Morton, 2013; Dafny, 2014; Vogt, Town, & Williams, 2006). However, mergers have led to complications including **not-for-profit** hospital closures, insufficient oversight (e.g., limitations of **Certificate of Need [CON]** programs), and rural and critical access hospital (CAH) closures.

Mergers may also be beneficial to patients if the facilities offer different services that will provide more comprehensive and centralized coordinated care for patients (Calem et al., 1999). However, with less competition, they have also led to an increase in price for consumers of health services, a trend that seems to be continuing regardless of anti-trust efforts (Gaynor & Town, 2012; Ginsburg, 2016).

In 1984, to control costs, the Centers for Medicare and Medicaid Services (CMS) instituted the Inpatient Prospective Payment System (IPPS) which dictated Medicare reimbursement levels to hospitals based on diagnosis-related groups (DRGs). The IPPS made hospitals financially responsible for the care provided related to specific diagnoses. Although initial reimbursements were high, by the 1990s, hospitals were losing money under this reimbursement structure. Around this same time, managed care became more prevalent, which gave insurance companies the power to negotiate lower rates that ultimately ended up hurting the hospitals' bottom line. These changes led to hospitals looking for innovative ways to gain market power and reduce costs—this opened the door to an increase in hospital mergers and acquisitions (Dafny, 2009).

From 2008 to 2016, the portion of hospitals that were part of a health system or an integrated delivery network increased by 10 percentage points, from 55% in 2008 to 65% in 2016 (**FIGURE 9.1**).

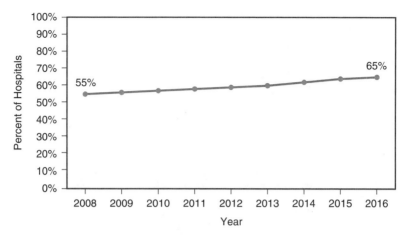

FIGURE 9.1 System Membership among U.S. Hospitals from 2008 to 2016

Data from The American Hospital Association Annual Survey 2008–2016.

▶ Hospital Classifications

Hospitals can be classified in many different ways including: how they are financed, specialty provided, teaching status, and ownership. In many cases, patients may not understand or feel the impact of how a hospital is classified. However, the type of hospital does serve a unique purpose and differs based on whether the focus is religious, academic, government, or critical access. Studies have shown that ownership type impacts the accountability hospitals provide in regards to their communities (Alexander, Weiner, & Succi, 2000).

Religiously Affiliated

The first hospitals were opened and run by religious organizations to care for the poor and those in need (Ferdinand, Epane, & Menachemi, 2014). Today, religiously affiliated hospitals account for almost 20% of hospital beds in the United States (Stulberg, Lawrence, Shattuck, & Curlin, 2010) and approximately 12% of hospitals in the United States (**FIGURE 9.2**). In addition to their operational duties, religious hospitals must also integrate their religious principles into their culture. One challenge these organizations face is the conflict that results as religious policy and clinical perspectives conflict. One study found that 19% of physicians had personally experienced this type of conflict (Stulberg et al., 2010). Religious hospitals are more likely to refuse certain procedures or treatments based on their moral beliefs (especially, reproductive health) (Bassett, 2001). However, although religious hospitals may not be ideal for those needing specific procedures, one study did find these organizations to be more involved in the communities they serve than other types of hospitals (Ferdinand et al., 2014).

Teaching Hospitals

Teaching hospitals tend to focus on biomedical research and development (Simpson, 2015). Teaching hospitals provide job and training opportunities to their

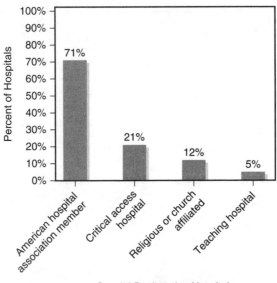

FIGURE 9.2 Special Designation Hospitals in the United States

Data from The American Hospital Association Annual Survey 2008–2016.

communities and, therefore, improve the communities in which they reside (Simpson, 2015). They account for approximately 5% of all U.S. hospitals (**FIGURE 9.2**) and have been leaders in trying new models of care, including focusing on proactive preventive medicine instead of reactive chronic care (Simpson, 2015). Hospitals affiliated with universities have a reputation for providing the best medical care; however, one study found that these types of institutions fell behind in quality of care in certain areas (Comparion Medical Analytics, Inc., 2013). This study found that teaching hospitals excel in cancer and overall medical care, but are less impressive in areas including orthopedic, neurological, general surgery, and cardiac care, when compared with nonacademic hospitals (Comparion Medical Analytics, Inc., 2013).

Critical Access Hospitals

CAHs were established as a part of the Balanced Budget Act of 1997 in response to hospitals closures, and are designed to improve access to healthcare services in rural areas (Health Resources and Services Administration, 2017). Hospitals with the CAH designation are eligible for increased Medicare reimbursement to reduce financial vulnerability of disadvantaged populations. These hospitals are certified by Medicare and must meet certain criteria, including being 35 miles (15 miles in mountainous region) from another hospital, maintaining an average length of stay of less than 96 hours for acute care patients, providing 24/7 emergency care, and having at least 25 inpatient beds (Gabriel, Jones, Samy, & King, 2014). CAHs face many challenges including Internet access, capital acquisition, and workforce shortages (Gabriel et al., 2014). Many CAHs are owned by a health system and are not-for-profit type and currently comprise approximately 21% of U.S. hospitals (Figure 9.2).

▶ Hospital Ownership

In the United States, most hospitals fall under three types of "ownership" categories: not-for-profit, **for-profit**, and government run (local, state, and federal) (Baltagi & Yen, 2014). With these comes perceptions, and the most predominate variations are with regard to trustworthiness. Both not-for-profit and government hospitals are eligible to receive tax exemptions and other financial advantages, and overall, they tend to provide more value to the patients in the community that they serve as compared to for-profit hospitals. For-profit hospitals, however, have financial motivations to provide superior care, therefore attracting more patients than not-for-profits (Bayindir, 2012). Regardless of ownership status, hospitals with a better reputation tend to influence patients' willingness to utilize their services.

Depending on the type of hospital ownership, there are different benefits for being a not-for-profit, for-profit, or government-run institution. For-profits are able to distribute dividends to shareholders, whereas not-for-profit and government-owned hospitals can take advantage of tax breaks (Horwitz, 2005). Although there are a few financial differences and incentives in these organizations, they still share many similarities in conducting business and providing care. These similarities include negotiating with the same insurance companies and government payers, as well as adhering to the same strict operational guidelines and regulations in providing care and operating the organization (Horwitz, 2005). Another similarity is that regardless of the classification, both not-for-profit and for-profit hospitals make a profit (Rushing, 1974). Additionally, all hospitals report providing community benefits such as health education classes on topics including nutrition and smoking cessation (Government Accountability Office [GAO], 2005). Regardless of ownership type, billions of dollars are spent on administrative expenditures (Woolhandler & Himmelstein, 1997).

Government

There are 983 local and state government-owned and 212 federally owned hospitals (American Hospital Association, 2017). Government-owned hospitals tend to provide the most unprofitable services compared with other types of hospitals (Horwitz, 2005). These facilities are most likely to serve the poor and under-insured compared with other ownership types (Horwitz, 2005). Currently, approximately 20% of U.S. hospitals are owned by a state or local government, while only 3% are owned by the Federal Government (**FIGURE 9.3**).

For-profit

As of 2017, there are 1,034 for-profit community hospitals in the United States (American Hospital Association, 2017), comprising approximately 27% of all hospitals (Figure 9.3). They provide more expensive procedures, including open heart surgery and are less likely to provide services such as emergency psychiatric care and obstetrics (Horwitz, 2005; Rushing, 1974). For-profits are more likely to provide services based upon their profitability. As one study found, for-profit hospitals varied greatly in their offering of home health services depending on the variability and ability to make a profit as a result of certain policies applicable to their location (Horwitz, 2005).

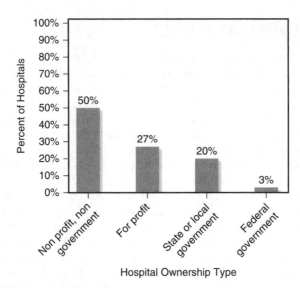

FIGURE 9.3 Hospital Ownership in the United States

Data from The American Hospital Association Annual Survey 2008–2016.

Not-for-profit

Not-for-profit hospitals have different affiliations including religious and academic. There are 2,845 nongovernment not-for-profit community hospitals in the United States (American Hospital Association, 2017), accounting for almost half of all hospitals (Figure 9.3). Not-for-profits tend to balance profit-making efforts and their efforts to serve the poor better than for-profits or government-owned facilities (Horwitz, 2005). Not-for-profits receive a federal tax exemption. This is based on a 1956 law that was created in response to the economic burden incurred from the government for being financially responsible for caring for individuals who did not have the ability to pay for their care. The law was intended to reduce the financial difficulty by placing the burden on not-for-profits in exchange for tax breaks (Ferdinand, Epane, & Menachemi, 2014).

However, there has been much debate as to whether not-for-profits actually provide a greater community benefit than their for-profit and government coun-terparts (Ferdinand et al., 2014). As an incentive for providing charitable care, the government provides tax breaks for not-for-profit hospitals. As a result, there have been dozens of federal lawsuits filed against these hospitals on the grounds of not keeping their charitable obligations, which has led Congress to consider changing accountability regulations (Horwitz, 2005).

▶ The Changing Landscape of Hospital Organizations

The changing landscape of the healthcare industry has created a myriad of continual challenges for hospitals and hospital systems. These include shifts in business prac-tices, such as a decline in not-for-profit hospitals, an insufficient CON program, and hospital closures affecting rural and CAHs.

Decline of Government-Owned Hospitals and Increase in For-Profit Hospitals

For-profit hospitals are the only growing type of hospital, while other ownership categories (e.g., government) have shown a decline over the last 15 years. Between 2008 and 2016, for-profit hospitals increased from 24% of all hospitals in the United States to 27% of hospitals. Government hospitals, including federal, state, and local, decreased from 26% to 23% of all U.S. hospitals (**FIGURE 9.4**). This growth in for-profit hospitals can have far-reaching consequences including the closure of service lines being downsized in order to turn them in to a profitable business (Horwitz, 2005).

Certificate of Need

The CON program was put into law in an attempt to control the cost of healthcare services by limiting the number of hospital beds in a community, thus ensuring hospitals were not spreading the patient population too thin, resulting in empty beds. Beginning in the 1960s, all 50 states had CON programs that were intended to evaluate their community's need before building a hospital or purchasing expensive equipment (Smith & Forgione, 2009). Currently, only 35 states and the District of Columbia (DC) still have CON programs which serve as a hospital oversight mechanism. CON laws are intended to protect consumers and ensure they have adequate access to health care to meet specific community needs (Khaikin, Uttley, & Winkler, 2016). Since the 1980s, many states have ended CON programs and existing programs are insufficient and many believe are a poor fit for the current healthcare landscape (Devers, Brewster, & Casalino, 2003). The original intent of the CON law was to limit hospitals' competition that result in costly duplication of services, and therefore, inefficiency in a given market (Rosko & Mutter, 2014). However, in some cases, it was found that CON had the opposite effect, and instead, resulted in higher hospital costs because they created barriers

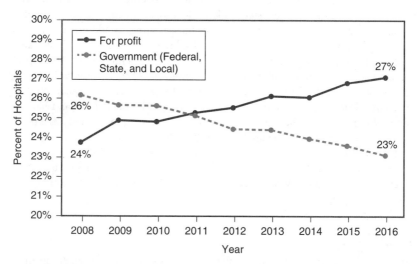

FIGURE 9.4 Trend of For-profit and Government-Owned Hospitals from 2008 to 2016

Data from The American Hospital Association Annual Survey 2008–2016.

to marketplace entry that deterred competitive rates among hospitals (Rosko & Mutter, 2014). Therefore, the usefulness of CON regulations and programs continues to be debated.

Rural Hospital Closings

Hospital closures impact communities and the health outcomes of their community members. When hospitals close, there is a risk of destabilizing the local economy (Succi, Lee, & Alexander, 1997). Hospital closures are defined as the cessation of acute inpatient services by a hospital (Kaufman et al., 2016); therefore, this is different than hospital mergers or ownership changes. Most often, hospital closures are a result of financial issues (Kaufman et al., 2016).

Hospital closures often result in access to care issues and financial adversity due to the loss of local health care; this is particularly true in rural areas (Holmes, Slifkin, Randolph, & Poley, 2006). Although hospital closures impact all communities, hospitals continue to close—specifically in rural areas. In 20 states, more than 60 rural hospitals have already closed since 2010 with more than 600 vulnerable to closures in 42 states (Ellison, 2016). Between 2010 and 2014, 47 rural hospitals closed (Kaufman, 2016).

According to the 2010 census, 19% of the U.S. population live in rural areas (United States Census Bureau, 2010). These communities are stricken with health challenges including limited health insurance coverage, chronic illness, and limitations to adequate healthcare access. CAHs were originally established as a demonstration project to bridge care to these rural communities and has expanded to include 1,328 systems across 45 states (Seright & Winters, 2015). A study concluded that when rural hospitals close, they reduce the per capita income and increase unemployment (Holmes, 2015).

It is estimated that states that have not expanded their Medicaid programs have put rural hospitals at greater risk for closure that could result in the loss of 99,000 jobs in rural settings and a $277 billion loss to gross domestic product (Ellison, 2016). By not expanding their states' Medicaid programs, more patients remain uninsured and unable to pay their hospital bills, leading to additional financial hardship on already resource-stretched rural facilities (Khaikin, Uttley, & Winkler, 2016). One study found that rural hospitals are a more central and integral part (e.g., only source of health care and a major employer) of their communities and, therefore, are supported by the community more strongly than their urban counterparts, which leads to more opposition to their closing (Mullner & McNeil, 1986). In addition to mergers, another strategy hospitals use to remain open is to align or be acquired by an insurance company (Mullner & McNeil, 1986).

For rural hospitals to reduce the chance of closure, one study recommends focusing on differentiation (Succi, Lee, & Alexander, 1997). Providing unique technological advances, procedures, and specialties will increase the likelihood of hospitals remaining open.

Technology

Healthcare facilities have promoted mergers as being positive by claiming their ability to improve their quality of care with tools such as electronic health records (EHRs) (Tsai & Jha, 2014). Currently, EHR systems only function internally with limited capabilities of connecting to systems outside of their organization. Therefore, mergers permit EHR systems to be more comprehensive and coordinate care effectively across different sites. Patient safety can be improved with proper use of EHR. The Obama Administration committed $27 billion to meaningful use of EHR systems with the aim of reducing patient risks through better communication and real-time accurate analysis of health records (Appari, Johnson, & Anthony, 2014).

Although technology can be an expensive undertaking, hospitals typically are rewarded with a high return on investment through improved patient care and reduced adverse events (Appari et al., 2014). For the EHR systems to be successful, organizations must ensure the interoperability of systems across all healthcare institutions. The software must be compatible and communicate with one another effectively and accurately, while also ensuring confidentiality. Effective coordination of EHR systems will lead to timely sharing of health information among all providers and organizations (Furukawa, Patel, Charles, Swain, & Mostashari, 2013).

One study found that hospitals have met meaningful-use criteria by improving the exchange of health information with patients and other providers during transitions in care (Adler-Milstein et al., 2015). This study also identified challenges with EHR implementation, which includes: the upfront and ongoing costs, the burden of meeting meaningful-use criteria, and the cooperation of providers (Adler-Milstein et al., 2015).

Although challenges persist, hospitals must tackle EHR adoption to avoid penalties enacted by the ACA, including penalties for not meeting meaningful-use criteria (Adler-Milstein et al., 2014). Most states have successfully integrated EHR into their hospital systems as a result of the Health Information Technology for Economic and Clinical Health (HITECH) Act of 2009 (Charles, Gabriel, & Searcy, 2015). Between 2008 and 2016, the percent of hospitals that have fully implemented an EHR grew from 17% to 78% (**FIGURE 9.5**).

Payment Reform Efforts

Hospitals are being tasked with accountability in their fee-for-service payment models. Advancement of value-based care requires mixed use of different care delivery and payment models. Adoption of the Patient-Centered Medical Home (PCMH)

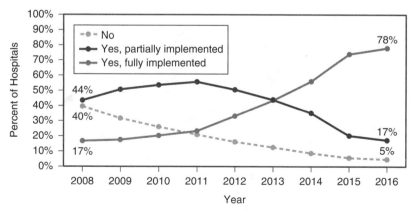

FIGURE 9.5 Trend of Electronic Health Record Adoption among Hospitals in the United States, 2008–2016

Data from The American Hospital Association Annual Survey 2008–2016.

care delivery model continues to expand as providers pursue quality improvement (QI) initiatives that drive value-based care delivery. Pursuit of quality-driven, value-based care is in response to stakeholder demand for medical services that associate with high-quality outcomes at lower costs (Thomson, Schang, & Chernew, 2014).

Currently, 26% of U.S. hospitals participate in a Medical Home program (**FIGURE 9.6**). Healthcare providers seek care delivery interventions that support patient care and satisfy payment requirements, such as the quality payment program through Medicare Access and CHIP Reauthorization Act (MACRA). Health payers also seek care delivery interventions that meet population needs without underutilization or overutilization of medical services.

Recent studies have shown that PCMH activities are related to improved health outcomes (Thomson et al., 2014). There is also growing evidence that medical costs and utilization rates are controlled better through the use of PCMH model activities (Nielsen, Buelt, Patel, & Nichols, 2016). These efforts to improve health outcomes while lowering costs have also led to the development of ACOs. ACOs are a network of healthcare providers that have partnered in an effort to reduce expenses while improving patient care in order to meet third-party payer stipulations (Dor, Pittman, Erickson, Delhy, & Han, 2016). The intention of ACOs is to create a continuum of care in a geographical region (Bazzoli, Harless, & Chukmaitov, 2017). One-third of hospitals in the United States are participating in some form of an ACO (Figure 9.6).

Other payment models are being piloted and tested by major payers, including Medicare to reward quality and value in health care including bundled payments. These models link otherwise unconnected payments for services provided by clinicians, hospitals, and other healthcare entities for a specific episode of care. Therefore, there is an incentive to reward hospitals for care that is not only efficient, but also coordinated. Although this is not a new approach to cost containment, these

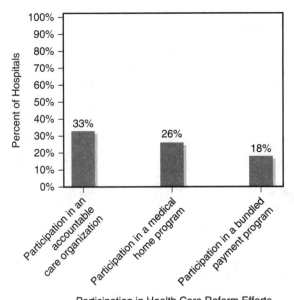

Participation in Health Care Reform Efforts

FIGURE 9.6 Participation in Payment Reform Efforts among Hospitals in the United States, 2016

Data from The American Hospital Association Annual Survey 2008–2016.

alternative payment models have been expanded to include longer episodes of care, more clinical services, and multiple clinicians across healthcare organizations. Approximately 18% of hospitals in the United States currently participate in this type of bundled payment program (Figure 9.6).

▶ Implications for the Future

Historically, hospital consolidation has proven to lead to higher prices for patients without an improvement in services or access, due to the increase in market power and reduced competition (Dafny, 2014). Additionally, there are anti-trust concerns with hospitals merging in a specific geographic area that may lead to monopoly-like power in controlling prices (Dafny, 2014).

Mergers have been proven to increase market power and the hospital's ability to negotiate with commercial insurers for higher prices which the insurance companies pass down to their members resulting in higher deductibles and co-pays (Haas-Wilson & Garmon, 2011). CON programs were created before the current trend of hospital mergers; therefore, these laws and regulations need to be updated and revised to ensure patient protections and respond to current market conditions (Khaikin, 2016). When hospitals are located in the same geographic region, they are more likely to merge than systems that are geographically separate.

Unless quality and altruistic strategic goals are set as part of the merger, quality and patient care will decrease in a merger in hopes of cost-containment efforts; therefore, quality measures need to be regulated to ensure they are included when the Federal communications Commission (FCC) approves any mergers between health systems (Brekke, Siciliani, & Straume, 2017). Regardless of ownership type, hospitals spend billions of dollars per year on administrative expenditures (Woolhandler & Himmelstein, 1997). It has been speculated that the savings from reduced administrative expenses would fund a national health insurance program and universal coverage (Woolhandler & Himmelstein, 1997).

▶ Conclusion

The current environment mergers pose a threat to the Institute for Health Improvement's (IHI) triple aim of affordability, access, and quality of care for patients. Oversight needs to be strengthened, potentially through CON programs, to ensure that mergers are conducted in a way that will benefit healthcare consumers—especially for vulnerable populations including rural areas. Without proper governmental oversight and regulation, the healthcare system will continuously be driven by profit acquisition and place the burden of increased costs on healthcare consumers.

Brief Chapter Summary

In its simplest form, a hospital system is composed of two or more hospitals owned, sponsored, or contract-managed by a central organization. Merged entities and systems have been developed for a variety of reasons: improved competitive ability, greater economies of scale, consolidation of technology, improved market share, and others.

Some hospital systems, such as those run by religious organizations, have existed for many years, but for the most part, systems of not-for-profit hospitals emerged largely within the recent five decades or so. System formation continues as more hospitals are brought into mergers with others and even some established systems are merged with other systems to comprise even larger systems. There are not-for-profit systems, many of which are formed about a central entity such as a teaching hospital; there are hundreds of governmental hospitals, many in systems such as that of the Veterans Administration; there are religiously affiliated systems; and there are for-profit hospital systems.

There have been numerous hospital closings related to mergers, affiliations, and system formation, including many rural institutions. People in many rural communities have had to rely on the closest urban centers for much of their health care.

There are anti-trust concerns with hospitals merging in specific geographic areas and thus limiting competition and causing higher costs, although to date there has not been a great deal of government pressure related to anti-trust issues. It is felt by some that due to the lack of effective government oversight and regulation, the greater healthcare system may be driven by the quest for increased revenue which in turn could increase the costs for taxpayers and healthcare consumers.

Questions for Review and Discussion

1. How did hospitals become widespread in delivering health care across the United States?
2. What factors caused mergers of hospitals and the evolution of large health systems?
3. What are the different classifications of hospitals and how are they unique? How are they similar?
4. What are the differences and similarities between not-for-profit and for-profit health systems?
5. What is a CON and how is it utilized? Why is it important in providing care?
6. What are emerging payment reform efforts that health systems are adopting?
7. Based on the nature of health care, should all hospitals, regardless of tax exempt status, be required to provide charitable care and community benefits in order to justify a tax break?
8. What are some alternative models of hospitals that you foresee emerging in the future to provide more cost-effective and efficient care? Are there other industries that healthcare might draw upon as a model?
9. Debate the pros and cons of CON? Should the CON process be federally legislated or should states be able to determine the use of such laws?
10. CAH were originally established as a demonstration project to bridge care to these rural communities. Should states abandon this approach and allow the free market to determine the viability of providing health services in different markets? Defend your position by including your rationale for eliminating or maintaining CAHs.
11. There have been many attempts at reducing costs through various payment reform efforts including: fee-for-service payment models, PCMH care delivery model, and ACOs. What other mechanisms, perhaps focused on the

consumer, can you think of that might help to reduce the cost of healthcare and reduce utilization of services?

12. Historically, hospital consolidation has proven to lead to higher prices for patients without an improvement in services or access, due to the increase in market power and reduced competition. Develop several solutions that reduce costs and expand access without passing the costs on to the patient.

References

Adler-Milstein, J., DesRoches, C. M., Furukawa, M. F., Worzala, C., Kralovec, P., & Jha, A. K. (2014). More than half of US hospitals have at least a basic EHR, but stage 2 criteria remain challenging for most. *Health Affairs, 33*(9), 1664–1671.

Adler-Milstein, J., DesRoches, C. M., Kralovec, P., Foster, G., Worzala, C., Charles, D., …Jha, A. K. (2015). Electronic health record adoption in US hospitals: Progress continues, but challenges persist. *Health Affairs, 34*(12), 2174–2180.

Alexander, J. A., Weiner, B. J., & Succi, M. (2000). Community accountability among hospitals affiliated with health care systems. *The Milbank Quarterly, 78*(2), 157.

American Hospital Association. (2017). *AHA hospital statistics: A comprehensive reference for analysis and comparison of hospital trends.* Retrieved from http://www.aha.org/research/rc/stat -studies/fast-facts.shtml

Appari, A., Johnson, M. E., & Anthony, D. L. (2014). Information technology and hospital patient safety: A cross-sectional study of US acute care hospitals. *American Journal of Managed Care, 20*, eSP39–eSP47.

Baltagi, B. H., & Yen, Y. F. (2014). Hospital treatment rates and spillover effects: Does ownership matter? *Regional Science and Urban Economics, 49*, 193–202.

Bassett, W. W. (2001). Private religious hospitals: Limitations upon autonomous moral choices in reproductive medicine. *The Journal of Contemporary Health Law and Policy, 17*(2), 455.

Bayindir, E. E. (2012). Hospital ownership type and treatment choices. *Journal of Health Economics, 31*(2), 359–370.

Bazzoli, G. J., Harless, D. W., & Chukmaitov, A. S. (2017). A taxonomy of hospitals participating in Medicare accountable care organizations. *Health Care Management Review.* doi:10.1097 /HMR.0000000000000159

Brekke, K. R., Siciliani, L., & Straume, O. R. (2017). Hospital mergers with regulated prices. *Scandinavian Journal of Economics, 119*, 597.

Calem, P. S., Dor, A., & Rizzo, J. A. (1999). The welfare effects of mergers in the hospital industry. *Journal of Economics & Business, 51*(3), 197.

Charles, D., Gabriel, M., & Searcy, T. (2015). *Adoption of electronic health record systems among U.S. nonfederal acute care hospitals: 2008–2014.* The Office of the National Coordinator for Health Information Technology, No. 23.

Comparion Medical Analytics, Inc. (2013). *2010 CareChex research study: An assessment of the quality of university hospital care in the U.S.* Retrieved from http://www.carechex.com/media /univhospstudy.aspx

Cutler, D. M., & Morton, F. S. (2013). Hospitals, market share, and consolidation. *JAMA, 310*(18), 1964–1970.

Dafny, L. (2009). Estimation and identification of merger effects: An application to hospital mergers. *The Journal of Law & Economics, 52*(3), 523.

Dafny, L. (2014). Hospital industry consolidation—Still more to come? *New England Journal of Medicine, 370*(3), 198–199. Science Citation Index.

Devers, K. J., Brewster, L. R., & Casalino, L. P. (2003). Changes in hospital competitive strategy: A new medical arms race? *Health Services Research, 38*, 447–469.

Dor, A., Pittman, P., Erickson, C., Delhy, R., & Han, X. (2016). Does ACO adoption change the health workforce configuration in U.S. Hospitals? GW Health Workforce Research Center Research Report.

Ellison, A. (2016). *The rural hospital closure crisis: 15 key findings and trends*. Retrieved from http://www.beckershospitalreview.com/finance/therural-hospital-closure-crisis-15-key-findings-and-trends.html

Ferdinand, A. O., Epane, J. P., & Menachemi, N. (2014). Community benefits provided by religious, other nonprofit, and for-profit hospitals: A longitudinal analysis 2000–2009. *Health Care Management Review, 39*(2), 145.

Fillmore, R. (2009). *The evolution of the US healthcare system*. Retrieved from http://www.sciencescribe.net/articles/The_Evolution_of_the_U.S._Healthcare_System.pdf

Furukawa, M. F., Patel, V., Charles, D., Swain, M., & Mostashari, F. (2013). Hospital electronic health information exchange grew substantially in 2008–12. *Health Affairs, 32*(8), 1346–1354.

Gabriel, M. H., Jones, E. B., Samy, L., & King, J. (2014). Progress and challenges: Implementation and use of health information technology among critical-access hospitals. *Health Affairs, 33*(7), 1262–1270.

Gaynor, M., & Town, R. (2012). *The impact of hospital consolidation—Update*. Robert Wood Johnson Foundation Synthesis Report. Retrieved from http://www.rwjf.org/content/dam/farm/reports/issue_briefs/2012/rwjf73261

Ginsburg, P. B. (2016). *Health care market consolidations: Impacts on costs, quality and access*. The Brookings Institution. Retrieved from https://www.brookings.edu/testimonies/health-care-market-consolidations-impacts-on-costs-quality-and-access/

Government Accountability Office (GAO). (2005). *Nonprofit, for-profit, and government hospitals: Uncompensated care and other community benefits*. Retrieved from http://www.gao.gov/new.items/d05743t.pdf

Haas-Wilson, D., & Garmon, C. (2011). Hospital mergers and competitive effects: Two retrospective analyses. *International Journal of the Economics of Business, 18*(1), 17–32.

Health Resources and Services Administration. (2017). *Critical access hospitals*. Rural Health Information Hub. Retrieved from https://www.ruralhealthinfo.org/topics/critical-access-hospitals

Holmes, G. M., Slifkin, R. T., Randolph, R. K., & Poley, S. (2006). The effect of rural hospital closures on community economic health. *Health Services Research, 41*(2), 467–485.

Holmes, M. (2015). Financially fragile rural hospitals mergers and closures. *North Carolina Medical Journal, 76*(1), 37–40.

Horwitz, J. R. (2005). Making profits and providing care; Comparing nonprofit, for-profit and government hospitals. *Health Affairs, 24*(3), 790–801.

Kaufman, B. G., Thomas, S. R., Randolph, R. K., Perry, J. R., Thompson, K. W., Holmes, G. M., & Pink, G. H. (2016). The rising rate of rural hospital closures. *The Journal of Rural Health, 32*(1), 35–43.

Khaikin, C., Uttley, L., & Winkler, A. (2016). When hospitals merge: Updating state oversight to protect access to care. The MergerWatch Project.

Mullner, R. M., & McNeil, D. (1986). Rural and urban hospital closures: A comparison. *Health Affairs, 5*(3), 131–141.

Nielsen, M., Buelt, L., Patel, K., & Nichols, L. (2016). *The impact of primary care practice transformation on cost, quality: Annual review of evidence 2014–2015*. Patient-Centered Primary Care Collaborative and the Robert Graham Center, pp. 1–40.

Rosko, M. D., & Mutter, R. L. (2014). The association of hospital cost-inefficiency with certificate-of-need regulation. *Medical Care Research and Review, 71*(3), 280–298.

Rushing, W. (1974). Differences in profit and nonprofit organizations: A study of effectiveness and efficiency in general short-stay hospitals. *Administrative Science Quarterly, 19*(4), 474–484.

Seright, T. J., & Winters, C. A. (2015). Rural settings. Critical care in critical access hospitals. *Critical Care Nurse, 35*(5), 62–67.

Simpson, A. (2015, January). Health and renaissance: Academic medicine and the remaking of modern Pittsburgh. *Journal of Urban History, 41*(1), 19–27.

Smith, P. C., & Forgione, D. A. (2009). The development of certificate of need legislation. *Journal of Healthcare Finance, 36*(2), 35–44.

Stulberg, D. B., Lawrence, R. E., Shattuck, J., & Curlin, F. A. (2010). Religious hospitals and primary care physicians: Conflicts over policies for patient care. *Journal of General Internal Medicine, 25*(7), 725–730. doi:10.1007/s11606-010-1329-6

Succi, M. J., Lee, S. D., & Alexander, J. A. (1997). Effects of market position and competition on rural hospital closures. *Health Services Research, 31*(6), 679–699.

Thomson, S., Schang, L., & Chernew, M. E. (2014). Value-based cost sharing in the United States and elsewhere can increase patients' use of high-value goods and services. *Health Affairs, 32*(4), 704–712.

Tsai, T. C., & Jha, A. K. (2014). Hospital consolidation, competition, and quality: Is bigger necessarily better? *JAMA: Journal of the American Medical Association, 312*(1), 29–30.

United States Census Bureau. (2010). 2010 *Census urban and rural classification and urban area criteria.* Retrieved from http://www.census.gov/geo/reference/ua/urban-rural-2010.html

Vogt, W. B., Town, R., & Williams, C. H. (2006). How has hospital consolidation affected the price and quality of hospital care? The Synthesis Project. Research Synthesis Report No. 9 MEDLINE.

Woolhandler, S., & Himmelstein, D. U. (1997). Costs of care and administration at for-profit and other hospitals in the United States. *The New England Journal of Medicine, 336*(11), 769.

World Health Organization (WHO). (2000). *The world health report 2000: Health systems: Improving performance.* Geneva: WHO.

CHAPTER 10

Mergers, Acquisitions, and the Government

Nancy J. Niles

CHAPTER OBJECTIVES

- Enable the student to define and discuss strategic planning.
- Outline the development of a SWOT analysis of a hospital.
- Introduce the concepts of mergers, acquisitions, joint ventures, and alliances.
- Identify the differences between horizontal and vertical mergers.
- Examine three reasons why mergers and acquisitions succeed and fail.
- Identify three major antitrust laws and their impact on merger activity.
- Discuss the role HR plays in post-merger activity.

KEY TERMS

Core competencies
Horizontal mergers
Mergers

SWOT (strengths, weaknesses, opportunities, and threats) analysis
Synergy
Vertical mergers

▶ Introduction

Any organization, regardless of the industry of which it is a part, needs to have a long-term or strategic plan to provide organization sustainability. With the rising cost of health care, healthcare organizations have had to assess diverse ways of minimizing their operating costs to maintain financial viability of the organization. With the changing patterns of healthcare consumers' preference for outpatient services, and considering economic trends and demographic changes, it is important that a hospital has a strategic plan. Part of their strategic planning process is to perform a **SWOT (strengths, weaknesses, opportunities, and threats)**

TABLE 10.1 SWOT Analysis of a Fictional Hospital	
Strengths/core competencies	Weaknesses
Reputation	Competitive market
Accreditation	Leadership turnover
Employee satisfaction	No outpatient services
Location	New healthcare legislation
Award winning services	Low occupancy rate
Opportunities	Threats
Merge with other healthcare facilities	Increased competition
Acquire outpatient facility	Labor shortages
Improve information technology	Economy
Expansion of patient services	Financial issues
	Accreditation issues

analysis which consists of an evaluation of both internal (strengths and weaknesses) and external (opportunities and threats) environmental factors that can have either a positive or negative impact on the hospital's operations (Griffin, 2012). To develop a strategic plan, it is important to capitalize on the strengths of the organization and to assess how the hospital's weaknesses can impact its success. In addition to the internal evaluation, it is also important to determine which opportunities in the environment can be beneficial to the hospital and which threats can hurt the hospital. Recent industry activity involving hospital closures increasing across the country indicates an increased focus on reducing the cost of care and increasing coordination of patient care while continuing to provide quality of care. In a 2013 Healthcare Financial Management Association survey of their senior financial executive members, more than 80% of respondents had expressed consideration of or are engaging in a merger and acquisition activity (An HFMA Value Project Report, 2013). One way to enhance the strengths of a hospital or to mitigate the weaknesses of a hospital is to develop formal or informal collaborative agreements with other healthcare facilities. The overarching goal is to create **synergy**, which means the result of the cooperative effort will be greater than the single operational effect of the organizations; in everyday terms, we could say this means *one plus one equals three*. **TABLE 10.1** presents an example of the SWOT for a fictional hospital that is considering a merger or acquisition as part of their strategic plan. The hospital had several strengths or **core competencies** that would be attractive to other healthcare facilities. These core competencies are clearly shown to have contributed to the success of the organization. Their weaknesses indicated they had no outpatient services, which could be turned into a strength if they opted to pursue a collaborative agreement with another facility. This choice would also satisfy their opportunity to expand their services. Ultimately, a SWOT analysis can be a valuable tool when developing a strategic plan.

▶ Collaborative Agreements

A **merger** is a formal and legal agreement between two organizations with the goal of creating a new organization, typically bearing a new name. This may also be called a merger or member substitution, resulting in a change in corporate membership.

The health system is the corporate owner of the acquired hospital. Instead of purchasing the hospital, the acquiring corporation makes financial commitments to the hospitals. There is shared decision-making between the entities. This is a typical arrangement when both hospitals are not-for-profit type.

There are two types of mergers: horizontal and vertical. A **horizontal merger** occurs within the same sector of an industry, meaning the companies involved offer the same product or service. An example of a horizontal merger is two hospitals merging into one organization. Such mergers are common in industries such as health care where there are fewer competitors, resulting in more intense competition. Thus, a horizontal merger potentially controls the industry market, which is often a concern for the federal government because it eliminates the opportunity for consumers to choose who their healthcare providers will be (five types of mergers).

A **vertical merger** is a type of merger that occurs within different sectors of an industry. The organizations offer various products or services, with the goal of creating efficiencies of operations and expand services. An acquisition is an unequal transaction, unequal because one organization absorbs the other organization. It is also referred to as an asset or stock acquisition, which is chosen depending on whether it is a for-profit or non-profit organization that is involved. With an asset acquisition, the assets are acquired for cash or a non-cash commitment. The acquirer can choose how much debt and liabilities are to be assumed. An example of an acquisition is CVS and Aetna; this is a vertical transaction because each company provides different health services (Thompson, Strickland, & Gamble, 2010).

If an organization decides not to pursue an organizational commitment to a collaborative arrangement, the involved organizations may opt for a joint venture. This type of collaborative operation is an agreement between two facilities. The facilities operate separately but the joint venture or hybrid is under the auspice of this type of alliance. This cooperative alliance can focus on different initiatives such as joint service programs or develop an initiative that focuses on patient quality assessments (Weiss, 2015). A more recent type of joint venture is a virtual merger; this may function as a merger without being legally structured as a merger. The agreement can be terminated after a specified period, providing more flexibility to terminate the agreement if both organizations feel it is not successful. These arrangements have been popular in Europe with, interest increasing in the United States within the last 15 years. Examples of joint venture models include Duke University Health Systems and LifePoint Hospitals and the Cleveland Clinic and Community Health Systems (Cohn, 2004).

According to Thompson et al. (2010), there are four reasons mergers and acquisition are considered by hospitals.

1. *Cost efficiency of operation*: When one healthcare organization acquires another organization having a similar operation, the operation can be streamlined. *For example, the operational departments such as finance and human resource management can be combined resulting in operational cost efficiencies.* In a recent study of mergers that occurred between 2009 and 2014, annual operating hospital expenses were reduced by 2.5 (Is this %?). The reduction in expenses was realized through clinical protocol standardizations, and upgrading facilities and services at the acquired hospitals (AHA News, 2017).

2. *Increased market share*: By combining forces with another organization is a rapid way to increase market share by either demographic or

geographic expansion. This type of agreement would be closely examined by the Federal Trade Commission (FTC) and the Department of Justice (DOJ) to ensure there was no major elimination of other competition.

3. *Expansion of products and services*: The merger or acquisition may provide an opportunity to offer more healthcare services. *Rather than developing a service internally, the hospital opts to merge or acquire another company that has successfully developed a service.*

4. *To gain access to other competitive capabilities*: The merger or acquisition may be an avenue to other competitive capabilities that the other organization possesses that are not present in the current situation. *This type of approach would occur because of a SWOT analysis indicating a hospital weakness that could be turned into a strength.*

According to Kamholz (2017), the following are suggested steps for successful acquisition of a hospital:

1. *Plan for planning.* Establish an overarching goal with specific strategic and financial objectives as the process proceeds.

2. Perform a macroenvironmental analysis to determine the best opportunities. A macroenvironmental analysis is influenced by both the macroenvironment and the industry environment. The macroenvironment is composed of the economic, government, technological, sociocultural, and demographic influences that impact the industry.

3. The industry environmental analysis analyzes the suppliers, competitors, the healthcare consumers, and the relative difficulty of entering the healthcare industry (Niles, 2012). Due diligence, or a comprehensive appraisal of the proposed agreement, should be performed for all viable mergers and acquisitions. It is also important to target any healthcare systems that are divesting or selling parts of their systems. *Assess a strategic and cultural fit with your hospital*: The possible acquisition or merger needs to fit into the strategic plan of the hospital in a positive manner which means there should be a discussion to ensure the plans can be integrated. It is also extremely important to assess the cultural fit with your hospital. Many mergers and acquisitions fail because the organizational cultures do not mesh well, resulting in a disconnection with senior management. According to Vartorella, a major trend in 2018 will be the lack of employee engagement due in part because of mergers and acquisitions (Vartorella, 2017). This could be extremely disruptive to the success of a hospital.

4. *Ensure that anti-trust regulations are reviewed.* The FTC has been vigilant within the healthcare industry. Both the DOJ and the FTC focus on the Herfindahl–Hirschman Index (HHI) which measures market competition and concentration in the industry. According to the DOJ, the HHI is a commonly accepted measure of market concentration. The HHI is calculated by squaring the market share of each firm competing in the market and then summing the resulting numbers. The index considers the relative size distribution of the firms in a market. It approaches zero when a market is occupied by many firms of relatively equal size, indicating choices for the consumer and reaching its

maximum of 10,000 points when a single firm controls a market which could indicate a possible monopoly.

5. *Implement a transparent process.* Develop a plan for integration of the two structures immediately. The plan should be transparent to all employees. When change occurs in an organization, there is often discomfort if employees are not informed during each step of the process.

6. *Review all types of collaborative agreements.* If a merger or acquisition is not feasible, examine other opportunities such as a vertical merger.

7. *Due diligence on price.* Paying the appropriate price is very important. The price should be based on comparative data of recent market transactions of similar hospitals.

8. *Review antitrust regulations.* Mergers and acquisitions are heavily scrutinized to ensure there are no issues with monopoly creation which reduces the consumer choice for their product.

▶ Legal and Regulatory Oversight of Mergers and Acquisitions

There are three major antitrust laws that remain in effect. The Sherman Act of 1890 was the first antitrust law as a "comprehensive charter of economic liberty aimed at preserving free and unfettered competition as the rule of trade." The Federal Trade Commission Act, passed in 1914, was created to protect consumers while promoting competition; this Act also established the FTC. The Clayton Act prohibits activities that are not specifically covered under the Sherman Act such as mergers. The Clayton Act was amended by the Robinson–Patman Act of 1936, which banned certain practices, and the Scott–Rodino Act of 1976 which required notice of proposed mergers. States also have antitrust laws.

The oversight of mergers and acquisitions is the responsibility of the DOJ and the FTC; however, the FTC is the only federal agency that protects the consumer and also has oversight of competition jurisdiction. Both federal agencies are responsible for ensuring that consumers could choose their products or services from different providers. They protect consumers by stopping unfair and fraudulent practices in the marketplace. The FTC challenges anticompetitive mergers and business practices that could harm consumers by resulting in higher prices, lower quality, or fewer choices. The U.S. Department of Justice, a federal agency established in 1870, is responsible for law enforcement and justice in the United States. It has an antitrust division that collaborates with the FTC to ensure consumers are protected. The Division prosecutes certain violations of the antitrust laws by filing criminal suits that can lead to large fines and jail sentences. In other cases, the Division institutes a civil action seeking a court order forbidding future violations of the law and requiring steps to remedy the anticompetitive effects of past violations. They also provide guidelines for **horizontal mergers**. For example, in 2016, the DOJ and attorneys general from multiple states sued to block Anthem's proposed acquisition of Cigna and Aetna's proposed acquisition of Humana, alleging that the transactions would increase concentration and harm competition across the country, reducing from five to three the number of large, national health insurers in the nation. Because of the suit and court decision to block the deal as it would lessen competition, the two companies ultimately called off the deal in 2017 (About the FTC, 2017).

The Hart–Scott–Rodino Act (amending the Clayton Act) established the federal premerger notification program, which provides the FTC and the DOJ with information about potential large mergers and acquisitions before they occur. The FTC's Bureau of Competition and the FTC's Bureau of Economics investigate market dynamics to determine if the proposed merger will harm consumers.

▶ Supply Chain Management

One goal of a merger or acquisition involving a hospital is to reduce operating costs. One way of analyzing where their operations are not cost-effective is to assess their supply chain management. **FIGURE 10.1** is an example of a generic supply chain of a hospital. According to Goodbaum (2015), there are five typical components of a hospital supply chain: (1) the payer for their services, including the government, the employer, and the healthcare consumer, (2) the intermediaries: the health insurance companies, including managed care organizations, (3) the suppliers of products and services, including wholesalers, purchaser organizations, and mail order distributors, and (4) producers, including medical device companies and pharmaceutical companies.

The payer in this supply chain consists of payment of healthcare services by federal and state governments, the healthcare consumer, and the employer who typically pays for a portion of the employee premiums. The intermediary in the supply chain consists of the health insurance companies and the managed care organizations that act as the intermediary for the payments. The hospital is the hub of the supply chain, responsible for providing the services to the patient. Suppliers can include the distributors and wholesalers of products and services.

Group purchasing organizations (GPOs) were developed to provide healthcare providers with cost savings through volume purchasing, enabling them to negotiate better rates with the suppliers for the hospitals (Eight Largest Purchasing Organizations, 2010). The supplier group accounts for 40% of hospital costs, and thus this is a target area for cost improvement strategies. There are also producers of

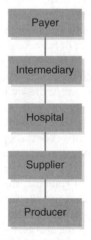

FIGURE 10.1 Generic Hospital Supply Chain

pharmaceutical products and medical devices which can be very costly to the hospital. Hospital financial managers are always assessing their supply chains for cost savings; they may at times determine it may be more efficient to manage a portion of the supply chain or merge with another facility that can manage that portion of the supply chain more efficiently. By using the SWOT analysis, the hospital can determine what strengths they have that can be used to internally manage a portion of a supply chain. For example, a hospital could decide to acquire a medical device company or another supplier so as to achieve more control over these costs. They could also expand their healthcare services by acquiring a physician's practice or surgery center. Each of these examples represents types of **vertical mergers** because they operate within different sectors of health care.

▶ Impact of Affordable Care Act on Hospital Merger Activity

The Affordable Care Act transformed the traditional reimbursement model for health services. The healthcare system now focuses more on pay for performance (P4P) or value-based models for provider reimbursement. These models focus on rewarding healthcare providers based on quality measurements (Niles, 2018). The Centers for Medicaid and Medicare Services' Triple Aim of improving patient outcomes, patient satisfaction, and reducing costs was part of the ACA initiative. The ACA provided incentives for increased use of electronic patient health records, representing a costly investment in infrastructure. The ACA focus resulted in vertical mergers between hospitals, wellness programs, and insurance programs. Research has indicated that joint ventures and other collaborative arrangements have helped in reducing costs while maintaining quality care and increasing patient satisfaction. In addition to the Triple Aim, Accountable Care Organizations (ACOs) were established that also focused on quality health care and cost reduction. ACOs are networks of hospitals, providers, and suppliers that collaborate to provide quality and cost-effective care. ACOs are a type of collaborative agreement (Niles, 2018). Providers felt that an integrated healthcare system resulting from vertical mergers is a way of accommodating this new focus (Kenen, 2013). As an example, there was a joint operating agreement in 2012 between Piedmont and Wellstar Health Systems, renamed the Georgia Health Collaborative Administrative Services Organization, a joint venture between an ACO and healthcare delivery (About Us, 2017; Vu, White, Kelley, Hopper, & Liu, 2016).

▶ The Role of HR in a Merger–Acquisition Activity

An important facet of a merger or acquisition that should not be ignored is the impact this major organizational change has on the employees. Post-merger acquisitions create a tense work environment. Employees are worried about whether their jobs will be eliminated or if they are reassigned, whether they can perform any new duties. There will be new policies and procedures, new organizational cultures to blend, new employees, and new bosses. Approximately 30% of employees may be eliminated because of a merger due to similar job responsibilities (Marks, Mirvis, & Ashkenas, 2017). Employees could be very distracted and underperform during a time when workloads will increase as the two companies merge. Typically, if the merger of the two structures and their organizational cultures are not handled appropriate, there may be high employee turnover. The human resource (HR) management department can play an integral role in the post-merger process. HR can oversee the communication that is needed to introduce the change in the organization. They can work with existing and new key management in developing new policies and procedures for the new organization that can introduce a new organizational culture that will include both sets of employees. HR will also assist those employees whose jobs will be eliminated by helping for new job training and job relocation if needed. HR can provide a more positive and stable environment as the merger moves forward.

▶ Conclusion

A merger is a formal and legal agreement between two organizations for the purpose of creating a new entity, typically with a new name. An acquisition is an unequal transaction between two organizations in which one organization absorbs the other organization; typically, the dominant hospital retains their name. Mergers and acquisitions have seen robust activity in the healthcare sector for several years. There have been both vertical and horizontal mergers in the healthcare industry as well as joint ventures and virtual mergers.

Successful merger and acquisition outcomes include cost efficiencies, increases in quality services and performance, increases in market share, and expanding core competencies. The Affordable Care Act has encouraged merger and acquisition activity in the hospital sector because elements of the industry felt these legal structures supported the ACA Triple Aim goals. The ACA and the federal government also have encouraged the increased use of information technology in health care by mandating electronic health records, and reimbursing telemedicine as a method of increasing healthcare access. Technology can be costly to hospitals, which is another reason hospitals are pursuing agreements with other hospitals to offset operating costs.

Any organization, regardless of industry, needs to develop a strategic plan to provide organizational sustainability. A key component of a strategic plan is a SWOT analysis providing information on both the external and internal environment of the hospital. Understanding the strengths and weaknesses of a hospital can assist with crafting an action plan for continuing organizational efforts revolving around their strengths and how to change their weaknesses into strengths. A way to support such a SWOT analyses is to assess whether a merger or acquisition is a way to enhance a hospital and to offset its weaknesses.

In addition to the SWOT analysis, a comprehensive analysis of the macroenvironment influences is needed. The economic influence can have a major impact on hospitals because if there is a downturn in the economy and people lose jobs, they will also lose their health insurance. The unemployed will use hospital emergency departments as their primary care provider. Although the Affordable Care Act's marketplace exchanges have eased some of the ED's traffic, under the current administration, these exchanges may be eliminated. Technological forces have become an integral component of healthcare delivery. Telemedicine uses technology as a means of providing healthcare services. If a hospital cannot afford to invest in technology, they may decide to merge or acquire another facility that has an excellent technology infrastructure.

Sociocultural influences are some of the most dominant influences because consumer preferences dictate service use, which is one of the reasons that outpatient services have become popular in the U.S. healthcare delivery system. A hospital may opt to acquire outpatient facilities to meet the demand of the sociocultural influence. The healthcare industry is one of the most heavily regulated industries in the United States; legal and governmental influences can influence how the hospital operates. To accommodate operational changes, they may merge with another hospital to offset operational expenses. Also, demographic influences can impact a hospital. Demographic statistics indicate the U.S. population is living longer, increasing the prevalence of chronic disease needs. This could change the specialty of the hospital. Rather than opting for an internal change, a hospital may opt to merge with another specialty hospital to complement their existing specialty areas (Niles, 2012).

Finally, once a merger is complete, it is vital for the new organization to include HR in the post-merger activities. For many employees, the merger is an exciting time of change. For other employees, it can be very uncertain. Morale could be low. Turnover could be high. HR can assist in creating a positive work environment by establishing an open communication with the employees, creating new policies and procedures, developing a new organizational culture with employee input and assist employees whose job will be terminated with job relocation and training.

With the rising cost of health care, healthcare organizations have had to assess diverse ways of minimizing their operating costs so as to maintain financial viability. The strategic plan must recognize the changing patterns of healthcare consumer's preference of outpatient services, as well as taking into account economic trends and demographic changes. If one hospital decides to merge with or acquire another hospital, it is necessary for senior management to address the issues of cultural fit between the two organizational cultures. Employee engagement with the new culture is imperative for success of the merger. Recent data indicate that mergers, acquisitions, and other collaborative agreements will continue to be active strategies for hospitals. However, hospital strategic planners need to perform due diligence to ensure that any activity of this sort will be successful.

Brief Chapter Summary

Central to strategic planning and consideration of an alternative organizational structure is a SWOT analysis examining the organization's strengths, weaknesses, opportunities, and threats. There are several forms of collaborative agreements: horizontal mergers, vertical mergers, joint ventures, and other affiliations. Such agreements are pursued for a variety of reasons including: improvement of cost efficiency, increased market share, expansion of products or services, and access to additional capabilities. Essentially all significant affiliations or combinations of existing organizations are subject to government scrutiny and must thus observe all pertinent legal and regulatory requirements.

Questions for Review and Discussion

1. Why does every hospital need a strategic plan?
2. What is the principal characteristic of a horizontal merger?
3. What is the fundamental difference between a merger and an acquisition?
4. What was the primary purpose of the Federal Trade Commission Act of 1914?
5. What is an Accountable Care Organization (ACO)? How are they impacted in a merger?
6. What are the principle government agencies that oversee mergers and acquisitions?
7. How do HR departments provide guidance during a post-merger period?

🔍 CASE STUDY ANALYSIS: CVS Health and Aetna

CVS (Consumer Value Stores) was founded in 1963 in Lowell, Massachusetts with the establishment of their first retail store. In 1969, it expanded its retail operations to include pharmacy departments in the northeast and was subsequently sold to the Melville Corporation in 1969. Throughout the 1970s, operations expanded with the acquisition of other drug stores. In 1983, they launched a national hemophilia home service, reaching one billion dollars in annual sales in 1985. CVS started a prescription benefit management service, a mail service pharmacy, and other healthcare services. In the 1990s, CVS launched a pharmacy benefit management company for employers and insurance companies. Caremark established CarePatterns, a disease management program. Caremark also entered the multiple sclerosis market. They established the pharmaceutical service as a core operation. In 1999, they launched CVS.com, the first online integrated pharmacy in the United States. In 2000, Minute Clinics, retail health clinics, were established; CVS partnered with them to open three clinics in their chain stores. Minute Clinics became the first to be accredited by the Joint Commission. In 2006, CVS acquired the Minute Clinics. In 2001, CVS/Caremark introduced the Extra Care Card, the first loyalty card for retail pharmacy chains. In 2007, CVS/Caremark and Rx officially merged, creating CVS Caremark. In 2009, the Minute Clinics became affiliated with several healthcare systems nationwide. In 2014, CVS Caremark changed its name to CVS Health. They also removed all tobacco products from their stores. In 2015, CVS acquired all of Target's pharmacies and clinics. In December 2017, the pharmacy chain, CVS/Caremark, announced their acquisition of Aetna Insurance for $69 billion. According to both companies, consumers will benefit from an integrated, community healthcare experience. Consumers will have access to Aetna's extensive network of providers with greater consumer access through CVS Health which includes nearly 10,000 CVS Pharmacy locations and more than 1,000 Minute Clinic walk-in clinics (CVS Health).

Please answer the following questions.

1. What was the primary strategy of CVS to expand its operations?
2. Go to https://cvshealth.com/about/company-history. Scroll down to the history section of the webpage. Identify three strategies that you feel are important to the growth of CVS Health.

3. Go to https://www.caremark.com/wps/portal/. Go to the bottom of the webpage. Click on the different icons that represent the different areas of CVS health. Summarize the focus of each of the areas and how they contribute to the mission of CVS Health.

4. Go to https://www.cvshealth.com. Provide a summary of their social responsibility activities.

5. According to the news release of December 3, 2017, CVS Health announced the execution of a definitive merger agreement under which CVS Health will acquire all outstanding shares of Aetna for a combination of cash and stock. According to the statement and the discussion in the chapter, what type of merger will this transaction be?

6. How could this transaction affect the hospital industry? Defend your answer.

7. Perform an Internet search regarding this transaction with Aetna. Based on the information, why do you think CVS Health made this decision?

References

5 Types of Mergers. Retrieved from https://www.mbda.gov/news/blog/2012/04/5-types-company-mergers

About the FTC. (2017). Retrieved from http://www.ftc.gov/aboutftc

About us. (2017). *Georgia collaborative*. Retrieved from www.georgiacollaborative.com

AHA News. (2017, January 26). Report finds hospital mergers reduce cost, enhance quality and services.

An HFMA Value Project Report. (2013). *Acquisition and affiliation strategies*. Retrieved from https://www.hfma.org/valueaffiliations/

Cohn, S. (2004). *The non-merger virtual merger: Is corporate law ready for virtual reality?* Retrieved from http://scholarship.law.ufl.edu/facultypub/315

CVS Health. History of CVS. Retrieved from https://cvshealth.com/about/company-history

Eight Largest Purchasing Organizations. (2010, September 2). Retrieved from https://www.beckershospitalreview.com/hospital-management-administration/7-largest-group-purchasing-organizations-for-hospitals.html

Goodbaum, B. (2015). *Streamlining the hospital supply chain: Just what the doctor ordered*. Retrieved from http://www.inboundlogistics.com/cms/article/streamlining-the-hospital-supply-chain-just-what-the-doctor-ordered/

Griffin, D. (2012). *Hospitals: What they are and how they work* (4th ed., pp. 283–286). Burlington, MA: Jones & Bartlett Learning.

Kamholz, K. (2017, October 11). *Interested in acquiring a hospital? 8 steps to follow*. Becker's hospital review. Retrieved from https://www.beckershospitalreview.com/hospital-transactions-and-valuation/interested-in-acquiring-a-hospital-8-steps-to-follow.html

Kenen, J. (2013). *Getting the facts on mergers and acquisitions*. Retrieved from https://healthjournalism.org/resources-tips-details.php?id=828#.WJG-79-nE2w

Niles. (2018). *Basis of the US healthcare system* (p. 374). Burlington, MA: Jones & Bartlett Learning.

Niles, N. (2012). *Basics of healthcare human resource management* (p. 316). Burlington, MA: Jones & Bartlett Learning.

Thompson Jr., A., Strickland III, A. J., & Gamble, J. (2010). *Crafting and executing strategy* (pp. 171–174). New York: McGraw-Hill Irwin.

Vartorella, L. (2017). *5 megatrends in that promise to shape healthcare*. Retrieved from https://www.beckershospitalreview.com/hospital-management-administration/5-megatrends-in-that-promise-to-shape-healthcare.html

Vu, M., White, A., Kelley, V., Hopper, J., & Liu, C. (2016). Hospital and health plan partnerships: The Affordable Care Act's impact on health and wellness. *American Health Drug Benefits, 9*(5), 269–278.

Weiss, M. (2015). Hospital-based medical group P acquisitions and alternatives the basics series for hospital based leaders.

Additional Resources

Healthcare Supply Chain 2015-Strategic Insights for the Distribution Channel. McKinsey & Company. Retrieved from http://www.hida.org/App_Themes/Member/docs/Press%20 Releases/HIDA_Thought-Leaders_White-Paper.pdf

Hospital M&A: When Done Well, M&A Can Achieve Valuable Outcomes. Deloitte Center for Health Solutions and the Healthcare Financial Management Association. Retrieved from https://www2.deloitte.com/content/dam/Deloitte/us/Documents/life-sciences-health-care /us-lshc-hospital-mergers-and-acquisitions.pdf

Marks, M., Mirvis, P., & Ashkenas, R. (2017, March–April). Surviving M&A: How to thrive amid the turmoil. Harvard Business Review, pp. 145–149.

Matthew, J., Joshin, J., & Kumar, S. (2012). *New trends in healthcare supply chain.* Retrieved from https://www.coursehero.com/file/22319415/New-trends-in-Supply-chain/

Patrick, M. (2014, November). *The 5 major entities of the hospital industry value chain.* Retrieved from http://marketrealist.com/2014/11/5-major-entities-hospital-industry-value-chain/

Spees, J. (2014). *Choosing the right affiliation structure.* Retrieved from https://www.hhnmag.com /articles/3951-choosing-the-right-affiliation-structure

Taylor, M., Porper, R., & Manki, S. (1995). The impact of horizontal mergers and acquisitions on cost and quality in health care. *Employee Benefits Journal, 95*(12), 16–19.

Vazirani, N. (2013). An integrative role of HR in handling issues post-mergers and acquisitions. *SIES Journal of Management, 9*(2), 88.

What Hospital Executives Should be Considering in Hospital Mergers and Acquisitions. (2013). *Dixon hughes goodman.* DHG Healthcare. Retrieved from http://www2.dhgllp.com/res_pubs /Hospital-Mergers-and-Acquisitions.pdf

CHAPTER 11

Structure, Organization, and Portals to Care

Claudia Neumann and Ashish Chandra

CHAPTER OBJECTIVES

- To identify common organizational structure concepts.
- To describe the typical organizational structure of an individual hospital.
- To address hospital line and staff functions, and administration and medical staff.
- To overview the governing body (board of directors) and its role as well as the management hierarchy from the top-down to the working supervisors.
- To address the means by which patients enter the acute-care hospital.

KEY TERMS

Entries to care
"Lean" management

Organizational chart
Organizational structure

▶ Common Organizational Structure Concepts

This section addresses some terminology and concepts from organization theory (Greenberg, 2012) to serve as background for understanding organizational structures utilized in hospitals. Organizational structures generally range from *mechanistic* to *organic*. Mechanistic structures are typified by a relatively narrow span of control, a high degree of centralization, specialization, and formalization, and a clearly defined chain of command. In contrast, organic structures typically exhibit a broad span of control, a limited degree of centralization and specialization, less formality than mechanistic structures, and sometimes an ambiguous chain of command.

Four common types of organizational structures, as utilized in both business and research, are listed in **TABLE 11.1** on descending order from most mechanistic to most organic (Alton, 2017).

Hierarchical structure is an **organizational structure** based on functions and their interrelationships. It is demonstrated by the arrangement of activities in a typical **organizational chart**. The advantages of this form are that it avoids redundancy, supports in-depth knowledge of skills, and clearly indicates interdepartmental relationships. Disadvantages are potentially unclear accountability of any particular sector of the business, and minimal understanding of details from the view of any particular product or service.

There are *divisional structures* assembled from smaller clusters of functional areas; and *product or service structures* aligned along a business's products or services. Advantages are in-depth product knowledge, ability to respond quickly, and a sense of identity, all potentially leading to enhanced commitment. Disadvantages of this type are loss of standardization and the chance of redundancy among functions.

Geographic (regional) structures are arranged along the lines of the regions or other geographic areas in which a business operates. For example, a hospital system that operates elements in different parts of a city, in different regions or states, and different countries. Similar structures may be aligned according to the various segments of the market the organization serves.

Matrix structures are based on the concept of matrix management. One axis of a matrix may show dimensions such as function, specific service, or other dimensions;

TABLE 11.1 Common Organizational Structures

Type	Characteristics	Flexibility
Functional Hierarchical	- High centralization, formalization, specialization - Many hierarchical levels - Small span of control	Least flexible type
Divisional	- Multiple, smaller functional structures - Hierarchical - More decentralized in terms of responsibilities than the functional structure	Less flexible type
Matrix	- Combined advantages of functional and divisional structures - Employees at medium and lower levels will have greater autonomy and be empowered to make decisions - Work in teams is supported	More flexible than the previous ones
Flatarchy	- Unnecessary levels are removed - Power is spread across multiple positions [9]	- More flexibility - Faster and better decision-making

the other axis is ordinarily a listing of the departments or managers responsible for certain accomplishments. The advantages of this arrangement are its flexibility, adaptability, capacity for more efficient utilization of resources, and its potential to provide dual career ladders. However, a significant disadvantage is its violation of the basic principle of unity of command (the "one boss" principle). In a matrix structure, an individual employee may be required to answer to multiple superiors.

Flatarchys are a hybrid of hierarchies and flat organizations. On the one hand, they utilize hierarchical elements; on the other hand, they often utilize teams and task-forces, often ad hoc, for particular tasks, or they may use a flat structure and occasionally form functional, hierarchical teams to accomplish certain objectives (Morgan, 2015).

Other organizational structures are:

Hybrid structures—In these structures, functional departments serve all areas, and at the same time specialization is maintained in certain dimensions.

The more organic organization structures may involve

- *Team-based structures*, which are usually meant for short-term tasks or projects, and have much higher flexibility. Members have more autonomy and their managers are meant to support and coordinate rather than control. Teams are sub-structures in the frame of the overall organizational structure (Faron, 2012).
- *Process (-based) structures*, which are also flat, decentralized, and foster equality instead of hierarchy. Number and tiers of managers are reduced (Faron, 2012).

A Word About "Lean"

Lean management is a process-improvement methodology and an important approach to management. It is intended to serve customer needs when and where they occur, reduce waste, and ensure defect-free products or services while continuously improving processes. In many respects, this approach is similar to that of total quality management (TQM). Lean concepts tend to lead to increased empowerment of staff, as Daniel T. Jones wrote in his Article "Four Lessons on Lean Healthcare" in 2015: "…what distinguishes Lean management is its focus on developing the capabilities of the front-line teams (doctors, nurses, and support staff) to manage and continuously improve their work."… which "results in highly motivated employees who feel a strong sense of ownership of "their" improvements." Lean management has to improve organizational design, and reduce bottlenecks and overprocessing. Implementing lean management in hospitals therefore seems to require rethinking and redesigning organizational structures to achieve flatter hierarchies or new concepts in matrix structures.

Why Is Organizational Structure Important?

1. *Organizational structure is the base of understanding reporting relationships and responsibilities.* The organizational structure of a hospital reveals the hospital's reporting structure, its chain of command, and the individuals or positions responsible for each activity.
2. *Organizational structure determines decision-making.* Organizational structure has a profound impact on how an organization is run. The way decisions are made and how people behave may differ considerably

from one hospital to another depending on organizational structure; for example, a hospital manager in an individual service area of one hospital might focus only on those departments that are enhancing his/her success, but a manager in the services sector of another hospital may be focused on making all the services perform well because he/she is responsible for all of them. Problem solving in steep hierarchies or highly centralized organizations may consume much time because of hierarchical overload.

3. *Organizational structure affects communication and coordination.* Depending on the type and details of organizational structure, the flow of information and the ways in which information exchange occurs will be different: one way, more unilateral, multilateral, two-way, top-down, or bottom-up. Structural support improves horizontal coordination, like liaisons, task forces, and project management in horizontally aligned projects.

4. *Organizational structure determines an organization's flexibility.* The capacity and flexibility to act depend, to a considerable extent, on organizational structure. Flat and lean structures empower employees to make more decisions on their own, shortening response times, while multi-layered organizations will require management to make most of the decisions, and approval processes through the organization's layers delay decision-making.

Organizational Structures in Hospitals—Overview

According to Shi and Singh (2016, p. 318), a hospital's organizational structure differs substantially from that of other large organizations (Alton, 2017; Faron, 2012). The authors describe a "dual" management structure of hospitals, constituted on the one hand by the general management of the organization, and on the other hand the organization of the medical staff, within a separate parallel structure. This dual structure provides the advantage of clearly assigned concerns and responsibilities of both administration and the medical staff, while at the same time it "presents numerous opportunities for conflict" (Shi & Singh, 2016) between these two chains of command. Especially the resulting (matrix-like) accountabilities, with staff being administratively accountable to one and professionally accountable to the other part of the organization, provide potential for both opportunity and conflict. Other sources (Shi & Singh, 2016) describe the organizational structure of hospitals as tripartite, with the CEO as a third pillar besides administration and medical staff.

Complex and Multi-layered Structures in Large Hospitals, Versus Much Simpler and Flatter Structures in Smaller Hospitals

According to the American Hospital Association (AHA), a hospital is an institution with at least six beds, the primary function of which is "to deliver patient services, diagnostics, and therapeutic, for particular or general medical conditions" (Shi & Singh, 2016, p. 290). Comparing this six-bed minimum requirement with hospitals within in the largest medical center in the United States, the Texas Medical Center in

Houston, with Memorial Hermann with a total of 3182 licensed beds (2013), Houston Methodist operating between 2108 (2013) and 2264 beds according to their own statistics (Corporate, n.d.), Texas Children's with 702 beds (2013), CHI St Luke's Episcopal Health with 1305 total licensed beds (2013), and others like the Tenet System, Kindred Healthcare, and Harris Health System all around 1000 beds, we can readily understand that the range of sizes—from 6 to 2000+ beds—will come with an equally broad range of organizational needs and requirements for an individual hospital's structure.

▶ Hospital Governance

Typical Organizational Structure of an Individual Hospital

Traditionally, in Hospital Governance, there is a *tripartite structure* (Shi & Singh, 2016).

CEO/Executive Level

- Perhaps also referred to as the President, Administrator, or Executive Director, the CEO is the public face of the hospital; this individual's job is to accomplish the organization's mission and objectives through leadership (Shi & Singh, 2016). The CEO has ultimate responsibility for day-to-day operations (Shi & Singh, 2016) and reports to the Board about the organization's progress with regard to mission and objectives. Therefore, the Board ordinarily appears at the top level of the organizational diagram.
- Further responsibilities of the CEO:
  - Create and maintain hospital policy
  - Recruit physicians
  - Provide liaison with medical staff
  - Ensure that the facility and its buildings are in working order
  - Make sure that the community receives the care it needs.

Board of Trustees

- This is also referred to as the Board of Directors or Governing Body. A number between 8 and 20 board members is not uncommon. Sometimes members are elected by the citizens, sometimes they are appointed by the system. Mostly, board members are influential business and community leaders (Shi & Singh, 2016). Hospitals with a religious affiliation often include clergy and congregational leadership on their boards. Teaching hospitals or other educationally affiliated hospitals are often overseen by universities (Shi & Singh, 2016).
- The Board is responsible for operations of the hospital, mission, policy guidelines, and the overall framework for day-to-day-operations (Shi & Singh, 2016). It approves long-term plans and budgets, appoints and evaluates the CEO, and has the power to remove the CEO (Shi & Singh, 2016). Usually, the Board also approves physicians' and other professionals' appointment to the medical staff.
- The board of directors has final authority overall in matters affecting the hospital organization.

Four Core Functions of the Board of Directors

1. Assures the community that the hospital cares for patients properly
2. Assumes financial responsibility
3. Exercises final approval over who is appointed to or removed from medical staff
4. Oversees all activities of the CEO.

Board members are commonly chosen every 2–3 years. In some instances, board members may be reelected and continue to serve. Insurance protects board members against financial liability in the event of lawsuits. Not-for-profit board members are ordinarily not financially compensated.

- A board of directors establishes a number of committees to oversee specific aspects of operations. These committees are the operative units of the Board; for example, Executive Committee, Finance Committee, Safety Committee, Long-Range Planning Committee, and so on.
- The board has ultimate fiduciary responsibility and can hire and fire the CEO and dictate the organization's policies. The board appoints and approves the members of the medical staff (credentialing and appointing).
- The Board of Directors is also the superior of the medical staff, and the body of providers (MD, DO, Podiatrists, DDS; Advanced NP and PA) who are credentialed for that hospital; staff, CEO, and the board of directors are expected to function cooperatively.
- The CEO and one or more physicians are ordinarily voting members of the Board.

Chief of Staff

A medical director ordinarily oversees all medical staff of a hospital. Depending on the size of the hospital, there will often be organizational structures for the different specialties. Medical staff is accountable to the CEO and the Board (Shi & Singh, 2016). Medical staff committees make decisions, are operative units of the medical staff, and oversee adherence to policies, documentation, rules, and regulations.

The chief of staff responds to provider requests to be credentialed for the hospital.

Other important structures—besides the tripartite structure—are:

Pyramid structure: with the board of directors on top level

- CEO reports to Board of Directors
  - Under the CEO: Medical staff office, Human Resources, CFO, CNO, etc.
  - Under individual executives, the directors of the departments:
    - Under the directors, the managers and supervisors within the department.

Matrix structure: Possessing multiple reporting lines, a matrix structure can be difficult to work with because of many responsible individuals than a single superior person to report to. In the Texas Medical Center, the Memorial Hermann System is one of the largest known examples of matrix structure.

Dyad structure: In this form, every leader has a designated partner; e.g., the Nursing leader and the Chief Medical Officer are often partners.

Balance of power. The balance of power among the elements of the governance structure has shifted throughout the history of hospitals. Power has been traversing between and among: the CEO as the representative and public face of the hospital; the Board of Trustees as the potential source of capital investment and prestige of the hospital; the physicians who are key to bringing patients into the hospital; and the Chief of Staff as the medical staff's authority. Presently, power is shifting more to the management side as hospitals and the entire healthcare environment become increasingly complex (Shi & Singh, 2016).

As a typical example of the divisional structure previously mentioned, hospital organization structures are commonly grouped into categories, as for example (Alzona, 2012):

- Administrative Services
- Informational Services
- Therapeutic Services
- Diagnostic Services
- Support Services

Another, perhaps more common way, is to categorize according to (Townsend, 2013):

- Financial
- Medical surgical
- Medical nonoperational
- Nursing
- Operations
- Human Resources

Hospitals vary in structure largely according to the presence of competitive hospitals nearby, the demographics of the region, and needs of the patient population (Townsend, 2013).

Types of Hospitals

For-Profit vs. Not-for-Profit Hospitals: Different organizational structures may result from different management requirements, according to their respective objectives.

For example, comparing for-profit with not-for-profit hospitals, in for-profit corporations, the CEO is often on the Board of Directors, and in some instances is even the president of the board (2008). On the other hand, in a great many nonprofit corporations, "Conventional wisdom often suggests that the Chief Executive Officer (often called the "Executive Director") not be on the Board" (2008).

TABLE 11.2 lists some key differences between for-profit vs. not-for-profit hospitals in the areas of Mission, Finance, and Executive (2008).

TABLE 11.2 Management Requirements for For-Profit Corporations versus Nonprofit Corporations (2008)

For-Profit Corporations	Nonprofit Corporations
Mission	
Mission important	Mission very important
Financial results	Cash-loss generator may be the key service
Nonfinancial metrics important	Nonfinancial metrics of mission performance very important
Finance	
Financial metrics of performance, P&I, stock price, and cash flow very important	Financial metrics of meeting budget and cash flow projections also important
Funds come from operations and financial capital markets	Funds come from operations, debts, grants, and philanthropy
Short-term goals very important	Deep focus on long-term goals (as long as cash is there)
Executive	
Small board—paid governance	Often large board—volunteer governance
Few board committees	Often many board committees
Combined chair/CEO plus lead director	Nonexecutive volunteer chair, plus CEO

Data from How Nonprofits Differ from For-Profits – and How They Are the Same. Authenticity Consulting, LLC. (2008). Retrieved from https://managementhelp.org/misc/Nonprofits-ForProfits.pdf; "Field Guide to Developing, Operating and Restoring Your Nonprofit Board," at www.authenticityconsulting.com

▶ Doorways into the Acute Care Hospital

The various means by which patients can be admitted to the hospital are frequently referred to as "entries to care." Generally, there are two ways to enter a hospital: a patient can directly access the hospital via *self-referral* or by way of the hospital's emergency service, or can access the hospital by *provider referral*, which involves admission from a primary physician, clinic, medical office, prison, or Federally Qualified Health Center.

Planned Hospital Entry

Entering a hospital via provider referral is a planned hospital entry. This ordinarily occurs when an individual's primary care physician or other involved provider with the authority to admit patients decides that hospitalization is necessary. A patient *must* be seen by a physician before admission to the hospital can be referred to as a planned entry.

Unplanned Hospital Entry

If a patient enters the hospital without being admitted via a physician who has admitting privileges at the hospital, this is an unplanned entry. Unplanned entries mostly result from acutely ill individuals entering by way of the emergency department, including persons brought to the hospital following accidents or other traumatic occurrence. Any patient arriving by means other than the referral of an admitting physician constitutes an unplanned entry.

More Means of Entry

The Emergency Medical Treatment and Active Labor Act (EMTALA) is a federal law enacted in 1986 to prohibit discrimination among patients presented for admission regardless of insurance status or ability to pay. It also provides that any patient coming to the emergency department must be seen and stabilized. To transfer any such patient to another facility, the hospital must have permission of both the patient and the accepting facility.

Varying means of entry can sometimes lead to unusual situations. For example, when an older patient arrives at a facility that does not participate in Medicare, one might call 911 for admission on an emergency basis. Or perhaps, the patient may be asked for upfront payment upon admission.

Patient access to the emergency department by way of first responders requires all of the usual permissions and paperwork but these may ordinarily be postponed until the patient is stabilized. The established order for physicians seeing patients in the emergency room is determined through *Emergency Department Triage*. The priority decision is based on seriousness:

- life threatening, seen first
- serious but not life threatening, seen later
- non-life threatening or routine

Life-threatening situations, of course, call for immediate attention any time of the day, including rapid access to tests and all other diagnostic and supporting services. However, as many individuals experiencing non-life-threatening problems or more routine illnesses or injuries have discovered, one can often expect long waits in the emergency departments.

Brief Chapter Summary

The chapter addresses some different types of organizational structures, including specifics of why organizational structures are important. There is a brief discussion of the various characteristics as well as the flexibility of different organizational structures. Another component included in the chapter is the concept of "Lean" organizations, which is increasingly becoming a critical part of each organizational structure. There is also a brief description about the various individuals involved in the hospital governance, including the roles that they play.

Questions for Review and Discussion

1. What are four common types or organizational structure? Include their advantages and disadvantages.
2. How can Lean Management influence a hospital?
3. Why is organizational structure important?
4. How does the type of a hospital, its ownership, length of stay of its patients, etc. affect its organization structures?
5. How does the hospital's organizational structure differ from that of other large organizations?
6. What typical structure do we traditionally find in Hospital Governance?
7. What are the four core functions of the Board of Directors?

References

Alton, L. (2017). *4 common types of organizational structures. All business.* Retrieved from https://www.allbusiness.com/4-common-types-organizational-structures-103745-1.html

Alzona, E. (2012). Organizational structure of a Hospital. *SlideShare.net.* Retrieved from https://www.slideshare.net/ealzona/organizational-structure-ofahospital-13374694?from_action=save

Authenticity Consulting, LLC. (2008). *How nonprofits differ from for-profits—And how they are the same.* Authenticity Consulting, LLC. Retrieved from https://managementhelp.org/misc/Nonprofits-ForProfits.pdf—Adapted from "Field Guide to Developing, Operating and Restoring Your Nonprofit Board", at www.authenticityconsulting.com

Corporate. (n.d.). *Houston methodist hospital system.* Retrieved from https://www.houstonmethodist.org/newsroom/facts-statistics/

Faron, A. (2012). *Relations between lean management and organizational structures.* University of Business, Wrocław, Poland. Retrieved from http://research.logistyka-produkcja.pl/images/stories/Numer_4/paper_9.pdf

Greenberg, J. (2012, December). *Behavior in organizations* (10th ed.). New Delhi: Prentice Hall of India Pvt. Ltd.

Houston Chronicle. (2013). Retrieved from https://www.chron.com/discoverhouston/article/Top-hospitals-in-Houston-4486856.php

Jones, D. (2015). *Four lessons on lean healthcare.* The Lean Enterprise Academy. Retrieved from http://www.leanuk.org/article-pages/articles/2015/february/19/four-lessons-on-lean-healthcare.aspx

Morgan, J. (2015). The 5 types of organizational structures: Part 4, Flatarchies. *Forbes.* https://www.forbes.com/sites/jacobmorgan/2015/07/15/the-5-types-of-organizational-structures-part-4-flatarchies/#189ec056707c

Shi, L., & Singh, D. A. (2016). *Delivering healthcare in America—A systems approach* (6th ed.). Burlington, MA: Jones & Bartlett Learning.

Townsend, M. (2013). *Quora.* Retrieved from https://www.quora.com/What-is-the-organization-structure-of-a-hospital

CHAPTER 12

Direct Patient Care: The Hospital Team

Charles R. McConnell

CHAPTER OBJECTIVE

- Provide a brief overview of the principal groups and functions involved in providing direct patient care; specifically, the Medical Staff, Nursing Services, Clinical Laboratory, Imaging, Physical Therapy, Respiratory Therapy, and Pharmacy.

KEY TERMS

Clinical laboratory
Diagnostic imaging and therapeutic
  Radiology
Medical staff

Nursing services
Pharmacy
Physical therapy
Respiratory therapy

▶ Introduction

The primary mission of the hospital, the provision of patient care, involves the applied efforts of a considerable number of people of broadly varying skills, capabilities, and qualifications. This chapter provides a concise overview of the services, departments, and activities that are brought together to fulfill that patient care mission of the hospital. The information that follows may be considered as representative of a "typical" hospital, if indeed there is such an entity as a typical hospital.

Not every function or activity cited in this summary will be present in every hospital. The very term "hospital" may, for some individuals, conjure up an image of a sprawling medical center of a thousand-plus beds affiliated with a medical school and including every conceivable form of healthcare service. Some, however, will ordinarily think of a hospital as a community-based facility of fewer than 100 beds that meets a few specific needs for the residents of a relatively limited geographic area. Other portions of this book will leave readers with the distinct impression, however, that the smaller, independent community hospitals are a dwindling resource as many of their numbers are either closed or caught up in mergers or in the formation of healthcare systems.

There are some fundamental services that are to be found in every hospital; there are some found only in specialized facilities or in larger centers of medical care.

▶ The Medical Staff

The hospital **medical staff** is an organized body composed largely of physicians, dentists, and osteopaths who have been granted specific rights to practice within the hospital, and who possess the right to admit patients to the hospital.

The medical staff has significant impact on the quality and quantity of care provided in the hospital. Its members have been authorized by the board of trustees to treat patients in the hospital and are accountable to this governing authority. The board of trustees appoints the medical staff. The staff formulates its own policies, rules, and regulations, and is responsible to the board for the quality of patient care.

Following appointment to the medical staff of the hospital, the individual is obligated to provide proof of participation in a program of continuing medical education (CME). The Joint Commission and all state medical organizations stipulate that the medical staff must participate in continuing education.

An individual's medical staff membership will ordinarily fall under one of the following categories:

Active or attending staff—medical staff members having full rights and privileges. Each physician with this designation may be required to admit a certain number of patients each year or lose active privileges.

Associate staff—medical staff members who have incomplete privileges and may be working toward active staff designation.

Provisional staff—ordinarily new staff members; there may be a probationary period during which they are supervised by other physicians for a certain number of cases.

Courtesy staff—ordinarily a physician does not often admit patients to that particular hospital.

Consulting staff—do not admit patients but rather are called upon to consult on particular cases.

Temporary staff—those accorded specific privileges for a designated time, often to treat a single.

The hospitalist—ordinarily an employee of the hospital, this is usually an internal medicine specialist who makes daily rounds and covers the entire hospital.

Allied health personnel—nonphysicians granted for clinical privileges in hospitals, including (but not limited to) podiatrists, chiropractors, physician assistants (PAs), nurse practitioners (NPs), nurse midwives, and psychologists.

The medical staff is divided into medical specialty departments and sections. Each clinical department has a physician designated as chief or director.

▶ Physician Extenders

The ever-expanding need for healthcare professionals has created a need for mid-level professionals such as PAs, NPs, and nurse midwives. These occupations have become important because of a chronic shortage of physicians in rural and inner city areas. These individuals are trained to perform routine medical procedures under the indirect supervision of a physician. They are able to work independently to diagnose and treat diseases.

Physician Assistants

PAs serve as extensions of the healthcare team in providing routine care, conducting physical exams, diagnosing and treating illnesses, ordering and interpreting tests, performing rudimentary surgical procedures, and prescribing medicine. PAs work in a variety of settings. In rural or inner city communities, PAs are often the only available primary care providers.

Nurse Practitioners

Like PAs, NPs are similar in that they also work under the supervision of a physician and treat both physical and mental conditions. An NP is a registered nurse (RN) who has earned an advanced degree and has been trained in a specific field. They focus on individualized care and may work with patients of all ages.

Midwives

NPs who work in obstetrics and gynecology can also provide specialized care in the field of midwifery. Midwives are healthcare professionals who provide prenatal care to expectant mothers, care for the infant during the birthing process, and assist both the infant and the mother with postpartum care. Midwives offer their services during normal pregnancies and deliveries, and if complications arise, they can ordinarily call upon a physician. There are different types of midwives based on training and education. Some gain the necessary skills by serving an apprenticeship with a midwife or physician, by completing an independent study, or by attending a midwifery school. Mid-level healthcare professionals hold the key to equalizing the shortage of healthcare professionals. PAs and NPs can reduce the burden of physicians by providing primary care, and midwives can provide a natural-care alternative in the field of gynecology and obstetrics.

▶ Nursing Services

A significant part of a hospital's mission is to ensure the delivery of quality, courteous, and considerate care from skilled, understanding personnel. The principal group involved in fulfilling this mission is the department of **nursing services**. Overall, nurses by far comprise the single largest healthcare professional group in the United States.

For many years, RNs were typically trained in the hospital setting in 3-year diploma programs that focused on clinical skills. As needs grew, shortages of professional RNs led to the development of the licensed practical nurse (LPN) and licensed vocational nurse (LVN). Becoming an LPN or LVN required about half the training time it took to become an RN, but by comparison, they were understandably limited in their scope of practice.

Meanwhile, educational programs for RNs underwent changes that became especially evident in the 1960s as nursing education began an orderly transition from hospital-based programs to nursing education at colleges or universities. The hospital-based diploma programs began to be phased out in favor of 2-year university baccalaureate degree programs or 2-year associate degree programs at community colleges. Educational programs continue to evolve.

Nursing Education

Already mentioned are the 2-year associate degree nurses (ADNs) versus 4-year baccalaureate degree nurses (BSNs). However, today's nurses are possessed of a variety of education-and-experience combinations. With additional education, usually 2 years, an RN can become an **advanced practice nurse** (APN or APRN). Advanced education in nursing may also lead to the role of **clinical nurse specialist** (CNS), NP, or certified registered nurse anesthetist (CRNA).

All RNs, LPNs, and LVNs must be licensed by the state board of nursing in the state where they will be practicing. All states have similar licensure eligibility requirements; and licensure is based on passing an examination. Each state's board of nursing is responsible for suspending and revoking licenses.

Modes of Nursing Care Delivery

Organizational structures today are moving away from vertical hierarchical structures with formal channels of communication and moving toward flatter organizations with collaborative teams, with a concomitant change in focus from product- to customer-centered care. This shift, along with the shortage of nurses, has been accompanied by an increase in outpatient care, self-care of chronic illness, and use of medical technologies, including electronic medical records.

Today there are several commonly used modes of nursing delivery: (1) case nursing, (2) functional nursing, (3) team nursing, (4) primary care nursing, (5) modular (or district) nursing, (6) case management, (7) collaborative practice, and (8) differentiated practice.

Case Nursing

The case method of nursing is one of the earliest forms of nursing care. In this system, the nurse or case manager individually plans and administers the care of a patient on a one-to-one basis.

Functional Nursing

Beginning in the 1920s and continuing into the 1950s, nurses became aware of studies about the functional division of labor in industry at large and applied some of these techniques to their own discipline. Functional nursing uses a pyramidal organization to designate the division of labor. Under such an arrangement, based on individual expertise, each unit member is given specific functions or tasks to perform, such as administering medications, taking vital signs, and such.

Team Nursing

Team nursing began around the time of World War II when there was a growing shortage of RNs. In the absence of RNs, hospitals had to use technicians, vocational nurses, and nurses' aides. Frequently, the less trained nursing personnel were put under the supervision of a more highly trained RN, who was called the team leader. A team would be asked to provide care to a group of patients in the nursing unit. Ideally, the team leader would be the best prepared person and could be expected to help the team formulate and carry out nursing care plans for every patient assigned to the team. Team nursing as a whole can be expensive because it requires more personnel.

Primary Care Nursing

Primary care nursing has some of the characteristics of the case method in that one RN is assigned to each patient. However, in contrast to the case method, the nurse assigned to the patient is not responsible for just one shift; rather, the primary care nurse is responsible for the patient's care for 24 hours a day, 7 days a week. The primary care nurse must assess a patient's nursing needs, collaborate with other health professionals, including the physician, and formulate a plan of nursing care for which he/she is held accountable.

Modular (or District) Nursing

Modular (or district) nursing is a form of both team nursing and primary nursing. Smaller teams care for the patient. An RN, with the assistance of a team, delivers care to as large a group of patients as possible. The RN functions as the coordinator of care. Sometimes, the same team will be assigned to the same patient rooms in a unit that experiences longer patient stays.

Case Management

Psychiatry and social work provided the model for case management in nursing. This method was initially utilized in community nursing and was introduced into inpatient settings in the 1980s. A specialized nurse coordinates the care of an episode of illness for a patient and their family. This work includes evaluating and monitoring services from the time of admission to the hospital to post-discharge.

Collaborative Practice

The American Medical Association and the American Nurses Association established a National Joint Practice Committee in 1972. The committee examined the effects of collaboration between physicians and nurses on such issues as nurse satisfaction and quality of care, and concluded that collaboration was beneficial. Collaboration gained in importance in the 1990s as health care moved from inpatient settings to outpatient and community settings. With this came the development of the NP role, visiting-nurse organizations, and methods to classify patient diagnoses as established by the North American Nursing Diagnosis Association (NANDA).

Differentiated Practice

The differentiated practice method of assigning work to nurses takes into account their credentials and levels of education. Nurses with graduate or bachelor degrees are assigned care and planning for patients who require more complex care, whereas nurses with a 2-year associate's degree are assigned patients who require less complex care in less structured settings. The educational level of the nurses may influence the strategy chosen for staffing.

Terms and Standards

The understanding of precisely which nursing standard was utilized when a nursing department's budget and staffing schedule was established is essential. A nursing standard or norm is defined as the amount of time and resources needed or considered desirable for each patient in a 24-hours period to provide the appropriate type of care. The American Hospital Association and the ANA identified various nursing standards as early as 1950. Financial managers should know that when nursing expenses are low or below budget, a detailed look at the staffing patterns may be required. The following possibilities must be considered: (1) non-nursing personnel were utilized in place of RNs, (2) nurses were attached to some other cost center and were used in place of regular staff nurses, (3) inadequate information was available at the time the budget was established, (4) the department was unable to fill all budgeted positions, and (5) the on-duty nursing staff is carrying an unfair load. To analyze all of these specific circumstances, a financial manager must understand certain nursing definitions and terms that are widely accepted in nursing service. The patient must be able to rely on a reasonable standard of care, meaning that the hospital must meet regulatory requirements and professional standards.

Staffing

Nurse staffing is accomplished by determining how many full-time equivalent (FTE) nursing personnel from each skill class (e.g., RNs, LPNs, and nurses' aides) are needed to properly operate each nursing unit. Given the variety of levels of nursing care required by different populations of patients, and the considerable labor needs of a nursing unit, staffing is a challenge. The key to determining the number of staff and the qualifications needed is to use patient acuity systems and nurse competence and expertise, guided by staffing policies. An initial consideration is whether staffing will be handled by one central office or delegated to each separate unit. Guidelines must also be established to determine how many weeks will be scheduled at one time. If hospitals tend to vary in the number of inpatients (census), it may be decided to staff for the minimum number of patients with additional staff of part-timers or *per diem* staff who are called upon as needed.

Hospitals may choose to use patient acuity systems to classify patients according to care categories and to quantify the nursing expertise and effort required. Generally, a patient's physical, technical, psychological, social, and teaching requirements are assessed in determining acuity levels. Care categories include routine care, moderate care, complete care, and continuous care. The nursing department quantifies the total nursing care time required for each patient-care category. Many patient acuity systems are computerized. Daily, weekly, and seasonal variations must be considered in the staffing arrangements.

Nurse Staffing Issues

Changes in the labor force in most areas of the nation have resulted in shortages of RNs as well as other health professionals. Because hospitals are labor-intensive, staff shortages can have a major impact on operations. Hospitals are addressing this issue by implementing creative strategies such as giving bonuses, using clinical career ladders to motivate and reward nurses involved in direct patient care, allowing nurses to budget for their unit, broadening job responsibilities and autonomy, providing in-service training, and offering child daycare services. In an effort to improve staff retention, hospitals have instituted programs to bring recognition to their institutions and make them desirable places to work.

Scheduling

Once the nursing leadership agrees on a staffing plan for each unit, and nursing administration determines the type of nursing modalities best suited to the hospital, the challenge is then scheduling nursing personnel so that patients receive the necessary care at the time they require it. Nurse scheduling is determining when each member of the nursing staff will be on duty and on which shift each will work. Scheduling should take into account weekends, the length of individual work assignments, and requests for time off. Scheduling is typically done for a period of 4 or 6 weeks, and is frequently tailored to each nursing unit. There are several commonly used approaches to nurse scheduling; which approach to use is determined by a unit's leadership based on knowledge of patient needs and staff capabilities.

Some nursing departments choose to schedule straight shifts; in other words, nurses are hired for the day shift, evening shift, or night shift. Some hospitals use rotating shifts so that all nursing personnel will have equal shifts divided among day, evening, and night shifts. Some hospitals have also utilized alternative arrangements such as a workweek of four 10-hour days or three 12-hour days.

Department Organization

Two general methods are used to organize the work of health professionals in an acute-care hospital, each centered on a function or a program. A functional organization revolves around the services to be provided, and workers report to a specific supervisor for their specialty area. This organizational form enhances relationships within a specialty area and can be cost-effective while promoting professional growth. However, this form of organization discourages collaboration and coordination among specialties and may fragment care.

Organization by program divides up work for a particular service or disease process, a multidisciplinary approach useful for integrating care; however, patients who require services from several programs may find it difficult to navigate the system. However, there can be duplication of services in separate programs that lead to inefficiency.

As many as 40%–50% of all hospital employees are found in the nursing department. The department may be organized in pyramidal fashion, much like the hospital itself. The primary responsibility for nursing functions rests with the top manager of the nursing department who may be referred to by one of several possible titles: director of nursing (DON); chief nursing officer (CNO); chief nursing executive; or vice president (VP) of nursing. The director may have one or two assistant directors. The title of supervisor is frequently given to an RN who oversees the activities of two or more nursing units or takes responsibility for a shift. Below this person, there may be nurse managers (formerly head nurses) who supervise individual units.

The Patient-Care Unit

Nursing departments may be organized in a decentralized fashion into patient-care units or nursing units. Units vary in size; they may be very small, with 8- to 10-bed units for specialized care, or they may contain many more beds. Most units fall in the range of 20–40 beds. Nursing units generally operate in three shifts covering a 24-hour period; a relative few units cover 24 hours with two 12-hour shifts.

In the past, most patient rooms were semiprivate and accommodated two patients; more recently, the trend has been to private or single-bed rooms. Most hospital units include rooms designed and reserved for patients with illnesses that warrant isolation. Units dedicated to respiratory disease may also have a negative-pressure room designed to eliminate outflow of air and are reserved for patients with tuberculosis.

Other Components and Technology in the Patient-Care Unit

A fundamental area in a patient-care unit is the nurses' station, ordinarily the focal point of administrative activity. The nurses' station is normally where patients' charts are kept. It is centrally located for all the activities of the nursing unit. It also ordinarily includes a designated area for physicians to update records and write orders. It may include computers dedicated to physician use. A quiet area may also be provided for physicians to dictate notes.

The nursing unit will also contain a medication room. Hospitals commonly use unit dosing, in which each unit of medication is separately packaged and usually bar-coded. In larger hospitals, nurses generally use a computerized system to administer medications. A computer is used to scan the patient's ID bracelet, and each medication is then scanned before it is given. The computer alerts the nurse if the medication must be adjusted and also alert the nurse if the wrong medication has been scanned for that patient or if a dose has been missed. The computer may be located permanently in the patient's room or on a rolling cart.

In larger hospitals, medications are stored in a pyxis, a computerized machine that dispenses unit-dose medications. This unit is located in a secure, separate room that may or may not also contain clean supplies, instruments, and equipment. In some hospitals, locked cabinets in each patient room contain scheduled medications for that patient, whereas other hospitals store all scheduled and PRN medications in a pyxis. Still others use rolling computer cabinets that contain locked drawers for each patient room in a hallway. Additionally, a separate room in the nursing unit is set aside for used, dirty, or hazardous items.

Often there is a small pantry or kitchen in the patient-care unit for use by patients and their visitors. There is a nurses' lounge where nurses take breaks, eat meals, receive in-service training, and give change-of-shift reports. Other rooms that might be found in nursing units are a toilet area for visitors, a consultation room where physicians can meet with the patients' families, and treatment rooms. Some units may also have a pleasant place for visitors to sit down with the patients outside of their rooms.

Special-Care Units

Special-care units have developed with increased technology and modern medical advances. Over the recent two decades, special-care units have multiplied and matured. The sophisticated modern hospital may have a variety of special-care facilities to manage and maintain patients with special illnesses and injuries. These facilities may include intensive-care units for medicine and surgery, special cardiac-care units, kidney dialysis centers, inpatient psychiatric units, inpatient alcohol and drug addiction units, inpatient rehabilitation units, obstetrics units, pediatric units, and skilled nursing facilities for long-term care. A special unit need not be based in the hospital; it may be constituted as a hospital home-care program or a hospice.

Intensive Care Units

The most common type of special care unit in the hospital is the general medical/surgical intensive care unit (ICU). These units were established to meet the clinical needs of hospitalized patients and their physicians. Critically ill patients who are in a precarious clinical state and require intense supervision are cared for in the ICU. In addition to sophisticated equipment and instrumentation, ICUs rely on a highly concentrated nursing staff; often, there is one nurse to each patient. Some hospitals further segregate their ICUs into specialty units based on the specific type of acute care needed; for example, cardiac critical care, neurological intensive care, neonatal intensive care, thoracic intensive care, and surgical intensive care.

Coronary Care Units

Today, nearly all medical/surgical hospitals in the United States have some CCU capacities. The CCUs do for cardiac patients what the ICUs do for severe medical and surgical patients. The CCU has had a dramatic impact on saving lives. Patients likely to require the services of a CCU are those who have had or are having a heart attack or a cardiac arrhythmia. The predominant care provided in this unit involves medication rather than surgery. Nurses in such units are generally certified in advanced cardiac life support (ACLS) and can attempt to resuscitate a patient requiring such action. One of the primary objectives of the CCU staff is to detect early signs of impending cardiac distress so that it can be treated before cardiac arrest takes place.

Thoracic Intensive Care Unit (TICU)

Patients admitted to the TICU have had either cardiac or pulmonary surgery. The protocols for their care include activities such as infusing blood that was lost during cardiac surgery into the patient. These patients have been placed on a ventilator to assist their breathing during surgery and come to the unit still being assisted by the ventilator. Certain parameters must be met before this machine is discontinued. The nurses in this unit must be familiar with these parameters and alert the physician when the patient is ready to have the ventilator removed.

Neurological Intensive Care Unit

Patients admitted to this unit have typically had a disruption in their neurological system (e.g., due to brain or spine injury, or brain surgery). These patients require special monitoring of cardiac and vital signs, such as the internal cranial pressure (ICP). Nurses in this area must know how to interpret changes in these signs and understand the standard of care required by these acute patients.

Surgical Intensive Care Unit

Patients who have had abdominal surgery and are unstable or require close surveillance may be sent to the surgical ICU. Nurses focus on postoperative conditions that require monitoring of returning bowel sounds and stability of vital signs. They must be familiar with the latest wound vacuum machines, which continually remove purulent material, as well as the specialized dressings that are required in this unit.

Non-acute Special Care Units

Some special care units are not intended for life-threatening situations, although all units must be prepared for such events. An example of a non-acute special care unit is a renal dialysis center. These centers have increased in number over the last decade. They provide artificial kidney support for patients whose kidneys have stopped functioning properly. These units may also serve patients who suffer from similar underlying disease processes such as diabetes.

Special care units also include psychiatric units and inpatient alcohol- and drug-related units. Currently on the increase are specialty units dedicated to rehabilitation. It is recognized that these units may provide the measures needed by patients prior to discharge that will allow them to return home.

Telemonitoring and Bedside Terminals

Along with burgeoning technological innovations and the use of patient acuity levels, telemonitoring equipment, bedside terminals, and automated clinical records are also being used by nurses. The type of telemonitoring equipment used may vary from hospital to hospital depending on unit complexity, the needs of the patients, and the resources of the hospital. This equipment can be used for routine evaluations of blood pressure, pulse, respiration, and temperature, as well as other physical and physiological conditions.

Unlike telemonitoring equipment, bedside terminals require interaction with the nursing staff. Nurses directly enter and retrieve patients' clinical data, such as vital signs, lab results, and medications given, using bedside computer terminals. This is an efficient and accurate way to capture data at the source or point of care. Ideally, the bedside terminals will be integrated with the hospital's information system. This facilitates communication between nurses and other allied health professionals, and results in more responsive patient care. Bedside terminals also produce an automated clinical record, a substitute for the traditional patient chart.

Older Patients in the Hospital: Geriatrics

The increasing presence of older adults in hospitals is consistent with the growing aging population in the United States. Compared with younger adults, older Americans use a disproportionately larger share of the services provided by physicians, nurses, and other practitioners. People older than age 65 consume one-third or more of all healthcare services.

Services to the Elderly

Hospital administrators must be mindful that elderly patients require additional services to aid the process of healing. Providing services that meet the specific needs of geriatric patients can reduce their length of stay in the hospital. These services can include geriatric case management, transportation, and physical or occupational therapy. The geriatric case manager plays an important role in the hospital setting.

In a perfect world, the families of inpatient geriatric patients would be available to provide added care. This would allow the hospital staff to rely on family members as mediators between patient and medical staff. In reality, however, members of the nursing staff bear the major responsibility for geriatric care. The nursing staff may complain of time constraints that prevent them from giving their patients the extra attention necessary to provide quality of care. In this situation, hospitals should provide competency training in the field of geriatrics to provide added support to the staff.

Hospitals can benefit by providing competency training to reflect the patient population they serve. In addition, job descriptions should reflect geriatric education, including continuing education and work experience specifically with older adults.

Hiring staff with no formal training in geriatrics can negatively impact direct patient care. In addition to acquiring staff with appropriate training, some hospitals have developed geriatric departments that focus on the needs of the older patients. These departments can provide a variety of services for older adults, ranging from transportation to social events. Services may include memory care, arthritis treatment, hospice, pain management, palliative care, geriatric psychiatry, eye institute, and wound-management services.

In the 21st century, nursing service is undergoing rapid changes centered on interprofessional collaboration and communication, increased safety awareness, activities to improve performance, standards of care, and evidence-based practice. Issues involving staff retention and efficient orientation and transition to practice for new nurses will continue to be a challenge.

▶ The Clinical Laboratory and the Pathologist

Structure and Function of the Clinical Laboratory

The standard **clinical laboratory** includes two basic divisions: anatomical pathology and clinical pathology. The anatomical division is overseen by a medical doctor or osteopathic physician who has graduated from an accredited academic program and is board certified in pathology. The pathologist and staff examine tissue and exfoliated cell samples collected from patients. The pathologist also performs autopsies to determine the cause and manner of death. The support staff assists with autopsies and prepares tissues and cells for microscopic examination by the pathologist.

In most instances, the clinical pathology division is also under the technical direction of the pathologist. This division is divided into functional sections or departments. For example, the hematology staff examines blood cells, the urinalysis staff analyzes urine samples, the clinical chemistry staff measures various analytes in plasma and serum, the coagulation staff examines the clotting properties of blood, the microbiology staff isolates and identifies microorganisms collected from patients, and the immunology staff analyzes the immune response of patients or uses immunological methods to measure other analytes. Technicians in the blood bank type patients' blood, select appropriate blood units, and prepare blood components for transfusion. Staff in the phlebotomy section collect blood samples from patients, although in some healthcare organizations, this responsibility is shared with nursing staff.

Clinical Laboratory Certification

Any laboratory that tests human samples to aid in the diagnosis or treatment of disease must be certified by the Department of Health and Human Services (DHHS). In 1988, Congress passed the Clinical Laboratory Improvements Act (CLIA) to establish minimum standards for clinical laboratories. This act was passed in response to several incidents in which Papanicolaou (Pap) smears were misread or mixed up, resulting in the misdiagnosis of many patients. The act established minimum educational and experience requirements for all clinical laboratory personnel and also clearly defined testing categories according to their level of complexity.

Clinical Laboratory Accreditation

Accreditation indicates that a clinical laboratory has met the stringent standards of the accrediting agency. Clinical laboratories can be accredited by various nongovernmental accrediting organizations. Accrediting agencies differ from governmental agencies in that they do not have enforcement powers and can only withdraw accreditation if a laboratory fails to comply with the accreditation standards. Many clinical laboratories are accredited by the College of American Pathologists (CAP). The Joint Commission (TJC) can also accredit clinical laboratories as well as other activities and operations of a medical treatment facility. Hospital blood banks can also be accredited by the AABB, formally known as the American Association of Blood Banks.

Laboratory Personnel

There are several different personnel positions in the clinical laboratory. The *laboratory director* must be a physician or possess a doctorate in a physical or biological science. Physicians must be board certified in pathology to perform tissue and cell examinations or autopsies. A nonphysician director must possess a PhD and be certified by the American Board of Microbiology, American Board of Clinical Chemistry, or the American Board of Bioanalysis.

A *technical consultant* is responsible for overseeing tests in the clinical division. This individual can be a qualified physician or a PhD scientist but is most often a clinical laboratory scientist (CLS) with a degree in clinical laboratory science.

The term "*medical technologist*" (MT) is an older title that was gradually replaced by the CLS title. Today, however, most often used for this position is medical laboratory scientist (MLS). The MT or MLS must possess a bachelor's degree in clinical laboratory science and must have passed a national certification examination. The MLS can perform any test in the laboratory regardless of complexity. In some states, the MLS must be licensed by the state. The MLS who wishes to specialize in one area of the laboratory can do so after receiving additional training and successfully passing a special certification examination.

Most clinical laboratories also employ *medical laboratory technicians* (MLTs). This position requires a 2-year associate degree in an accredited program and certification. The MLT generally does not perform tests of high complexity.

The *phlebotomist* is trained to draw blood specimens from patients for laboratory analysis. Phlebotomy training can be obtained at a technical school or on the job.

The *laboratory assistant* supports the activities of the clinical laboratory by washing glassware, cleaning the area, inventorying supplies, and filing reports. The laboratory assistant is usually trained on the job and no certification or specific education is required.

In the anatomical division of the laboratory, *the histologic technician* cuts, stains, and mounts tissues on slides for review by the pathologist. This technician must have graduated from an approved program and must have passed a certification test. The *cytology technologist* examines exfoliated cells for disease and forwards questionable samples to the pathologist for review. The cytology technologist must have graduated from an approved program and must have passed a certification examination. An additional position in the anatomical division is the *pathology assistant*, who assists the pathologist on autopsy cases and other anatomic pathology procedures. This also requires successful completion of a special academic program and a certification process.

Quality Improvement

Clinical laboratories are required to have a quality improvement system that promotes the highest standards of quality regarding patient test results, employee qualifications, management, training, and services provided to the patient and physician. Laboratory tests must be timely and accurate, as clinical laboratory results play a critical role in the diagnosis of many disease states.

The Future of the Clinical Laboratory

Like other fields of medicine, the clinical laboratory is evolving rapidly. Many new tests are being developed in the areas of molecular diagnostics and biomarkers. In the *molecular diagnostics* approach, a patient sample is searched for specific RNA/DNA base sequences or other regulatory molecules associated with cell functions. Analysis at the molecular level can detect disease and even the potential to develop a specific disease in the future.

The *polymerase chain reaction* (PCR) test is becoming commonplace in clinical reference laboratories. This is a molecular diagnostics test that searches for a specific DNA or RNA base sequence to detect the presence of a species bacteria or virus in a patient sample. This type of test can greatly reduce the time it takes to get results, which can significantly improve patient care.

The Professional Laboratorian

It is apparent that the professional laboratorian must be a highly educated and skilled individual. Today's laboratorian must have a thorough knowledge of quality improvement, medical ethics, biology, microbiology, parasitology, chemistry, biochemistry, anatomy, physiology, pathology, and molecular biology.

▶ Diagnostic Imaging and Therapeutic Radiology Departments

Diagnostic imaging and therapeutic radiology departments offer a wide array of services ranging from an initial diagnosis of injury or disease to treatment for diseases such as cancer. The umbrella of radiologic services covers all specialties that use ionizing (and in some cases, nonionizing) radiation to view and treat internal anatomy. Ionizing radiation has been in use since 1895, when William Roentgen first discovered the x-ray. Today, the uses of radiation are ever increasing and technological advances are allowing for more accurate and prompt treatment of patients, holding out the hope fora cure for many suffering from a variety of cancers and debilitating diseases.

Mission of the Departments

The mission of diagnostic imaging and therapeutic radiology departments is to provide patients with high-quality, cost-effective imaging and therapeutic services to aid in the diagnosis and treatment of disease. It is important to educate patients about the procedures they will undergo, including risks and benefits, before they receive ionizing radiation of any type. Education is vitally important because of the potential risks associated with exposure to ionizing radiation such as genetic damage and the development of cancer. Because of the potential risks, employees in this field must undergo extensive training in radiation safety and protection, for their own safety as well as that of the patients.

Diagnostic Imaging Department

Diagnostic imaging is used to reveal, examine, and diagnose what is ailing the patient and determine the proper treatment. Diagnostic imaging encompasses a large variety of modalities, each of which requires a unique set of skills from the people performing the procedures and the physicians interpreting the images.

Radiography, or the use of diagnostic x-rays, is the best-known procedure in the imaging department; it was the first imaging modality available in modern medicine. With radiography or traditional x-ray, the output is a two-dimensional black and white image, or radiograph, of the body part under investigation.

Fluoroscopy is also used in diagnostic imaging. This technique is similar to radiography, but instead of taking a "snapshot," it uses a continuous flow of x-rays to visualize the anatomy in real time.

Radiologists

The radiologist specializes in interpreting images produced by modalities such as x-ray, computed tomography (CT) scans, and ultrasound. The radiologist is a medical doctor who has completed residency in diagnostic radiology.

Radiologic Technologists

The personnel who perform diagnostic imaging examinations are *radiologic technologists*. After completing a course of study, students must pass a credentialing examination administered by the American Registry of Radiologic Technologists to become certified and licensed to perform radiography procedures. Many radiologic technologists go on to seek certification in other specialized areas of diagnostic and therapeutic radiology, such as CT, magnetic resonance imaging (MRI), nuclear medicine (NM), mammography, or radiation therapy.

Specialties within the Diagnostic Imaging Department

CT scans provide a three-dimensional view inside the body. In contrast to traditional x-ray machines, CT scanners produce multiple x-rays from a variety of angles at the same point in the body. A computer then processes these x-rays to produce a detailed image that allows physicians to see the patient's anatomy from many different directions, and to identify a disease or injury that might go undetected by traditional x-ray imaging.

MRI is an imaging technique that was first used in the late 1970s. Unlike certain other imaging modalities, MRI scans do not use ionizing radiation to produce images; instead, images are produced by means of a powerful magnet that interacts with different molecules in the body. Like CT scans, MRI produces a variety of images that allow physicians to see the body in three-dimensional views.

NM, also known as scintigraphy, uses radioactive materials to diagnose and treat disease. Radioactive isotopes are combined with chemical compounds or pharmaceuticals to form radiopharmaceuticals. These radiopharmaceuticals are administered internally (orally or intravenously injected); they differ according to which organ or body part is under investigation.

Other Specialties of Diagnostic Imaging

Three additional modalities that should be mentioned are mammography, ultrasound, and interventional radiology. *Mammography* is a diagnostic screening procedure that is used to examine the breast, and has had great results in decreasing the mortality rates of breast cancer patients. *Ultrasound* is another nonionizing form of radiation that is used routinely in obstetrics. *Interventional radiology* provides guidance during minimally invasive procedures so that physicians can see what they are doing inside the patient's body.

Therapeutic Radiology

Therapeutic radiology, also known as radiation therapy, is used to treat cancer with high-energy radiation. It is one of the three main treatment modalities for cancer patients alongside surgery and chemotherapy. Patients may be treated with radiation therapy alone or with any combination of these treatment modalities. Radiation therapy delivers high doses of radiation to the inflicted body part. The radiation interacts with the cells of the body and prevents the cancer cells from multiplying. The purpose is to deliver a high enough dose of radiation to control the tumor while sparing as much of the surrounding normal tissue as possible. The *radiation oncologist* is the physician in charge of prescribing a regimen of radiation for the cancer patient. *Radiation therapists* are the individuals who carry out the course of treatment as prescribed by the radiation oncologist.

The diagnostic imaging and therapeutic radiology departments are vital components of the healthcare system. Diagnostic imaging is a common, early step in identifying patient problems, and is found in facilities from group practices and urgent care centers to hospitals of all sizes. Radiation oncology is present in essentially all hospitals that treat various forms of cancer.

▶ Physical Therapy

Physical therapy, known also as physiotherapy in some contexts, is a healthcare occupation in the pursuit of which practitioners diagnose and manage movement dysfunction and endeavor to restore, maintain, and promote optimal physical function and fitness and quality of life as related to movement and health. In brief, the physical therapy mission is to restore and improve mobility in peoples' lives. *Physical therapists* play a key role in caring for many patients in the hospital setting whose mobility has been affected by an incident such as joint replacement surgery, stroke, or amputation. The PT performs an assessment of patient functional status to determine how much assistance the patient needs to be able to recover as much as possible of former or desired physical capability.

Services Provided by the Physical Therapy Department

The broadly stated primary service provided by the physical therapy department is patient care. Physical therapists often work in concert with other rehabilitation professionals, including occupational therapists and speech therapists. Because of the complex nature of health care, particularly in the hospital environment, PTs must communicate and coordinate not only with other rehabilitation providers but also with physicians, nurses, and other members of the healthcare team. Such communication and coordination ensures that each member of the healthcare team has a complete picture of the patient's status, which in turn ensures that the patient will receive optimal care.

In addition to patient care, PTs often provide staff training in activities such as proper body mechanics for back safety during heavy-lifting tasks, and proper techniques for performing patient transfers. They may also participate in teams managing clinical outcomes for particular types of patient problems or diagnoses, or participate in clinical outcomes research. Finally, PTs may also fill roles other than patient care, such as administration, research, community education, and consultation.

Personnel

The physical therapy department is staffed by PTs and support personnel, including *physical therapy assistants (PTAs)* and aides. Physical therapists are licensed professionals who provide physical therapy services and supervise the support personnel; PTAs are licensed providers who provide selected physical therapy interventions under the direction and supervision of a physical therapist. Aides are unlicensed support staff members who perform designated and supervised routine tasks related to physical therapy services.

Requirements for Education and Licensure

Most entry-level PT education programs offer a clinical doctorate degree (doctor of physical therapy [DPT]) which generally requires 3-years study beyond a bachelor's degree. The curriculum includes supervised clinical experience in a variety of clinical settings. After graduation, the student must pass the National Physical Therapy Examination for Physical Therapists licensed.

PTAs must complete a 2-year associate's degree program that includes supervised clinical experience following which they are eligible to sit for the National Physical Therapy Examination for Physical Therapist Assistants to become licensed; in most states, PTAs are licensed, certified, or registered. Licenses must be renewed periodically, typically every 2 years.

▶ Respiratory Therapy

All accredited healthcare facilities in the United States are required to include credentialed, qualified, and properly trained respiratory therapists as part of their ancillary services. The vast majority of **respiratory therapy** departments are centralized units within the organizational structure of the hospital; however, some respiratory therapy units are decentralized according to service areas provided throughout the facility. Regardless of the configuration used, the delivery of all respiratory therapy-related patient care and diagnostic services should be consistent. Known in most facilities is "respiratory therapy"; in some settings, it may be described as cardiopulmonary services, respiratory care, or pulmonary services.

The central focus of respiratory care services is the patient. Respiratory practitioners directly assist physicians and other members of the healthcare team in determining the most appropriate care to be delivered. Traditionally, respiratory therapy department has been defined by two major service areas: general care and critical care. General care refers to therapy provided to the general medical/surgical areas of the hospital and includes services such as oxygen therapy, treatment modalities, and specific oxygen-monitoring diagnostics. Critical-care services include advanced interventions provided in critical care units, such as mechanical ventilator implementation and management, ACLS, oximetry, and specialty diagnostics (e.g., bronchoscopy).

Personnel

Staffing of the respiratory therapy department is directly related to the mission of the facility and the services it offers. Facilities providing a larger variety of services and specialty diagnostics require a larger and more diversified staff. The Joint Commission's requirements for hospital accreditation require the director or manager of respiratory therapy to be nationally credentialed and state-licensed as a *respiratory care practitioner* (RCP). All staff personnel in the department must be minimally licensed by the state or hold a national credential before they can provide patient care.

In the United States, RCPs must be credentialed and licensed before they can deliver patient care. All therapists must complete an accredited educational program and sit for national board exams. The national credentialing process permits respiratory therapists to be recognized in Canada, Europe, and all 50 states of the United States.

There are three levels of respiratory therapy related to extent of education and training. Individuals who have completed a 1-year respiratory therapist (RT) program in a community college are eligible to sit for the *certified respiratory therapist* (CRT) exam administered by the National Board for Respiratory Care (NBRC), following which the therapist must apply for a state license. The entry-level credential for patient care in respiratory therapy is a CRT credential with an RCP state license.

Echoing the registered nurse model of education, individuals seeking to earn a *registered respiratory therapist* (RRT) national credential must attend either a 2-year associate degree program or a 4-year baccalaureate degree program, followed by the national board exam, the CRT entry-level exam, the RRT written board exam, and the RRT clinical simulation exam before earning the RRT credential. Once passing all three national board exams, one must also obtain a state RCP license before directly providing patient care.

▶ Pharmacy

The hospital **pharmacy** is responsible for dispensing and compounding drugs (i.e., mixing drugs to fit the needs of a particular patient) and other diagnostic and therapeutic chemical substances that are used in the hospital. The hospital pharmacy is usually located within the facility itself and often includes outpatient services as well as inpatient services. Some hospitals have decentralized pharmacy systems, with one main pharmacy and satellite pharmacies in each nursing unit. In larger hospitals, the emergency department may also have pharmacy services.

Hospital pharmacies serve different functions including inpatient and outpatient pharmacy, dispensing facilities, and medication counseling. Very small, usually rural, hospitals (a gradually vanishing entity) will not have a regular pharmacy department, may purchase items from a local pharmacist, and maintain a limited supply of pharmaceuticals under supervised security. It is sometimes difficult to recruit pharmacists to work in rural areas.

Telepharmacy is a relatively new concept that offers 24-hours pharmacy coverage for small hospitals. The process is simple: A physician writes an order for a medication, a nurse enters the order into a computer, and a pharmacist at a contracting hospital then reviews the order, ensures there are no drug interactions, and authenticates the order after which nurse can dispense the medication.

Pharmacy Staff Activities

In most hospitals, a full-time pharmacist is available to supervise and coordinate the activities of pharmacy assistants, pharmacy technicians, and other staff. *Pharmacy technicians* assist the pharmacist in prepackaging drugs, controlling inventory, distributing floor stock items, and other activities that do not require professional judgment. Pharmacy technicians may be trained on the job or in a hospital-based program. Currently, with pharmacists in short supply, many hospitals contract with an outside pharmacy company to supply personnel and manage the department.

The pharmacist oversees or personally performs inpatient and outpatient pharmacy services and the preparation of a wide range of sterile products for the medical facility. The pharmacist is responsible for providing services in accordance with the policies and procedures of the hospital and accepted pharmacy practice. The duties of the pharmacist include interpreting medication orders written by physicians, providing information and consultative advice to prescribing doctors regarding the contraindications and side effects of drugs, selecting drugs, compounding drugs, and dispensing appropriate medications. Hospital pharmacists are also responsible for the special preparation of IVs, nutritional solutions, chemotherapeutic agents, and radioactive medications. Pharmacists may be involved in medication counseling for cardiac rehabilitation or cancer patients. Some hospital pharmacists are allowed privileges that include assessing patients and adjusting medications accordingly. Hospital pharmacists may work rotating shifts, including evenings, weekends, and holidays.

Pharmacist Education

Pharmacists trained in the United States must earn a PharmD degree from an accredited college or school of pharmacy. Before being admitted to a PharmD program, an applicant must have completed at least 2 years of studies, including courses in mathematics, chemistry, biology, and physics. While completing the 4-year program, students are allowed to practice with licensed pharmacists before moving on to the 1-to 2-year residency program required for hospital pharmacists. Students must pass all examinations required by the state in which they plan to practice before they are granted a license.

Brief Chapter Summary

This chapter provides an extremely concentrated view of the functions, activities, and personnel primarily involved in providing direct patient care; consider this chapter an overview of what may be encountered on the medical or clinical side of a patient's hospital stay. Of course, depending on the nature of one's ailment, not all of those services addressed may be encountered, but surely most of them will. What has been provided here is simply an overview of the principal medical services that one is likely to encounter during a hospital stay; nursing service is of course always present, as is clinical laboratory to some extent. One may or may not encounter the others depending on one's specific need.

The departments described in this chapter are *line* departments in that they involve direct, usually hands-on patient care; a line function is one that advances the mission of the function in providing care. There are also other activities, functions that do not advance the completion of care but are important in that they support the provision of care by the line departments. These are *staff* activities; they do not advance the provision of care but they are essential in support of patient care. These hospital support activities are discussed in a subsequent chapter.

Questions for Review and Discussion

1. What is "telepharmacy?"
2. What is a "physician extender?" Describe at least two occupations that fit the description of a physician extender.
3. Describe the essential purposes of including "respiratory therapist" on the patient care team.
4. What is the principal domain of expertise of the "physical therapist?"
5. What are the principal differences between the two principal divisions of the "clinical laboratory?"
6. Why is "geriatrics" a major concern of today's nursing service departments?
7. How does a physician become a member of a hospital's "medical staff?"
8. What was the primary force leading to the development of the "licensed practical nurse (LPN)" and "licensed vocational nurse (LVN)?"
9. Briefly explain the mission of the "diagnostic imaging department."
10. What is a "medical laboratory scientist (MLS)" and what is involved in becoming one?

CHAPTER 13

Staffing Shortages: Then, Now, and Continuing

Susan Young and Laura Reichhardt

CHAPTER OBJECTIVES

- To overview staffing needs in nursing, physical and occupational therapy, respiratory therapy, pharmacy, and allied health.
- To review the time line of and causes for nursing and allied health profession shortages presenting in geographic areas.
- To overview the changes in nursing education and employment.
- To overview the changes in physical, occupational, respiratory therapy, and pharmacy education and the need for these specific skills.
- To overview the role of allied health.

KEY TERMS

Advance practice registered nurse (APRN)
Allied health
Interprofessional practice
Licensed practical/vocational nurse (LPN/VN)
Nursing

Occupational therapist
Pharmacist
Physical therapist
Registered nurse (RN)
Respiratory therapist

▶ Health Industry Changes

The healthcare industry continues to undergo changes in labor force requirements, skill sets, advanced technology, and additional services for patients. Over time, the relationships among these changes have required a shift toward advanced education and knowledge for the healthcare workforce. Other considerations that influence the healthcare industry are cost, quality, policymakers, and consumer expectations.

This chapter provides a view of the environmental changes that have affected **nursing** practice related to need, education, and advanced practice requirements. With advancing technology, strict regulations, and complex services required to treat patients in a variety of settings, the need for expanded roles in physical, occupational, and respiratory therapy and pharmacy has emerged as well. State licensing laws for registration and certification vary state to state and continue to require healthcare workers to update credentials. Finally, the field of **allied health** is emerging as a means for augmenting healthcare careers and assisting with changing trends affecting shortages in the healthcare professional roles.

▶ Nursing

Nursing is the art and science of caring for individuals of all ages, families, groups, or communities in all settings in which that health care may be offered. Nursing includes health promotion, disease prevention, care of ill, disabled, and dying people and may include direct patient care, education, research, and policy. Modern-day nursing is attributed to Florence Nightingale (1820–1910). Throughout her career, she led innovation in practice and education and was able to demonstrate improvement in both through meticulous documentation and data collection. Her first breakthrough in nursing care was improvement in sanitation. Working as a nurse during the Crimean War, Nightingale concluded that the high death rate of wounded soldiers was attributed to the unsanitary condition in which they were living. This led to greatly improved survival rates for the wounded soldiers under her care. She went on to innovate in nursing education, founding nursing training institutions that standardized nursing training and forged a pathway for professional nursing (Steele, 2017).

Today, nurses are the largest group of healthcare providers in the nation and work in all settings where health care is delivered (Institute of Medicine, 2011). Nurses must complete nursing education and pass an entrance-to-practice examination in order to become licensed to practice nursing. In addition, nurses pledge to adhere to the nursing code of ethics, which helps a nurse determine whether her/his practice is grounded in supporting the welfare of the patient, family, and the community (American Nurses Association, 2015).

Education of Nursing Workforce

A **licensed practical or vocational nurse (LPN or LVN)** is an individual who has completed a state-approved practical or vocational nursing program and is licensed by a state board of nursing to provide patient care. LPN and LVN nurses work under the supervision of a **registered nurse (RN)**, advanced practice registered nurse (APRN), or physician (Definition of Nursing Terms, n.d.).

An RN is an individual who has completed nursing education at the diploma, associate's degree, or baccalaureate degree level and is licensed by a state board of nursing to provide patient care. Today, there is an increasing trend for nurses to enter practice with baccalaureate degrees in nursing. In addition to education, RNs must pass an entry-to-practice exam and maintain licenses in the states in which they practice (Definition of Nursing Terms, n.d.). Nurses who hold an RN may choose to continue their education to the Master's Degree (MSN), Doctor of Philosophy (PhD), or Doctor of Nursing Practice (DNP) to achieve advancements in their career, including nursing administration, leadership, and advanced clinical practice and research (Definition of Nursing Terms, n.d.; American Nurses Association, n.d.).

An **APRN** must hold a bachelor's degree in nursing or equivalent and be a licensed RN who has completed additional education at the master's or doctorate level in nursing. The DNP is increasingly becoming the degree of choice for nurses seeking to become APRNs. In addition, to become an APRN, one must pass an entry-to-practice examination, hold a certificate in specialty areas, and be licensed as an APRN in the state or states in which one chooses to practice (Definition of Nursing Terms, n.d.). There are four categories of APRNs recognized in the APRN consensus model developed by the National Council of State Boards of Nursing. These include certified nurse practitioner (CNP), certified nurse–midwife (CNM), clinical nurse specialist (CNS), and certified registered nurse anesthetist (CRNA; APRN Consensus Work Group, 2008; Definition of Nursing Terms, n.d.).

Today there are more pathways into nursing than ever before. There are accelerated programs for individuals who have completed baccalaureate degrees in disciplines other than nursing; they may complete their nursing coursework in a condensed timeframe. There are also graduate entry programs for individuals who have at least nonnursing bachelor's degrees and are seeking graduate degrees in nursing. These are two avenues that enable people with some education to enter into nursing with something of a head start. In addition, there is a national movement to engage nurses in academic progression with the focus primarily on supporting nurses with an associate's degree in nursing in attaining their baccalaureate degree in nursing (Institute of Medicine, 2011).

Practice Settings and Other Services

LPNs and LVNs primarily provide care in gerontology, home health, primary care, or other specific specialties. Locations these nurses work in include home health, nursing homes, and hospitals. There is an apparent trend for long-term care facilities to increasingly hire LPNs and LVNs, whereas employment opportunities for these nurses in other settings are decreasing (Budden, Moulton, Harper, Brunell, & Smiley, 2016). With more career ladder opportunities afforded through advanced licensure, nurses are using the LPN or LVN role as a stepping-stone in their nursing careers to achieve higher licensure (Hawaii State Center for Nursing, 2017).

RNs work in hospitals, long-term care, public health nursing, and in the community. Nursing roles are also expanding into other sectors of involvement in health care. Although approximately half of RN jobs remain primarily in hospitals, patient care is becoming more patient-centered and community-based, with ambulatory care, home health, and nursing homes emerging as the next most common work sites (Budden et al., 2016).

Meanwhile, the patient population is both aging and becoming more complex, requiring advanced clinical reasoning skills in all settings of health care, from home health to hospital-based nursing to care coordination (Advisory Board, 2017). The movement to achieve a more highly educated nursing workforce supports these nurses as they work with more complicated care requirements for patients and in more diverse roles.

Nearly half the states in the nation allow APRNs to work to the full scope of their education and training, allowing them to assess, diagnose, treat, and coordinate care for patients on their own patient panels (American Association of Nurse Anesthetists, 2017a). APRNs may care for patients, including performing health promotion, assessment, diagnoses of illnesses, management of chronic and acute illnesses, and prescribing of treatments and medications (APRN Consensus Work Group, 2008; Definition of Nursing Terms, n.d.).

Nurse practitioners are the most common type of APRN; they most commonly work in provider's offices, outpatient care settings, and hospitals. CNMs provide women's health and reproductive health care, including the management of pregnancies and delivery of babies; these APRNs are most likely to work in labor and delivery wards of hospitals, birth centers, and women's health clinics. CRNAs provide advanced pain management and anesthesia in inpatient and outpatient surgical centers, labor and delivery units, and pain management clinics. CNSs often serve in specialty roles in areas, such as behavioral health, oncology, or adult-gerontology acute care, also providing advanced clinical oversight in the use of evidence-based practice (EBP), as well as mentorship of fellow nurses, patient education and advocacy, and nursing education. The APRNs are more likely than other advanced practice healthcare providers to provide care in rural areas or to underserved populations (Budden et al., 2016; Buerhaus, Skinner, Auerbach, & Staiger, 2017).

Future Needs in Nursing

The healthcare industry is expected to grow by more than 5% per year over the next 10 years, outpacing the nation's overall average economic growth rate of 3% (Keehan, 2017). The two major causes of this continued growth are the aging population, all Baby Boomers having reached 65 years of age by 2025, and continued economic growth of our nation (Advisory Board, 2017). Additionally, within healthcare utilization overall, a few themes or trends are evident. First, health care is increasingly being provided in the community rather than in hospital settings. Second, personal health care, including home health care and prescription drug utilization, is steadily increasing. Third, as the age of the population increases, Medicare and Medicaid utilization will increase, shifting payment models from private insurance to public payment for medical and healthcare services (Advisory Board, 2017).

To keep up with the demands, more healthcare professionals are needed. Fortunately, healthcare jobs presently constitute the fastest growing employment option in the nation (Bureau of Labor Statistics, 2017a).

The Patient Protection and Affordable Care Act

In 2010, President Barack Obama signed into law the Patient Protection and Affordable Care Act, also referred to as the ACA or "Obamacare." Among many provisions, this Act required all Americans to carry health insurance coverage. Five years after the enactment of this legislation, health insurance coverage had increased from approximately 85% of all Americans to nearly 91% of the total population. It is expected that if this law remains in place, health insurance coverage will remain relatively stable and that health insurance spending, specifically the medical and healthcare services paid by a person's health insurance coverage, will increase (Keehan, 2017). Though insurance rates may remain stable, as Baby Boomers near retirement age, utilization is likely to shift from private insurance to Medicare and Medicaid (Holahan, Blumberg, Clemans-Cope, McMorrow, & Wengle, 2017; Keehan et al., 2017). This will affect how these individuals utilize medical care and how healthcare facilities and providers are reimbursed for the services they provide. At the start of the Trump Presidency, efforts were undertaken at the Federal Government level to repeal elements of the ACA, including mandated health insurance coverage. Should this happen, a decline in the number of insured Americans will result, with estimates of up to 32 million uninsured individuals by 2026. Additionally, characteristics of health service utilization may shift and the overall health of the insured population may decline. This would require the nursing workforce to become increasingly skilled in caring for patients with complex healthcare needs (Congressional Budget Office, 2017).

Interprofessional Practice

Interprofessional practice is the provision of patient care by a team of healthcare professionals of several fields, with understanding of the all team members' roles and recognition that using the strengths of each role will result in improved patient outcomes and more safe and efficient care. As patient care becomes more complicated, regulation and oversight increase, and electronic medical records allow for increased timeliness of consultation feedback and transparency between practice providers. Once healthcare professionals engage in interprofessional practice, there is increased preference for working in such settings. Further, a major objective of healthcare delivery remodeling is to achieve improved outcomes with improved efficiency. Interprofessional models are expected to be the solution to healthcare delivery remodeling efforts. Nurses often lead or are involved in healthcare interprofessional teams, as they work closely with all other healthcare professions and allied health roles and serve as patient and family advocates (Cox, Naylor, & FAAN, 2013).

Evidence-Based Practice

EBP involves utilizing a large body of research, or many research findings that support a common conclusion, plus a clinician's clinical expertise and the patient's values and preferences, to determine patient care plans and processes. This concept leads to improved patient outcomes, improved decision-making capacity for all healthcare team members, and decreased healthcare costs. Nurses often lead EBP initiatives in practice. This requires a nurse or an interprofessional team driven by a nurse to move through the following steps: asking clinical questions related to patient care; seeking the answers from research; appraising the research; working to develop policies and procedures or a treatment plan based on the body of research; and then applying the plan to practice. The final step is to evaluate the outcome with the patient. The movement lies squarely within the goal of providing optimal health care and allows a clinician to both provide culturally competent, patient-driven care, and care that is supported by current and consistent research findings (Siminoff, 2013; Titler, 2008).

Nursing Employment Outlook

Health care is a steadily growing field. However, the skills required to fill the needs in health care are always changing. As populations change, different types of healthcare workers are needed, creating differing levels of demand. In addition, changes in enrollment in healthcare occupation programs, retirement rates, and people exiting the workforce for various reasons all contribute to the status of the supply of healthcare professionals at any given time. The balance between the supply of healthcare workers and the demand for healthcare workers reveals workforce shortages or gluts. In the decade of 2000–2010, it was determined that because the population is both growing and aging, more people are diagnosed with more chronic illnesses than ever before; thus, health insurance coverage will increase because of ACA regulations and the demand for health care will rise exponentially (Keehan et al., 2017). At the same time, we will have fewer nurses than we need because Baby Boomers will be retiring soon, resulting in a loss of one million experienced nurses from the workforce (Buerhaus et al., 2017). To balance this expectation of fewer nurses available than are needed, efforts to increase nursing school enrollment and advance the education of working nurse have been undertaken to respond to the expected shortage and close the gap between needed nurses and available nurses (Auerbach, Buerhaus, & Staiger, 2017).

However, nursing shortages are not uniformly distributed about the country; some states may at times have more than enough nurses, and some states may not have nearly enough. Some nurses may need to travel to other states to gain employment, and some communities may need to recruit nurses from other states to meet their healthcare needs. And although a given area may have enough nurses in total, these nurses may not represent the specialties most needed in any specific community, particularly as healthcare reform focuses on increased accountability of interprofessional teams, quality outcomes, costs, and population health.

As health care shifts from the hospital setting to the community setting, nurses may need to seek additional education or training to deepen or develop skills in new specialties, such as ambulatory care, community nursing, home health nursing, or care management, to continue to meet the changing needs of their community or of nursing in general (PlumX Metrics, 2016). Importantly, cycles of nursing workforce shortages repeat as populations grow and large groups of nurses move toward retirement or as delivery models change. Maintaining flexibility within the field by continuing to diversify skills, or willingness to move to other communities or take other roles within health care, are some options for nurses with regard to changing demands for their skills (Auerbach et al., 2017; Buerhaus et al., 2017).

Employment Outlook

TABLE 13.1 shows the estimates provided by the Bureau of Labor Statistics (Bureau of Labor Statistics, 2017b) of both current jobs and the expected growth in jobs over the next 10 years. Physical therapists and nurse practitioners are expected to experience the greatest growth by percentage of current numbers, whereas RNs and nursing assistants are expected to experience the greatest number of job openings. The many factors enumerated in this chapter and text will also affect job openings and availability, and by the time one graduates, there may be new healthcare roles that do not yet exist. Health care, however, is a reliable job market. Of the 30 fastest growing jobs in the nation, 22 are in health care (Bureau of Labor Statistics, 2017a). Further, health care and social assistance jobs outpaced all private service industries in 2015, with the greatest growth in services for the elderly and disabled, home healthcare services, and health care and social assistance services (Sullivan et al., 2016).

TABLE13.1 JobOutlook, Healthcare Occupations

	2014 National Employment Matrix title and code	Employment number, in thousands	Employment change, 2014–2024 (%)	Job openings due to growth and replacements, 2014–2024 by number of jobs	Median annual wage, 2016
Nursing	Licensed practical/vocational nurses	719.9	16	322.2	$44,090.00
	Registered nurses	2751	16	1088.4	$68,450.00
	Nurse anesthetists	38.2	19	16.4	$160,270.00
	Nurse midwives	5.3	25	2.5	$99,770.00
	Nurse practitioners	126.9	35	74.7	$100,910.00
Allied health	Pharmacists	297.1	3	78.4	$122,230.00
	Pharmacy technicians	372.5	9	71.6	$30,920.00
	Physical therapists	210.9	34	128.3	$85,400.00
	Physical therapist assistants and a des	128.7	40	88.7	$45,290.00

(continues)

TABLE 13.1 JobOutlook, Healthcare Occupations   (continued)

2014 National Employment Matrix title and code	Employment number, in thousands	Employment change, 2014–2024 (%)	Job openings due to growth and replacements, 2014–2024 by number of jobs	Median annual wage, 2016
Respiratory therapists	120.7	12	43.3	$58,670.00
Respiratory therapy technicians	10.7	–19	1.1	$49,780.00
Nursing assistants	1492.1	18	599	$26,590.00
Medical assistants	591.3	24	262.1	$31,540.00
Medical transcriptionists	70	–3	14.6	$35,720.00
Phlebotomists	112.7	25	51.6	$32,710.00

Bureau of Labor Statistics (2017a).

Reproduced from U.S. Bureau of Labor Statistics. (2017). Occupational employment, job openings and worker characteristics. Retrieved August 18, 2017, from https://www.bls.gov/emp/ep_table_107.htm.

▶ Physical Therapists

Physical therapists (PTs) diagnose and treat individuals from newborns to the elderly who have medical problems or other health-related conditions that limit their ability to move and perform functional activities in their daily lives. These professionals actively work with patients to prevent progression of impairments enabling optimal performance and enhancing health, well-being, and quality of life (American Physical Therapy Association, 2014a).

Today's healthcare environment requires collaboration with medical, nursing providers, and other professional therapists in planning care for rehabilitation, performance enhancement, and risk-reduction services. PTs participate in development of current and updated standards for their practice ensuring healthcare policies for physical therapy are evidence based.

Practice Setting and Other Services

PTs may practice in the hospital, clinic, rehabilitation center, or private care setting. In addition, PTs participate in research, serve in health administration roles, and provide educational training for PT students. Along with PTs, support personnel, such as physical therapy assistants (PTAs), provide specific physical therapy to patients under the supervision of the PT. The educational requirements are distinct for each of these levels.

Educational Requirements and Degree Requirements

There are several types of degrees a therapist may hold in the field of physical therapy. In the past, prior to 1990, the bachelor's degree in physical therapy was the requirement for PTs. Over the years, requirements have moved to a master's degree and now a doctorate physical therapy degree.

Currently, all new students in the United States are required to obtain a doctorate-level degree to become a PT. The American Physical Therapy Association (APTA) has a goal that all PTs will enter the profession with a doctorate degree by the year 2020 (American Physical Therapy Association, 2014a).

The direct entry to doctorate in physical therapy (DPT) applies to those who have completed their bachelor's degree. An additional 3 years will be required to earn a doctorate degree. Specific coursework is required as well as clinical experience under a licensed PT. The final step after graduation requires passing the National Physical Therapy Examination for PTs to obtain licensure as a PT (American Physical Therapy Association, 2014b).

In addition to the direct entry DPT, a transitional DPT (tDPT) exists for PTs who already have a physical therapy bachelor's or master's degree. The PT may continue working while completing the coursework required for the doctoral degree.

The current requirement for PTs to sit for licensure is a doctorate-level degree. However, there exists a grandfather clause allowing PTs who have earned degrees prior to this requirement to continue to practice under their current degree and licensure. Presently, PTs covered under the grandfather clause are not required to return to school and earn a doctorate level degree but are encouraged to do so (American Physical Therapy Association, 2014b).

Physical Therapy Assistants and Physical Aides

Assisting the PT is PTA who are certified/licensed or the physical therapy aide. The PTA is directed by the PT to assist in selected therapy treatments. The PTA must be a graduate of a 2-year associate degree accredited program and then may take the national physical therapy examination for physical assistants in order to obtain licensure, which is required in all 50 states. The physical therapy aide is a staff member who has received training from a PT and performs tasks under the direction of the PT and is not licensed (Bureau of Labor Statistics).

Employment Outlook

According to the 2017 Bureau of Labor statistics, employment of PTs is projected to grow 25% from 2016 to 2026 and projected growth for physical assistants and aides is projected to grow 30%. The demand for physical therapy can be attributed to aging baby boomers and medical issues that require mobility training (Bureau of Labor Statistics).

▶ Occupational Therapist

Occupational therapists (OTs) treat injured, ill, or disabled patients so that optimum function of everyday activities can be achieved. OTs evaluate patients and develop plans of care to assist in recovery, improve function, and optimize work skills.

Treatment plans may include exercises, adapting to new skills and evaluating environments at home and work for safety and accessibility (Bureau of Labor Statistics).

Practice Setting

OTs work in a variety of settings, such as rehabilitation centers, healthcare facilities, schools, or in the home. As with PTs, OTs may purse employment within a research center. Occupational therapy assistants and aides are the support staff for OTs. Under supervision of the OT, activities and duties can be assigned. Training and education for these occupations are specific to requirements of the patient.

Educational Requirements and Degree Requirements

OTs are required to have a master's degree in occupational therapy and all states require OTs to be licensed. There are doctoral programs available; however, this is not a requirement. Occupational therapy assistants must complete a 2-year accredited school. Then, a national certification examination conducted by the American Occupational Therapy Board must be taken and passed. The occupational therapy aide is required to have a high school diploma with training under an OT (Bureau of Labor Statistics).

Employment Outlook

Employment of OTs is projected to grow 21% from 2016 to 2026, faster than the average for all occupations. The expected growth is due to treatment for people with various illnesses and disabilities, such as Alzheimer's disease, cerebral palsy, autism, or the loss of a limb (Bureau of Labor Statistics).

▶ Respiratory Therapists

Respiratory therapists (RTs) care for patients who have breathing disorders and provide treatment for a variety of respiratory diseases. Patients range from premature infants to elderly patients. In addition, RTs may provide emergency care to patients suffering from heart attacks, drowning, or shock (Bureau of Labor Statistics).

Practice Setting

Most RTs work in clinical settings, such as hospitals, long-term care facilities, clinics, or physician offices. Providing care to patients with pulmonary disorders will usually be in the confines of these service areas (Bureau of Labor Statistics).

Educational Requirements and Degree Requirements

RTs must complete a minimum of 2-year associate degree, with specific competencies designated by the American Association for Respiratory Care (AARC). A 4-year bachelor's degree is not required but is encouraged by employers.

RTs are licensed in all states except Alaska; requirements vary by state.

There are no requirements or positions for respiratory assistants or aides (Bureau of Labor Statistics; Definition of Nursing Terms, n.d.).

Employment Outlook

Employment of RTs is projected to grow 23% from 2016 to 2026. This is attributed to growth of the elderly population and increased birth and survival of premature infants. Both of these populations have delicate respiratory systems that often need support (Bureau of Labor Statistics).

▶ Pharmacist

Pharmacists dispense prescription medications to patients and provide instruction in the safe use of prescriptions. Education is an important role pharmacists provide, explaining the interaction of medications and side effects that may occur.

Practice Setting

Pharmacists may work in a variety of settings, for example pharmacies, including those in pharmacy stores in general merchandise and grocery stores. They also work in hospitals, clinics, and military settings. Pharmacists play a role in quality care management by participation in discharge planning from acute and post-acute departments (Bureau of Labor Statistics).

Education and Degree Requirement

Pharmacists must have a 4-year bachelor's degree followed by a 4-year Doctor of Pharmacy degree (Pharm.D.). They must also be licensed, which requires passing two exams (APRN Consensus Work Group, 2008). The role of the pharmacy technician assists pharmacists in dispensing prescription medication to customers or health professionals. They may also package and label prescriptions, and process payments and insurance claims. Pharmacy technicians work under direct supervision of a licensed **pharmacist**. Employers may require a certification through the National Health Career Association, who provides the Pharmacy Technician Certification (CPhT) program.

Employment Outlook

Employment of pharmacists is projected to grow 6% from 2016 to 2026, and employment of pharmacy technicians is projected to grow 12% from 2016 to 2026 (Bureau of Labor Statistics). As the role of the pharmacist continues to become an important collaborator in quality and safety initiatives, this profession will continue to grow.

▶ Allied Health

Allied health professionals provide services to patients who follow the plan of care set forth from the physician or nurse responsible for the patient. The use of evidence-based principles in treatment for patients is the basis of medical and nursing diagnosis and plan of care as well as treatment by allied health professionals.

The ACA (P.L. 111-148) defines allied health professionals as follows: *ALLIED HEALTH PROFESSIONAL.—The term "allied health professional" means an allied health professional as defined in section 799B(5) of the Public Health Service Act (42 U.S.C. 295p(5)) who has graduated and received an allied health professions degree or certificate from an institution of higher education and shares in the responsibility for the delivery of health care services or related services including identification, evaluation and prevention of disease and disorders, dietary and nutritional services, health promotion services, rehabilitation services and health service management. In addition allied health professionals are further identified as not receiving a degree of doctor of medicine, doctor of osteopathy, degree of doctor of dentistry, a degree of doctor of veterinary medicine, a doctor of optometry, doctor of podiatric medicine, a degree of bachelor of science in pharmacy, a degree of doctor of pharmacy a graduate degree in public health, a degree of chiropractic, a graduate degree in health administration doctoral degree in clinical psychology, a degree in social work, a degree in counseling or any equivalent degree to those professions stated above* (The Patient Protection and Affordable Care Act (ACA), 2010).

The Association of Schools of Allied Health Professions (ASAHP) defines allied health as the segment of the healthcare field "that delivers services involving the identification, evaluation and prevention of diseases and disorders; dietary and nutrition services; and rehabilitation and health systems management." The allied health worker's role as a team member can be invaluable as the United States experiences workforce shortages in the medical and nursing fields.

Education of Allied Health Workforce

The allied health professions are employed as technicians (assistants) and therapists or technologists. Technicians are trained to perform procedures, and their education lasts less than 2 years. They are required to work under the supervision of technologists or therapists. Examples include medical assistants, ophthalmic technicians, and cardiovascular technicians.

The educational process for therapists or technologists is more specific and includes acquiring procedural skills. Students learn to evaluate patients, and develop treatment plans with assistance of the health supervisor while evaluating the patient's progress and response to therapy. Examples of allied health therapists and technologists include anesthesiologist assistant, neurodiagnostic technologist, and pathologists' assistant.

Future Needs in Allied Health

Careers may include medical assistance, rehabilitation, dietary and nutrition services, dental health, physical therapies, and technical services, such as X-ray techs and scans. The Georgetown University Center on Education and the workforce predicts the demand for healthcare workers will grow twice as fast as the national economy, now at 18%; the jobs in the industry are predicted to grow to 19.8 million by 2020 (ASAHP).

Brief Chapter Summary

The professions rendering care to our population continue to become increasingly more sophisticated. Nurses are the largest group of healthcare providers in the nation and work in all settings where health care is delivered.

Healthcare professions, such as nursing, physical therapist, occupational therapists, respiratory therapists, and pharmacists, work in various healthcare settings in collaborative practice taking care of the nation's sickest patients. The complexity of health care has increased requiring additional education and expertise in care.

Finally, we see the field of allied health assisting healthcare professionals to supplement where staffing may not be optimal. Today's healthcare teams continue to collaborate in practice by reviewing evidence-based practice for new models of care.

Questions for Review and Discussion

1. Who is considered the founder of modern nursing practice and how did she save the lives of soldiers?
2. What are the three license types in nursing? What are the four categories of the highest level of nursing?
3. Describe some of the places nurses work?
4. What is a future trend in nursing?
5. What made the Pennsylvania Hospital different from previous hospitals?
6. Why is Florence Nightingale important to the history of hospitals?
7. Discuss early infection-control efforts by environment for allied health personnel.
8. What is the difference in educational and training requirements of physical therapists and physical therapy aides?
9. Which healthcare providers must be licensed?
10. Can physical therapy and occupational therapy aides render care without oversight? If not, who is responsible for the oversight to care of the patient?
11. What are some of the functions of the pharmacist?
12. What important role do pharmacists provide in patient safety?

References

Advisory Board. (2017). CMS: US health care spending to reach nearly 20% of GDP by 2025. Retrieved from https://www.advisory.com/daily-briefing/2017/02/16/spending-growth

American Association of Nurse Anesthetists. (2017). Certified registered nurse anesthetists fact sheet. Retrieved from https://www.aana.com/patients/certified-registered-nurse-anesthetists-fact-sheet

American Physical Therapy Association. (2014a). *Guide to physical therapist Practice 3.0.* Alexandria, VA: American Physical Therapy Association. Retrieved from http://guidetoptpractice.apta.org/

American Physical Therapy Association. (2014b). *Introduction to the guide to physical therapist practice. Guide to physical therapist Practice 3.0.* Alexandria, VA: American Physical Therapy Association. Retrieved from http://guidetoptpractice.apta.org/content/1/SEC1.body

American Nurses Association. (2015). *Code of ethics for nurses with interpretive statements.* Retrieved from http://nursingworld.org/DocumentVault/Ethics-1/Code-of-Ethics-for-Nurses.html

American Nurses Association. (n.d.). *How to become a nurse.* Retrieved from http://www.nursingworld.org/EspeciallyForYou/What-is-Nursing/Tools-You-Need/RegisteredNurseLicensing.html

APRN Consensus Work Group, & National Council of State Boards of Nursing APRN Advisory Committee. (2008, July 7). *Consensus model for APRN regulation: Licensure, accreditation, certification & education.* Retrieved from https://www.ncsbn.org/Consensus_Model_for_APRN_Regulation_July_2008.pdf

ASAHP. Retrieved from http://www.asahp.org/definition.htm. https://static1.squarespace.com/static/57a64a023e00beb95af13929/t/57f59d17e6f2e1b801ff50c8/1475714327542/Health-Professions-Facts.pdf

Auerbach, D. I., Buerhaus, P. I., & Staiger, D. O. (2017). How fast will the registered nurse workforce grow through 2030? Projections in nine regions of the country. *Nursing Outlook, 65*(1), 116–122. doi:10.1016/j.outlook.2016.07.004

Budden, J. S., Moulton, P., Harper, K. J., Brunell, M. L., & Smiley, R. (2016). The 2015 nursing workforce survey. *Journal of Nursing Regulation, 7*(1 Suppl.), S1–S90.

Buerhaus, P. I., Skinner, L. E., Auerbach, D. I., & Staiger, D. O. (2017). Four challenges facing the nursing workforce in the United States. *Journal of Nursing Regulation, 8*(2), 40–46.

Bureau of Labor Statistics, U.S. Department of Labor. *Occupational outlook handbook, physical therapists, physical therapist assistants & aides on the internet.* Retrieved from https://www.bls.gov/ooh/healthcare/physical-therapists.htm

Bureau of Labor Statistics, U.S. Department of Labor. *Occupational outlook handbook, occupational therapists, on the internet.* Retrieved from https://www.bls.gov/ooh/healthcare/occupational-therapists.htm

Bureau of Labor Statistics, U.S. Department of Labor. *Occupational outlook handbook, respiratory therapists, on the internet.* Retrieved from https://www.bls.gov/ooh/healthcare/respiratory-therapists.htm

Bureau of Labor Statistics, U.S. Department of Labor. Occupational outlook handbook, pharmacists, on the internet. Retrieved from https://www.bls.gov/ooh/healthcare/pharmacists.htm

Bureau of Labor Statistics. (2017a). *Fastest growing occupations.* Retrieved from https://www.bls.gov/emp/ep_table_103.htm

Bureau of Labor Statistics. (2017b). *Occupation employment, job openings and worker characteristics*. Retrieved from https://www.bls.gov/emp/ep_table_107.htm

Congressional Budget Office. (2017). Cost Estimate: H.R. 1638 Obamacare Repeal Reconciliation Act of 2017: An Amendment in the Nature of a Substitute [LYN17479] as Posted on the Website of the Senate Committee on the Budget on July 19, 2017. Retrieved from https://www.cbo.gov/system/files/115th-congress-2017-2018/costestimate/52939-hr1628amendment.pdf

Cox, C., & Naylor, M. (2013). *Transforming patient care: Aligning interprofessional education with clinical practice redesign.* Retrieved from http://macyfoundation.org/publications/publication/transforming-patient-care-aligning-interprofessional-education-with-clinica

Definition of Nursing Terms. (n.d.). Definition of nursing terms. Retrieved from https://www.ncsbn.org/nursing-terms.htm

Hawaii State Center for Nursing. (2017). *2017 Hawaii Nursing Workforce* (Research Reports). Retrieved from http://www.hawaiicenterfornursing.org/wp-content/uploads/2017/11/2017-Summary-Final.png

Holahan, J., Blumberg, L. J., Clemans-Cope, L., McMorrow, S., & Wengle, E. (2017). *The evidence on recent health care spending growth and the impact of the affordable care act*. Retrieved from www.healthpolicycenter.org

Institute of Medicine. (2011). *The future of nursing: Leading change, advancing health: Health and medicine division*. Retrieved from http://www.nationalacademies.org/hmd/Reports/2010/The -Future-of-Nursing-Leading-Change-Advancing-Health.aspx

Keehan, S. P., Stone, D. A., Poisal, J. A., Cuckler, G. A., Sisko, A. M., Smith, S. D., ... Lizonitz, J. M. (2017). National health expenditure projections, 2016–25: Price increases, aging push sector to 20 percent of economy. *Health Affairs, 36*(3), 553–563. doi:10.1377/hlthaff.2016.1627

PlumX Metrics. (2016). Registered nurse results. *Journal of Nursing Regulation, 7*(1), S12–S53. doi:10.1016/S2155-8256(16)31058-4

Siminoff, L. A. (2013). Incorporating patient and family preferences into evidence-based medicine. *BMC Medical Informatics and Decision Making, 13*(Suppl. 3), S6. doi:10.1186/1472-6947-13-S3-S6

Steele, N. M. (2017, March). A time to celebrate: Florence nightingale. *Urologic Nursing, 37*(2), 57–59.

Sullivan, K. (2016). Workforce growth in community-based care. *Monthly Labor Review*. Retrieved from https://www.bls.gov/opub/mlr/2016/article/pdf/workforce-growth-in-community-based -care.pdf

The Patient Protection and Affordable Care Act (ACA). (2010). Title 42, Chapter 6A, Subchapter V, Part F, Sec. 295p of the Federal Code.

Titler, M. G. (2008). The evidence for evidence-based practice implementation. In R. G. Hughes (Ed.), *Patient safety and quality: An evidence-based handbook for nurses*. Rockville, MD: Agency for Healthcare Research and Quality (US). Retrieved from http://www.ncbi.nlm.nih.gov/books /NBK2659/

CHAPTER 14

The Physical Facility

Camonia R. Graham-Tutt and Lisa K. Spencer

CHAPTER OBJECTIVES

- To overview the physical facility of hospitals and the codes, regulations, requirements, and laws that govern its design.
- To overview the environmental services department and its role in hospitals.
- To overview the plan engineering and maintenance department and its role in hospitals.
- To overview the biomedical engineering department and its role in hospitals.
- To overview the safety and security department and its role in hospitals.
- To overview the physical needs of hospital facilities in the 21st century.

KEY TERMS

Biomedical engineering
Environmental services

Facility security
Plant engineering and maintenance

▶ Introduction

The physical facility of a hospital is designed with guidance from local, state, and federal legal and regulatory requirements. On the federal level, International Building Codes, National Electrical Codes, the Americans with Disabilities Act (ADA), OSHA, and the National Fire Protection Association (NFPA) govern how a building is designed and what requirements must be implemented (International Code Council, 2018; National Fire Protection Association, 2018c; United States Department of Justice, 2018; United States Department of Labor, 2017; United States Environmental Protection Agency [EPA], 2017). At the State level, State Health Planning may be involved, such as state licensing agencies, state fire codes, and state building codes. This chapter can be divided into two main sections. The first section includes the codes, regulations, requirements of hospitals, and the laws that govern the hospital's design. The second section includes the departments that cover a range of areas relevant to the physical facility: (a) plant- and environmental-related departments and services, (b) **environmental services** department, and (c) **plant engineering and maintenance** department in hospitals. This chapter ends with an overview of the physical needs of hospital facilities in the 21st century.

▶ Laws, Codes, and Standards

International Building Codes (IBC) (International Code Council, 2018) provides the minimum requirements to ensure the safety of occupants of buildings. IBC (International Code Council, 2018) is required for all buildings, including hospitals; however, some family dwellings and townhouses do not qualify. IBC includes guidelines for fire and smoke protection (i.e., fire codes), structural design, accessibility (i.e., ADA requirements), materials used (i.e., plastic, glass, steel, and masonry), and systems (i.e., electrical, mechanical, and plumbing). Hospitals must meet these minimum building code requirements, and many more not listed above, before, during, and after hospitals are constructed and patients, visitors, and employees enter the facility.

National Electrical Codes (NEC) (National Fire Protection Association, 2018c) provides standards for safe installation of electrical wiring and equipment in the United States, including in hospitals. The NEC, published as NFPA 70, is adopted by individual states and locales at different levels and editions. NEC is not federal law but standards that must be adopted by individual states as best practices for electrical installations. When installing electrical wiring and equipment in hospitals, construction and plant engineers must be familiar with the NEC standards for the specific state and type of building.

The Americans with Disabilities Act (ADA) Standards for Accessible Design (Title III) (United States Department of Justice, 2018) includes standards, enforced by the federal government, for medical care and long-term care facilities. Part 36 of the ADA Title III regulations guides construction and plant engineers in ensuring nondiscrimination on the basis of disability in public accommodations, including hospitals, during design, construction, and alterations (United States Department of Justice, 2010). While the accessible design is provided as a separate standard (United States Department of Justice, 2018), all ADA standards must be followed including public accommodations and equal access to goods, services, and benefits. ADA standards relate to all patients, visitors, and employees who meet the definition of "disability," and therefore, all personnel working with any of these groups must be familiar with how ADA standards are followed and enforced.

Occupational Safety and Health Administration's Regulations (Standard - 29 CFR), Part 1926, Safety and Health Regulations for Construction (United States Department of Labor, 2017) provides safety and health standards for workforce safety. Construction standards include general safety and health provisions, occupational and environmental controls, personal protection and life safety empowerment, and fire protection and prevention (United States Department of Labor, 2017). The standards also include proper signage, signals, and barricades, materials handling, storage, use, and disposal, and other potential hazards such as welding and cutting, electrical, steel, and concrete (United States Department of Labor, 2017). OSHA standards for construction deals primarily with constructing and altering of the hospital; however, other OSHA standards provide guidelines for employees working under hazardous conditions (i.e., plant and engineering maintenance working in poor air-quality areas), with hazardous items (i.e., housekeepers or laundry staff working with disinfectants and chemicals), or as part of their everyday job responsibilities (i.e., patient-care providers wearing Personal Protective Equipment [PPE]) (United States Department of Labor, 2017). All members of the hospital must be familiar with OSHA standards to protect personal health and safety in the workplace and the health and safety of patients and visitors.

The NFPA provides codes and standards to prevent fire, electrical, and related hazards (National Fire Protection Association, 2018b). The Centers for Medicare and Medicaid Services (CMS) requires its providers to follow the requirements established under NFPA, including following the 2012 editions of NFPA 101 and NFPA 99. CMS also requires its providers to develop emergency preparedness plans. According to CMS, hospitals (among others) must evaluate their emergency and standby power systems and inspect, test, and maintain the said systems according to NFPA standards (Centers for Medicare & Medicaid Services, 2016).

▶ Plant- and Environmental-Related Departments and Services in Hospitals

Environmental Services

The goal of the environmental services department in a hospital is to provide a safe, sanitary, and comfortable environment and to help prevent the development and transmission of disease and infections (Becker's Clinical Leadership & Infection Control, 2015). Environmental services departments include housekeeping services and, in some hospitals, laundry services. Environmental services maintain standards regulated by laws, codes, regulations, and policies and procedures of the hospital.

Housekeeping

Housekeeping's primary responsibility is maintaining cleanliness throughout the hospital, thereby controlling the spread of infections (Becker's Clinical Leadership & Infection Control, 2015). Proper cleaning, disinfecting, and sanitizing of areas in the hospital, including patient rooms, restrooms, waiting areas, and departments, ensure a safe, hygienic, and healthy environment for patients, visitors, vendors, and employees (Becker's Clinical Leadership & Infection Control, 2015). The Asia-Pacific Society of Infection Control [APSIC]'s Guidelines for Environmental Cleaning and Disinfecting recommends good housekeeping practices that are performed on a routine and consistent basis, effective use of disinfectants and sanitizers for specific environment(s), and cleaning schedules "reflecting whether surfaces are high-touch or low-touch, the type of activity taking place in the area and the infection risk associated with it; the vulnerability of the patients housed in the area; and the probability of contamination" (Asia-Pacific Society of Infection Control [APSIC], 2013, p. 48).

The United States Environmental Protection Agency (EPA)—epa.gov—and the Occupational Safety and Health Administration (OSHA)—osha.gov—provide guidelines and lists of disinfectants hospitals can use to meet Centers for Disease Control and Prevention (CDC)—cdc.gov—criteria as appropriate and approved (Becker's Clinical Leadership & Infection Control, 2015; Rutala, Weber, HICPAC, 2008; United States EPA, 2017). Hospitals must ensure the disinfectants used are effective against those infections and diseases that are seen throughout the hospital such as HIV, Hepatitis A, B, and C, Methicillin-Resistant Staphylococcus Aureus (MRSA), Vancomycin-Resistant Enterococcus (VRE), and *Clostridium difficile* (Becker's Clinical Leadership & Infection Control, 2015; Rutala, Weber, HICPAC, 2008; United States EPA, 2017). As new infections or diseases are seen in a hospital, such as Ebola, or new criteria or regulations are incorporated, hospitals must review their use of specific disinfectants and purchase new products should the need exist. Housekeeping staff is knowledgeable of the different disinfectants, when and how to use them, how long the product must be left on the surface to be effective, and any rinsing instructions if necessary (Becker's Clinical Leadership & Infection Control, 2015; Rutala, Weber, HICPAC, 2008; United States EPA, 2017). Development of hospital policies and procedures guiding the housekeeping staff in the proper use of housekeeping supplies (i.e., disinfectants) following written manufacturer's guidelines, having a Hazardous Communication Program, and educating the housekeeping staff in its use ensures safe use and proper cleaning and sanitizing of the hospital environment. More information on a Hazardous Communication Program will be provided later in this chapter.

Laundry

Laundry departments have their own set of rules and regulations within the hospital environment. The proper choice and use of laundry soaps, detergents, and bleach, and the temperatures in washing machines and dryers must meet standards for killing germs found in linens and garments, either provided by the hospital or brought in by patients (Sehulster & Chinn, 2003). Basic laundry tasks such as collection of soiled items; sorting, washing, and drying; sorting, folding, and distribution of clean items are designed to decrease the spread of infection and disease throughout the hospital. Similar to housekeeping, the laundry department personnel also follow policies and procedures designed by the hospital to prevent contamination and ensure a clean environment for the patient, visitors, vendors, and employees.

While all facilities may not have in-house laundry departments, all potentially contaminated linen and garments must be handled with appropriate measures to prevent cross-contamination (Sehulster & Chinn, 2003). For routine handling of contaminated laundry, minimum agitation is recommended to avoid the contamination of air, surfaces, and persons (Sehulster & Chinn, 2003). The risk of environmental contamination may be reduced by having personnel bag or contain contaminated linen at the point of use, and not sorting or prerinsing in patient care areas. If laundry chutes are used, no loose items in the chute and bags should be closed tightly before tossing into the chute. The CDC—cdc.gov—provides recommendations for hospitals with laundry departments that prevent the spread of infections and disease from linens and garments (Sehulster & Chinn, 2003).

Waste Management

Disposal of both general and hazardous waste is a responsibility of environmental services. General waste can be disposed of in a trash dumpster and hauled off to a general refuse center. Hazardous waste (i.e., solid, liquid, sharps, or pathological) must be disposed of following OSHA and EPA standards (Centers for Disease Control and Prevention [CDC], 2017). Hospital policies and procedures that address the safe handling and disposal of hazardous waste must include prevention of cross-contamination from infected materials, prevention of needlestick and sharps injuries, and proper storage and disposal of infected materials and equipment (CDC, 2017). Most hospitals will contract out the final disposal of all hazardous waste products to the company specializing in hazardous waste.

▶ Plant Engineering and Maintenance

Plant engineering and maintenance is the "fix it" department. Whenever there is a problem with the physical parts of the hospital (i.e., air conditioning, heating, elevators, plumbing, or building maintenance) or the equipment used (i.e., biomedical equipment, wheelchairs, and gurneys, or beds and toilets), the plant engineering and maintenance personnel are notified. Personnel in this department must be familiar with carpentry, engineering, electricity, plumbing, heating and ventilation, and medical equipment. While most hospitals have contracts with vendors who specialize in specific areas of the physical plant (i.e., elevators, or air conditioning), personnel must have a minimal working knowledge to resolve issues that have easy fixes.

Hazard Communication Plan and Lock-Out, Tag-Out

In order to ensure chemical safety in hospitals, labels and signage must be posted throughout the facility to identify potential hazards. OSHA provides standards hospitals must follow when using hazardous chemicals (United States Department of Labor, OSHA, 2017). In an OSHA brief entitled, Hazard Communication Standard: Safety Data Sheets (2012), "chemical manufacturers, distributors, or importers [must] provide Safety Data Sheets (SDSs) for each hazardous chemical to downstream users to communicate information on these hazards" (Occupational Safety & Health Administration [OSHA], 2012, para. 1). OSHA requires hospital personnel be trained in Hazard Communication, including understanding labels and SDS and how to safely handle hazardous chemicals (United States Department of Labor, OSHA, 2017). Hospitals must ensure education is conducted annually, SDSs are easily accessible to staff using or potentially coming into contact with hazardous chemicals, chemicals are labeled properly, and proper signage is posted conspicuously, to ensure a safe workspace (United States Department of Labor, OSHA, 2017).

Lock-Out, Tag-Out is another OSHA standard related to the physical environment of hospitals. With the majority of hospital departments using electrical equipment, electrical currents pose hazards for the plant engineering and maintenance team. Lock-Out, Tag-Out follows the OSHA standard for The Control of Hazardous Energy (Lockout/Tagout), Title 29 Code of Federal Regulations (CFR) Part 1910.147 (OSHA, 2002). This standard guides policies and procedures of the hospital to prevent the release of hazardous energy and protect employees when working on electric circuits and equipment (OSHA, 2002).

Life Safety

The NFPA's 101 Life Safety Code for Healthcare Occupancies—nfpa.org—provides strategies that minimize the effects of fire and related hazards in hospitals (National Fire Protection Association, 2018a). The Life Safety Code provides provisions for fire alarms, emergency lighting, and fire-suppression equipment; stipulates distances from exits, fire pull stations, and fire extinguishers; governs smoke barrier requirements; and determines fire and smoke ratings required for most aspects of the hospital and some furnishings, such as wall and floor coverings and some fabrics (National Fire Protection Association, 2018a). Healthcare providers (i.e., hospitals) that participate in federal reimbursement programs (i.e., Medicaid and Medicare) are required to meet the Certificate of Participation (COP) expectations for life and fire safety programs (National Fire Protection Association, 2018a).

Life Safety and Emergency Preparedness programs are required for hospitals to ensure the safety of the patients, visitors, vendors, and employees. Life safety programs include fire safety and emergency preparedness. Hospitals must develop a written fire plan for employees to follow. Using a plan such as the R.A.C.E. protocol and training employees in how to use a fire extinguisher, the P.A.S.S. protocol, guide employees' actions, should a fire occur. Regularly scheduled fire drills provide employees with opportunities to practice the fire plan process and revise any processes and equipment that may not be working properly (National Fire Protection Association, 2018a). Fire extinguishers and fire and smoke alarms must be inspected at least monthly by the plant engineering and maintenance team and annually by the fire protection company contracted by the hospital (National Fire Protection Association, 2018a).

Disasters whether internal (i.e., fire, power failure, water disruption, or elevator stoppage) or external (i.e., hurricane, earthquake, tsunami, or flood) can compromise a hospital's structural integrity, resulting in injuries to patients, visitors, or employees, threaten the hospital's ability to care for patients, or cause explosions, transportation disorder, or civil disorder. An Emergency Preparedness Plan, also referred to as a Disaster Plan, will guide employees on what to do should an emergency occur. To be effective, emergency preparedness plans should include regularly scheduled inspection—preventive maintenance—of the structural integrity of the building and the systems (i.e., water, medical gas, ventilation, and electric) or equipment (i.e., ventilators, dialysis machines, and pumps) in which failure may cause major injury or death. Any issues should be addressed and resolved immediately by the plant engineering and maintenance team.

▶ Biomedical Engineering (Medical Equipment)

Biomedical engineering is primarily responsible for installing, calibrating, maintaining, and repairing medical equipment used in the hospital. Biomedical equipments include electronic monitoring devices, patient lifts and trapeze, infusion and transfusion pumps, surgical and radiology machines, ventilators, incubators, and laboratory and dialysis machines. Biomedical engineers and technicians perform scheduled preventive maintenance on medical equipment evaluating the safety and efficacy of use and train hospital personnel on the proper use and, in some cases, how to troubleshoot the medical equipment. Biomedical engineering works closely with nursing, plant engineering and maintenance, and other patient care departments (i.e., surgical services and radiology) to provide needed assistance with medical equipment used on or for patients.

▶ Safety and Security

The safety and security department has the primary role of protecting patients, visitors, and employees from harm and keeping the hospital and its property secured. Safety and security personnel may confront persons due to unauthorized entry, patrol hospital grounds for unauthorized access, escort hospital visitors or personnel to and from parking areas, participate in emergency management activities, and monitor security-sensitive areas such as cash handling, pharmaceutical, and medical supply departments, emergency departments, and infant and pediatric departments. Safety and security personnel are also responsible for ensuring security laws and regulations are being followed; policies and procedures are developed to decrease safety and security risks, and security risk assessments are conducted regularly to identify security hazards. To protect patients, visitors, and employees from harm and property secured, safety and security personnel are on duty 24 hours a day, 7 days a week.

▶ Physical Needs of Hospitals in the 21st Century

Hospitals

The future of hospitals will revolve around technology and patient empowerment, and patient-centered care. Future technology trends will include e-health for communication between patients and providers improving access to care, social media sites with increased security and encryptions (HIPAA, HITECH), hybrid imaging devices for patients, consultants, and providers to access images and participate in care planning, remote or virtual ICU monitoring centers where providers away from the hospital can have immediate access to patient information and address issues or modify care plans remotely, and robots be seen, not only in surgery centers, but in patient care areas to improve quality of care and address cost. Technology and patient-centered care together will provide a service environment that enhances patient satisfaction and well-being.

Patient-Centered Hospitals

Hospitals will be viewed as centers of healing with environmental designs adapting to the needs and wants of its users, primarily the patients. A change of focus from institutional designs to more tranquil, homelike designs may aid in improving patient healing and outcomes. In a seminal paper by Robert Ulrich, Ph.D., EDAC (1984) entitled, "View through a window may influence recovery from surgery," he showed patients with a view of nature through their windows had shorter surgical stays, took less moderate–severe pain medications, and had fewer complications from minor surgery (Ulrich, 1984). Bigger windows that let in more ambient (natural) light, private rooms with window views of nature and open spaces with gardens and seating areas for patients, families, and visitors to enjoy during a visit will enhance the psychosocial needs of patients and aid in healing. Spiritual and cultural spaces where patients, families, and visitors can go to conduct or participate in personal practices and beliefs will enhance care interventions and improve a patient's feeling of well-being and autonomy, the choice to participate in activities that, to the patient, are important.

Patients will request technology of their own in 21st-century hospitals. Communication will be a priority. Access to providers, medical records, health information, blogs, and social media sites through computers, tablets, and phones, whether personal or hospital provided, will require modifications of hospital designs. Network infrastructures may need to be added or redesigned to meet the needs of the patient population and offered services. Privacy areas for communicating with providers and others (i.e., family, spiritual leaders, and cultural advisors) to ensure confidentiality may also need to be addressed.

Green and Sustainable Facilities

Conserving the environment and focusing on renewable resources is the wave of the future in facility design. Non-toxic or recycled materials that have the low impact on the environment, longer lasting, more durable products that do not need to be replaced as often, and the use of renewable resources and recycling will be common place in these hospitals. Hospitals will use both natural and artificial light to increase the patient's well-being. Facilities will be flexibly designed to meet the changing demands of the healthcare environment and the changing needs of consumers. Gary L. Vance, FAIA, FACHA, LEED AP (2017) states, "As the occupants and users of health care facilities age, it is important to utilize design principles and respond appropriately with the comprehensive products and materials of interior design" (Vance, 2017, para. 33).

Brief Chapter Summary

The physical facility of a hospital is highly integrated. Each department has been established to ensure that facilities are regularly maintained for hospital patrons, employees, and visitors. In the future, the physical facility of a hospital will include better technologies for better maintenance, service delivery, and overall care for patients.

This chapter has provided an overview of each of the essential departments of the physical facility of hospitals. Environmental services such as housekeeping, laundry, and waste management; plant engineering and maintenance services such as hazard communication plans, Lock-Out, Tag-Out, and life safety; biomedical engineering services such as maintenance of medical equipment; and **facility security**, parking, and fire safety were outlined.

Hospitals in the 21st century will continue to grow and improve, thereby increasing the codes, regulations, and laws that govern its design. Technological and "green" services will continuously add to the ever-changing nature of the physical facility of hospitals.

Questions for Review and Discussion

1. What are the main plant- and environmental-related departments and services in hospitals? List them and provide definitions of each.
2. What is the goal of the environmental services department, and what are the services provided in this department?
3. Identify at least three regulations mandated for hospital environmental services.
4. What is patient-centered care and how does this affect hospital design?
5. Name three characteristics of "green" hospitals?
6. Why are safety and security important to the development of hospital facilities beyond the 21st century?
7. Discuss the relevance of infection control measures in hospitals. What is the NFPA's Life Safety Code and what provisions does it recommend for the physical facility?

References

Asia-Pacific Society of Infection Control (APSIC). (2013). APSIC guidelines for environmental cleaning and decontamination. Retrieved from http://apsic-apac.org/wp-content/uploads/2016/09/Environmental-Cleaning-APSIC-Guideline-14-Jan-2013.pdf

Becker's Clinical Leadership & Infection Control. (2015). Infection prevention and housekeeping: A collaboration of equals. *Becker's Hospital Review*. Retrieved from https://www.beckershospitalreview.com/quality/infection-prevention-and-housekeeping-a-collaboration-of-equals.html

Centers for Disease Control and Prevention (CDC). (2017). Guidelines for environmental infection control in health-care facilities. Retrieved from https://www.cdc.gov/infectioncontrol/guidelines/environmental/background/medical-waste.html

Centers for Medicare & Medicaid Services. (2016). Medicare and medicaid programs; fire safety requirements for certain health care facilities. Retrieved from https://www.federalregister.gov/documents/2016/05/04/2016-10043/medicare-and-medicaid-programs-fire-safety-requirements-for-certain-health-care-facilities

International Code Council. (2018). 2012 international building code. Retrieved from https://www.iccsafe.org/content/2012-international-codes/

National Fire Protection Association. (2018a). National Fire Protection Agency (NFPA)'s 101 Life Safety Code for Healthcare Occupancies.

National Fire Protection Association. (2018b). Codes & standards. Retrieved from https://www.nfpa.org/Codes-and-Standards/All-Codes-and-Standards/List-of-Codes-and-Standards

National Fire Protection Association. (2018c). *National electrical code, 2017 edition*. Retrieved from https://www.nfpa.org/NEC

Occupational Safety & Health Administration (OSHA). (2002). Lockout/Tagout. OSHA Fact Sheet. Retrieved from https://www.osha.gov/OshDoc/data_General_Facts/factsheet-lockout-tagout.pdf

Occupational Safety & Health Administration (OSHA). (2012). Hazard communication standard: Safety data sheets. Retrieved from https://www.osha.gov/Publications/OSHA3514.html

Rutala, W., Weber, D., & HICPAC. (2008). *Guideline for disinfection and sterilization in healthcare facilities, 2008*. Centers for Disease Control and Prevention (CDC). Retrieved from https://www.cdc.gov/infectioncontrol/pdf/guidelines/disinfection-guidelines.pdf

Sehulster, L., & Chinn, R. (2003). *Guidelines for environmental infection control in health-care facilities*. Recommendations—Laundry and Bedding. CDC & HICPAC. Retrieved from https://www.cdc.gov/mmwr/preview/mmwrhtml/rr5210a1.htm

Ulrich, R. (1984). View through a window may influence recovery from surgery. *Science, 224*(4647), 420–421.

United States Department of Justice. (2010). Americans with Disabilities Act Title III Regulations. Nondiscrimination on the basis of disability by public accommodations and in commercial facilities. Retrieved from https://www.ada.gov/regs2010/titleIII_2010/titleIII_2010_regulations.pdf

United States Department of Justice, Civil Rights Division. (2018). ADA standards for accessible design. Retrieved from https://www.ada.gov/2010ADAstandards_index.htm

United States Department of Labor, OSHA. (2017). Hazard communication. Retrieved from https://www.osha.gov/dsg/hazcom/index.html

United States Department of Labor, Occupational Safety, and Health Administration. (2017). Regulations (Standards – 29 CFR) Part 1926. Construction. Retrieved from https://www.osha.gov/pls/oshaweb/owasrch.search_form?p_doc_type=STANDARDS&p_toc_level=1&p_keyvalue=Construction

United States Environmental Protection Agency (EPA). (2017). Pesticide registration. Selected EPA-registered. Retrieved from https://www.epa.gov/pesticide-registration/selected-epa-registered-disinfectants

Vance, G. (2017). Healthcare design for boomers and beyond: Universal design concepts can aid patient of all ages. *Health Facilities Management*. Retrieved from https://www.hfmmagazine.com/articles/2633-boomers-and-beyond

CHAPTER 15

Business Activities and the Business of Medicine

Randall Garcia and Ashish Chandra

CHAPTER OBJECTIVES

- To address hospital activities related to conducting business and creating, maintaining, and storing records.
- To provide an overview of health information management systems.
- To distinguish the difference between electronic medical record (EMR) and electronic health record (HER).
- To review the history and purpose of the Health Insurance Portability and Accountability Act (HIPAA) and its importance to health care.
- To identify and describe the four conditions of a HIPAA breach.

KEY TERMS

Accountable Care Organizations (ACOs)
Chief Executive Officer (CEO)
Chief Financial Officer (CFO)
Chief Information Officer (CIO)
Chief Operating (or Operations)
   Officer (COO)

Electronic health records (EHRs)
Electronic medical records
   (EMRs)
Health Insurance Portability
   and Accountability Act (HIPAA)

▶ The Business of Medicine

This chapter explores the purpose of the business office and how hospital activities relate to conducting normal business functions while creating and maintaining records. The business office is responsible for many activities within a hospital, including accounting, payroll, budgeting, health information systems

(HIMs), and **electronic health records (EHRs)**. There are many governmental requirements dictating when, how, and by whom patient records can be accessed (to be addressed in a later section). Patient records are utilized or reviewed in various areas, such as quality management (or quality assurance), billing, risk management, and documentation of all activities, that play a pivotal role in supporting patient care every day. Many people are required to operate a hospital efficiently and properly, and a considerable number of such employees are involved day to day in maintaining the hospital's business functions.

Hospital Leadership

There is no denying the reality that healthcare professionals are the backbone of any healthcare organization, but it is imperative to recognize that it is actually a team of professionals of diverse backgrounds and experiences that makes for a strong and successful healthcare organization. While an argument is often made as to whether a physician should oversee all hospital functions on a daily basis (and in some instances, often large centers of care, physicians are indeed top managers), the majority of healthcare institutions employ nonphysician hospital administrators, today often called **Chief Executive Officer (CEO)**. This top manager is responsible for all aspects of running the hospital. This is the individual ultimately responsible for day-to-day operations of the organization, who is usually experienced in several important areas, including operations, fund-raising, operations, planning, managing, and public speaking. Unless being a physician, the administrator is never involved in the clinical aspects of patient care. The leadership in clinical medicine and hospital administration operates in two quite different languages, the clinician dealing in a more clinical or "medical" language and the administrator dealing with a "business-oriented" language. This chapter focuses on the business activities of a healthcare organization.

Whether running a small private practice or functioning as part of a large healthcare system, the administrator needs to be able to understand where to go to solve problems of business, management, personnel, or operations. Mainly by the sheer size and the number of people involved in running a hospital, an administrator has several colleagues who assist in daily operations. Even if the organization is a small entity with relatively few personnel, this does not mean that there will be fewer business challenges. It is also likely that in smaller organizations, the distinction between the roles of the clinician and the administrators can become blurred, and the clinicians may become more involved in the administrative aspects than they would be in a larger healthcare organization.

The **Chief Operating Officer (COO)** is responsible for overseeing all aspects of daily nonclinical operations in a hospital organization. This can include housekeeping, cafeteria, transportation, maintenance, and security. Depending on the structure of the organization, the COO may also be responsible for clinical areas. One popularly used organizational model has the CEO on top with three direct-reporting executives: Chief Financial Officer (CFO), COO, and Medical Director, with all other functions, including nursing and other clinical areas, reporting to the COO.

In most organizations, accounting is found within the responsibility of the **CFO**. This person is responsible for all accounting functions, including payroll, budgeting, accounts receivables and payables, billing, and collections from all entities. The paying entities can include Medicare, Medicaid, public and private insurance companies, and self-pay patients.

The responsibility for computer systems and all related equipment usually falls under the auspice of the **Chief Information Officer (CIO)**. This person's responsibility is overseeing all aspects of computer operations and ensuring that data entered, accessed, retained, and stored in compliance with federal and state regulations. The role of the CIO has become extremely important in healthcare organizations, and in many instances, the CIO may also have to work closely with healthcare professionals in identifying, implementing, and running appropriate clinical information systems.

Depending on the size and complexity of the organization, there are often other managers and specialists who figure prominently in the operations of the hospital.

▶ In the Matter of Budgeting and Budgets

Hospital administrators face a difficult time each year during the essential budgeting process. Budgeting is financial planning, projecting the likely resource needs of each department for the coming operating cycle, usually a calendar year or fiscal year. There are different approaches to budgeting, the most commonly used process today involving all department managers and supervisors drafting their own budget requests according to guidelines and negotiating a final budget with the finance division in the face of limited funds (and there are nearly always "limited" funds). The practice of finance or a budget committee dictating departmental budgets without department management input is a relic of the past to be abandoned in favor of participative budgeting.

A budget is a must; it must be developed to ensure the most effective use of resources in covering all essential needs in support staff and departmental needs while also providing for the level of care patients need. And this must all be accomplished while adhering to restrictions placed by government and other sources of funding. To exacerbate the problem, changing technology and increasing healthcare costs, coupled with government budget restrictions, make budgeting for any healthcare organization a significant annual challenge.

In the long run, no organization, public or private, will be successful if budgeting is not a serious annual activity that takes into account all the realities, financial and others, of the environment in which the organization works. Without budgeting, an organization cannot properly plan how to allocate limited resources or determine what services can be offered in the future. The larger the entity, whether it is an individual hospital or a multifacility system, the more important it becomes for every manager to actively participate in budgeting.

Once a budget has been approved, it is the obligation of the department manager to ensure expenditures do not exceed amounts budgeted. A properly run organization will plan for contingencies by establishing a rainy day or contingency fund. These could include replacement or repair of equipment that breaks down unexpectedly, is damaged in hurricanes, floods, or other natural disasters, or perhaps is rendered inoperable by an organized labor action.

▶ Challenges in Health Care

For decades, the single largest budget item for hospitals has been labor costs, which can represent as much as 50%–60% or more of the total expense budget. Over the past several years, there has been a dramatic increase in pharmaceutical costs, creating even more pressure on the bottom line. A recent study showed that overall, hospitals' average annual inpatient drug spending jumped by more than 23% between 2012 and 2016 (Kamal & Cox).

Pharmaceutical costs create a significant challenge as more healthcare organizations move further into a population health model with more of the bottom line at risk. This is particularly challenging, since most often the best setting for chronic disease management is in the outpatient setting—where reimbursement is low as compared with the inpatient setting.

Therefore, reimbursement needs to become better aligned with the objective of keeping people of all ages healthy and out of the hospital.

One of the biggest budgetary challenges for hospital administrators is the transformation from volume to value, the shift from hospital-based to community-based services, decreased lengths of stay, and growing consumerism with providing patients more involvement in their health care. These conversions in health care have an impact on revenue, level of service which eventually affects the bottom line.

Care options and difficult cost containment measures are being expanded and developed. The advent of Meaningful Use and **Accountable Care Organizations (ACOs)** places healthcare organizations at greater risk for the very few additional dollars that make up already thin operating margins. ACOs are groups of healthcare professionals, hospitals, and other healthcare providers who come together to give coordinated high-quality care to their Medicare patients. Medicare is the fastest growing and lowest performing payer in terms of revenue per patient. While expansion of the Patient Protection and Affordable Care Act, most often shortened to Affordable Care Act (ACA) or sometimes referred to as Obamacare, has provided coverage to many previously uninsured patients. Patients are utilizing the delivery system more than expected—which is straining hospital financial performance and the healthcare markets.

The shift to community-based centers for outpatient surgery, imaging, and other outpatient services also affects an organization's revenue. Community-based service centers are being aggressively embraced by patients by providing the right care at the right place by the right clinician at the right price and at the right time. This model results in a decrease in patient volume and has been accepted by insurance plans, employers, physicians, patients, and the communities in general. Only time will tell if this business model will succeed.

Technological advancements are also changing the entire healthcare arena. For better or worse, technology is expected to play a major part in reducing the high costs of health care; however, implementing and maintaining new technology is expensive at the hospital level.

At the patient level, there has been a proliferation of new devices for tracking our everyday overall well-being. These devices include watches and apps that can monitor physical activity, sleep patterns, calorie intake, and much more. The future is exciting with the potential that healthcare technology can bring to improve patient care. A working model of the *Star Trek* tricorder has now been developed that can track 12 bodily activities. This is an exciting new frontier with a great deal of potential for improving patient care. It will be exciting to see the impact this trend has on improved patient engagement.

▶ Hospital Information Systems

A hospital or healthcare information system (HIS) is a computer system that manages all the information to allow healthcare providers and hospital staff to perform their jobs effectively. Computer systems in healthcare facilities have been around since the 1960s and have evolved as computers have advanced. The computers were large and expensive and provided the level of information in real time as computers do today. The equipment was used primarily for billing and inventory. Current hospital information systems integrate all clinical, financial, and administrative applications.

▶ Healthcare Information Management

Healthcare information management (HIM) professionals possess skills and competencies in health data management, information policy, information systems, and administrative and clinical work flow. HIM is focused on operations management, which is essential to ensuring an accurate and complete medical record and cost-effective information processing.

In acute care hospitals, HIM personnel are often part of the team, including the Information Technology (IT) staff and clinical informatics professionals who oversee EHRs.

HIM skills are critical to continuous quality improvement, regulatory requirements, and revenue cycle processes, ensuring the availability and accuracy of health data. The role of HIM in helping medical practices adopt EHRs is expanding.

HIM is a value-added connection between clinicians, payers, regulators, patients, consumers, and technology (EHRs and personal health records), with critical skills and competencies essential to building the nationwide health information network (NHIN) and health information exchanges (HIEs) (Grandia, 2017). One hindrance in the implementation of HIE is the lack of a national data format for all electronic health or medical records and regarding who will maintain the records.

▶ Electronic Medical Records Versus Electronic Health Records

There is much confusion between these two terms that are casually used interchangeably by many people; they should therefore be first defined.

Electronic medical records (EMRs) are digital versions of the paper charts in the clinician's office. An EMR contains the medical and treatment history of a patient in one practice. EMRs have advantages over paper records. For example, EMRs allow clinicians to:

- Track data over time
- Easily identify which patients are due for preventive screenings or checkups
- Check how patients are doing on certain parameters—such as blood pressure readings or vaccinations
- Monitor and improve overall quality of care within the practice.

But the information in EMRs does not travel easily out of the practice. In fact, the patient's record might even have to be printed out and delivered by mail to specialists and other members of the care team. In that regard, EMRs are not much better than paper records.

EHRs focus on the total health of the patient, going beyond clinical data collected and inclusive of a broader view of a patient's care. EHRs are designed to reach out beyond the health organization that originally collects and compiles the information. They are built to share information with other healthcare providers, such as laboratories and specialists, so they contain information from all the clinicians involved in the patient's care. The information moves with the patient—to the specialist, the hospital, the nursing home, the next state, or even across the country.

In comparing the differences between record types, the EHR represents the ability to easily share medical information among stakeholders and to have a patient's health information follow the patient through the various levels of care. This link makes all the difference. When information is shared in a positive and secure way, health care becomes a team effort; shared information supports that effort. The derived value from the healthcare delivery system results from the effective communication of information from one party to another and, ultimately, the ability of multiple parties to engage in interactive communication of information (Eisen & Gulick, 2002).

Electronic Health Records

Implementing EHRs or upgrading antiquated systems are two possibilities that many healthcare institutions will have to deal with to comply with government mandates. Operational efficiencies are predicted to follow, but they may not be evident immediately, making the ROI (return on investment) in switching EHRs more difficult to ascertain.

Unlike other industries, where IT advancements and automation can reduce personnel needs, implementation of an EHR will often increase healthcare technology staffing needs. And before a new EHR system is rolled out, work flows must be examined so improvements can be made; however, there is not a large return on the EHR investment. Nonetheless, falling behind technologically is not an option and usually results in organization's reduced market share to competitors.

Switching or upgrading EHR systems must plan accordingly to ensure staffing needs ahead of time to ensure an efficient rollout. Implementing a new system can deliver cost savings, but only if you understand your training needs, establish clear goals, and adapt the work flow with careful planning.

▶ Health Insurance Portability and Accountability Act

History

The **Health Insurance Portability and Accountability Act**, better known as HIPAA, first introduced in 1996, is a comprehensive legislative act integrating the requirements of several other legislative acts, including the Public Health Service Act, Employee Retirement Income Security Act, and the Health Information Technology for Economic and Clinical Health (HITECH) Act. HIPAA is best known for protecting the privacy of patients and ensuring patient data are properly secured. These requirements were added by the HIPAA Privacy Rule of 2000 and the HIPAA Security Rule of 2003. The requirement for notifying individuals of a breach of their health information was later introduced in 2009 in the Breach Notification Rule.

Purpose

The main purpose of the privacy portions of HIPAA was to restrict the permissible uses and disclosure of protected health information (PHI), stipulating when, by whom, and under what circumstances, health information could be shared. An additional purpose of the HIPAA Privacy Rule was to give patients access to their health data on request. Furthermore, the purpose of the HIPAA Security Rule is to ensure electronic health data are appropriately secured, access to electronic health data is controlled, and an auditable trail of personal health information (PHI) activity is preserved.

HIPAA also introduced further standards that were intended to improve efficiency in the healthcare industry, requiring healthcare organizations to adopt the standards to reduce the paperwork burden. Code sets had to be used along with patient identifiers, which helped pave the way for the efficient transfer of healthcare data between healthcare organizations and insurers, streamlining eligibility checks, billing, payments, and other healthcare operations.

Importance to Health Care

Every time a patient visits a new provider or goes to the hospital, the individual is given a release form to sign stating the patient understands the institution observes HIPAA guidelines. The form also allows communication with other medical professionals in regard to patient health care.

A critical aspect of HIPAA is the right of the patient to designate who can speak on behalf of the patient. The patient has the right to designate as many people as he/she may choose.

Another important aspect of HIPAA is the right of patients to obtain copies of their medical records. A patient cannot be denied the copies; however, a fee maybe incurred in obtaining the copies. Under HIPAA, a hospital or healthcare professional's office is allowed to charge for copies. A patient must be informed how long it will take to acquire copies of the requested documents. All or just only certain specific parts can be requested. A patient may also designate what part of the records can be sent to other medical professionals or institutions; this section was enacted to protect the patient.

▶ HIPAA Breach

A breach of "PHI" is defined as the acquisition, access, use, or disclosure of unsecured PHI in a manner not permitted by HIPAA, posing a significant risk of financial, reputational, or other harm to the affected individual. For a breach to occur, there must be: (1) an access to, or use or disclosure of unsecured PHI; (2) a use, access, or disclosure that violates the "Privacy Rule" (i.e., Subpart E of 45 C.F.R. 164); (3) a significant risk that such access, use, or disclosure will cause financial, reputational, or other harm to the patient; and (4) no exceptions that apply. If any of these four criteria are not met, the incident is not a breach, as defined in the Breach Notification Rule, and notifications do not need to be sent or reports made to the Office for Civil Rights (OCR) (Eisen & Gulick, 2002).

In summary, the purpose of HIPAA is to improve efficiencies in the healthcare industry, to improve the portability of health insurance, to protect the privacy of patients, and to ensure health information is kept secure and patients are notified of breaches of their health data.

Brief Chapter Summary

This chapter explores the purpose of the business office and how hospital activities relate to conducting normal business functions while creating and maintaining records. It takes many people to efficiently run a hospital. The CEO or hospital administrator is responsible for all aspects of running a hospital. This person usually has experience in several areas which include fund-raising, operations, planning, managing, and public speaking. Unless this person is a physician, the administrator is never involved in the clinical aspect of patient care. The CEO is usually assisted by the CFO, COO, and CIO in running a hospital. This chapter briefly reviews budgeting and the challenges within health care.

The evolution of HIMs is provided in addition to the differences between an electronic medical record and EHRs.

Finally, the history, purpose, and the conditions of a HIPAA breach are discussed and why HIPAA is important to health care.

Questions for Review and Discussion

1. Who is the person responsible for overseeing all aspects of daily operations in a hospital system? What areas is the person usually responsible for?
2. Describe the evolution of HIMs.
3. What is the difference between EMR and EHR?
4. What is the history, purpose of HIPAA, and why is it important to health care?
5. What are the four conditions to be considered a HIPAA breach?

References

Eisen, J., & Gulick, S. (2002). What is a breach under the HITECH breach notification regulations? Retrieved from https://www.americanbar.org/content/newsletter/publications/aba_health _esource_home/aba_health_law_esource_0512_eisen.html

Grandia, L. (2017). Healthcare information systems: A look at the past, present, and future. Retrieved from https://www.healthcatalyst.com/wp-content/uploads/2014/11/Healthcare-Information -Systems-A-Look-at-the-Past-Present-and-Future.pdf

Kamal, R., & Cox, C. What are the recent and forecasted trends in prescription drug spending? Kaiser Family Foundation, Peterson-Kaiser Healthsystem Tracker. Retrieved from https:// www.healthsystemtracker.org/chart-collection/recent-forecasted-trends-prescription -drug-spending/#item-start

© sudok1/Getty Images

CHAPTER 16

Unions in Healthcare Organizations[1]

Charles R. McConnell

CHAPTER OBJECTIVES

- Examine the present state of unions and union organizing in the United States and explore possible reasons for the success of some union organizing drives.
- Address the fundamental management errors that have been repeatedly shown to lead to unionization.
- Examine the circumstances that presently make some healthcare organizations appear to be fertile ground for union organizing.
- Explain why today's practices of merging provider organizations and combining various entities into larger systems can increase vulnerability to union organizing.
- Describe the typical union organizing approach.
- Address the roles of all levels of management in the presence of union organizing and specifically examine the role of the first-line manager in maintaining communication with employees in the presence of a union.

KEY TERMS

Bargaining election   Collective bargaining agreement
Bargaining unit   Decertification

▶ Can Unionization Be Avoided?

A close examination of union organizing campaigns and their results over the recent decades would likely lead to the following three conclusions, often verified through experience:

1. Most past organizing campaigns focused on economic issues, at least into and through most of the 1990s, when union emphasis on job

security and quality of work life began to increase noticeably. Usually, most initial demands have been unreasonable, reflecting ignorance or indifference concerning the organizations' true financial positions. In many instances, the unions won their bargaining elections because of apparent management indifference to complaints, no response to employees' problems, and lack of credibility with employees in regard to costs and true operating circumstances.

2. In the majority of union victories, antimanagement sentiment initially arises from working conditions that include poor organizational communication or arbitrary or seemingly uncaring management.

3. In many cases, the anxiety produced by widespread lack of knowledge about what is truly happening concerning the organization's status and likely future provides a boost to the union cause.

In essentially all instances of elections lost to unions, it is possible to identify serious and usually long-standing morale problems among employees. Also, in all such instances, management will be found to have been operating in something of a vacuum with respect to true employee feelings and opinions.

In assessing the potential for unionization, it is simply not enough for top management to have managers talk with employees and report back on how the employees seem to be feeling about the state of the organization. True antimanagement sentiment, nearly always beneficial to union organizers, is determined only through carefully listening to employees on an ongoing basis. Many employees—quite likely the majority—would prefer to be loyal to the organization, but the organization's seeming indifference to upward communication can discourage such loyalty. Also, the price of management indifference can be extremely high: If a union loses a bargaining election, it may try again after 1 year has elapsed, and go on to try again and again until it succeeds, but management need lose only once. It has been proven time and again that if management does not listen to employees, the union organizers will.

There are three fundamental errors commonly committed by management in assessing the potential for success of union organizing efforts:

1. There is a widely prevalent management notion that most reasons for worker dissatisfaction involve concerns for wages, benefits, and other economically related issues. However, more often than not initial organizing activity springs from noneconomic matters involving issues that are not readily quantifiable in dollar amounts. Employee dissatisfaction will ultimately be expressed through a union in the form of financial demands; a specific financial package can be obtained by contract, but there is no contractual way to obtain less tangible items, such as sympathetic listening, open communications, and humane and respectful treatment.

2. Many top managers automatically assume that all supervisors—those first-line managers of the people who perform the hands-on work—are on the side of management. However, the majority of supervisors came up from the ranks within the functions they supervise and as such often remain an integral part of the same work group. Also, in many institutions, first-line supervisors have been kept out of participation in real management decision-making.

3. Frequently, nobody at the top of the organization has any solid idea of what, if anything, is really troubling the rank-and-file employees. It is not uncommon for top management to interpret the silence of the workforce as indicating the absence of problems; this has been a significant error leading to union victories when top management was confident of union defeat.

Commission of any of these fundamental errors in one form or another can pave the way for a successful union organizing drive. More specifically, an organization can push its employees closer to a union by engaging in the following practices:

■ introducing major changes in organization structure, job content, equipment, or operating practices without advance notice or subsequent explanation
■ giving employees little or no information about the financial status of the organization or about its plans, goals, or achievements
■ making key decisions in ignorance of the employees' true wants, needs, and feelings
■ using pressure (authoritarian or autocratic leadership) rather than true leadership (consultative or participative approaches) to obtain employee performance
■ disregarding or downplaying instances of employee dissatisfaction

In addition to the three fundamental management errors and the foregoing acts of managerial shortsightedness, there are some factors encouraging unionization that are unique to health care. For a number of years, health care and industry in general appear to have been moving in opposite directions in their appeal and suitability for union organizing, with interest in organizing increasing in health care while unions are finding fewer organizing opportunities in other industries. Present circumstances suggest that healthcare organizations will continue to be choice organizing targets for some time to come.

▶ Health Care: More and More a Special Case

It is no secret that the total number of jobs available in the manufacturing sector of the U.S. economy has been steadily declining for a number of years as competition and the "globalization" of business cause the relocation of an increasing number of jobs to foreign countries. Manufacturing was long the source of most union membership. However, as manufacturing jobs have been lost, the unions have shifted much of their focus to service industries. The service sector of the economy now employs more than 75% of the workforce. Thus, it comes as no surprise that many unions, having seen their membership dwindle for several years, have diversified and turned their attentions to the service industries.

Healthcare organizations represent fertile ground for union organizing and should continue as such for a number of years to come. From the 1970s to the present, total union membership dropped while union membership in health care continued to increase. The Department of Labor reported that during the year 2000, the percentage of American workers belonging to unions fell to 13.5%, the lowest in six decades (McConnell, 2015). As of this writing, the percentage of the total workforce that is unionized remains the smallest it has been since the late 1940s; however, the percentage of the healthcare workforce that is unionized is presently the largest it has ever been.

Health care as an employment arena began to change dramatically during the late 1960s. Pressures intended to stem the steady increase of healthcare costs— which have gone up at twice or more the "normal" rate of inflation for years— continue to the present. Along the way, specifically in 1975, the National Labor Relations Act (NLRA) was amended to include hospitals and other healthcare organizations that had previously been excluded from coverage under the Act. In 1975, when much of the industry was starting to see the effects of cost-containment efforts, unions were given new opportunities in this significant segment of the service economy.

With much of health care in turmoil or at least in a chronic state of change, employees are feeling more and more uncertain about the future. In some parts of the country where hospitals have been severely underutilized, many employees perceive a threat to their continued full-time employment. As healthcare providers attempt to meet shifting demands in the most economical fashion by adopting more staffing variations—more part-time employment, flextime and other nontraditional approaches, and job sharing and the like—employees are further threatened by the perceived uncertainty of their situation.

The survival-oriented remedies of many provider organizations have included staff cuts, mergers, downsizing, and corporate reorganizing. As a partial result, employees perceive a direct threat to the quality of the care they can provide and to their job security. The effects of healthcare organization restructuring—mergers, downsizing, and the rest—emerged as the number one human resources concern that hospitals faced in 1987 (Fallon & McConnell, 2014). These effects remain at the forefront of employee concern nearly three decades later; healthcare workers remain concerned for their jobs and their futures in health care. And while job security remains a critical issue targeted by healthcare union organizers, at the same time, wages and benefits are becoming increasingly important to the predominantly female healthcare workforce.

Tangibles, such as pay and benefits, are always prominent in the presence of labor unrest, but the turmoil in the healthcare industry drives far more than these economic concerns. When employees feel that their concerns are not being adequately addressed by management—and healthcare management is faced with some nearly overwhelming concerns, many of which seem to defy all attempts at resolution because of outside pressures and restrictions—these employees will turn to someone else who will seem to listen. Often this "someone else" is a union.

Direct caregivers, particularly nurses, are especially susceptible to organizing pressures. Dissatisfaction with pay and stressful working conditions, aggravated by a shortage of nurses, are spurring job actions and the formation of nursing unions. The Department of Health and Human Services predicts a shortage of 400,000 nurses by the year 2020. Although the number of registered nurses is slowly increasing at present, many are choosing to work in settings other than hospitals or nursing homes. Approximately two of every five new nurses are opting for positions with health maintenance organizations, pharmaceutical companies, or other health-related organizations, such as urgent care centers and clinics and other free-standing providers. Such jobs are often less physically demanding and higher paying when compared with hospital positions.

▶ System Growth and Increased Vulnerability

As hospitals and other provider entities come together to form health systems, these ever-larger collections of what were once smaller organizations sometimes present larger and more attractive organizing targets. Depending on the particular union that is interested in organizing within a healthcare system, the target group may be small and fairly well defined. For example, a union serving skilled maintenance workers may target just that specific group within one or more elements of the larger system; this organizing interest is not likely to spill over into other occupational groups. However, if the organizing interest happens to be registered nurses, it is possible that all member elements of the entire system that include nurses will be subject to organizing pressure. In other words, the larger the system, the more attractive it may be as an organizing target. However, much will depend on the occupational group or groups sought by a particular union.

In 1975, the NLRA was amended to bring not-for-profit hospitals under federal labor law; prior to this time, only state labor laws, if any, applied to such organizations. Recognizing that hospitals needed to be treated differently from other kinds of businesses, specific rules were established governing the relationship between a union and a not-for-profit hospital. All of the details of the 1975 amendments are not relevant to this discussion, but of interest are the potential "bargaining units" that apply to unions, a potential bargaining being a designated employee grouping that could be served by a union.

Multiplicity of Bargaining Units

A major point in the congressional intent of the 1975 amendments to the NLRA was the wish to avoid fragmentation of bargaining units in healthcare institutions, that is, avoiding having numerous small units working with and bargaining within the same institution. However, in spite of this wish, in the middle to late 1980s, the National Labor Relations Board (NLRB) moved decidedly in the direction of proliferation of bargaining units by issuing new rules for determining bargaining unit boundaries in hospitals. To be applied in nongovernmental acute-care hospitals (nursing homes and psychiatric hospitals excluded), these rules would leave hospitals very limited flexibility with which to challenge proposed units. After some haggling and negotiating, the proposed rules underwent some modest modifications but continued to call for a multiplicity of bargaining units. The proposed rules were vigorously opposed by the American Hospital Association and other interests. The rulemaking authority of the NLRB came under legal challenge, culminating in an April 1991 decision by the U.S. Supreme Court favoring the NLRB.

The decision of April 1991 officially established eight separate bargaining units as appropriate in acute-care hospitals:

1. registered nurses
2. physicians
3. all other professionals
4. technical employees
5. skilled maintenance employees
6. business office clericals

7. security guards
8. all other nonprofessionals (service, clerical, etc.)

Previously, units were determined on a case-by-case basis, and a hospital, especially a small one of fewer than 100 beds, stood a good chance of having to deal with perhaps only two or three unions at most. Present rules, however, mean that a hospital of any size could conceivably have to deal with as many as eight separate unions. Concerning bargaining unit proliferation, the NLRB went far afield from the congressional intent of the 1975 amendments.

Although petitions filed for NLRB-supervised elections increased in the months following the Supreme Court ruling, there was not the flood of petitions that some had predicted. The groups that were initially most affected of the eight designated units were registered nurses, all other professionals, and skilled maintenance employees. This came as no surprise; the previous long-standing combination of nurses and other professionals had inhibited organizers for a number of years; for example, the individual state units of the American Nurses Association sought units of professional nurses only. And the skilled trades have long been associated with union membership; in separating them from all others, the NLRB essentially encouraged them to organize. In past years when bargaining unit determinations were made on a case-by-case basis, skilled maintenance employees had been grouped with the larger body of service employees.

What all of the foregoing really means for today's emerging and expanding healthcare systems is that a system could conceivably have to deal with several sizable bargaining units or a mix of a number of both larger and smaller bargaining units.

▶ The Potential for Communications Problems

There are some simply described characteristics that more or less govern much communication in complex organizations whether single large entities or systems or conglomerations composed of numerous elements both large and small:

■ the more levels there are in any organized entity, the more opportunities there are for errors to occur in information flow both downward and upward;
■ since management controls the means of disseminating information, information flows downward far more effectively than upward;
■ upward flow of information—that is, information from employees—is generally weak for a variety of reasons and may be very nearly nonexistent without deliberate stimulation by all levels of management;
■ horizontal dissemination of information—that is, information flow between and among system elements—must depend more on conscientious communication between and among managers than on rules and procedures.

In other words, the larger a system becomes—or, for that matter—the larger a single corporate entity grows, the more opportunities there are for errors and omissions in communication. And take it as given that effective union organizers are skilled at seeking out and capitalizing on such errors or omissions as the genuine weak spots they often are.

▶ The Supervisor's Position

It is possible, however, for the nonunionized institution to remain that way; all managers, and especially the individual first-line manager, have an important role in keeping the institution union-free.

The supervisor of any working group is the single member of management that the group's employees know best. The supervisor may indeed be the only member of this mysterious entity called management most of the employees know on a first-name basis or even know on speaking terms at all. Thus, as the employees see their supervisor, so too are they likely to see all of management and the organization itself. If they see the supervisor as unconcerned, uncaring, distant, or indifferent, some of them, perhaps even most of them, are likely to view the organization as a whole that way.

It follows, then, that the supervisor is in a key position when it comes to dealing with the threat of unionization. The supervisor is the link that ties the employees to higher management and thus to the organization. The supervisor's long-term behavior will have a great deal to do with whether this department is a fertile ground for union organizing activity, and the supervisor's conduct and actions during an organizing campaign will exert a significant influence on the employees' reaction to an organizing drive.

▶ The Organizing Approach

In considering what the first stages of a union organizing campaign might look like, one might be inclined to identify one of the first visible signs of union activity—"leafleting," or the distribution of union literature to employees at walkways, driveways, and parking lot entrances. However, although serious leafleting is an undeniable indication of union activity, it is ordinarily not the first step in an organizing campaign. Chances are the union has been studying the institution for weeks or even months to judge its organizing potential before the first literature appears.

When organizing activity actually begins, management may well know nothing about it. In fact, during the earliest stages, the union may take considerable precautions to prevent management from learning about their interest. The union may send organizers into the institution simply to loiter and listen and pick up what they can from conversations in the cafeteria, snack bar, parking area, employee lounge areas, and other such places where employees congregate informally. Outsiders can move freely in many institutions, and such infiltration is especially easy in an institution that does not require or enforce the use of employee identification badges or passes for visitors and vendors. The organizers will simply merge with the crowd and listen, picking up gripes, locating supervisory weaknesses and departments with obvious morale problems, and identifying informal leaders among the employees. They will try to learn as much as possible about the institution before revealing themselves.

The still-unannounced organizers will also attempt to pinpoint employees who have the potential to serve as internal organizers, looking especially for those employees who are popular, knowledgeable, reasonably articulate, and in some way unhappy with the organization.

Should their silent survey raise serious doubts that the institution could possibly be unionized, the organizers might simply withdraw without ever announcing their presence. However, if they believe the union stands a chance of succeeding, they will likely identify themselves to a few selected employees and begin preparations to carry their message to others. Leafleting is likely to begin at about this stage.

The major exception to the usual significance of leafleting occurs in a practice sometimes referred to as a "pass-through." In a pass-through, the union will devote a day or two to distributing literature at perhaps several institutions in the same general area. These are generally "cold" visits—no advance investigation has taken place. The union will simply "pass through" the area and drop off as much literature as possible with the employees of as many institutions as they can readily reach and follow up only if they receive expressions of interest from employees. (The pass-through literature usually includes a reply card to be returned for more information.)

When the organizers are out in the open and their purpose is generally known, they will step up their activities in meeting with employees and contacting them in other ways. Somewhere along the way, possibly through sympathetic employees, they will attempt to obtain a list of the names and addresses of all the institution's nonmanagerial employees. The union will most certainly be contacting many individual employees by telephone and will seek to visit the homes of others.

In talking with employees, the union will attempt to uncover issues to use as rallying points for employee sympathy and support. The organizers will attempt to identify martyrs and victims of "the system" and will effectively play on emotions in spotlighting incidents of alleged unfair treatment and discrimination.

The union organizers will go to great lengths to impress on employees their right to be treated as individuals. This may seem elementary; most of us will normally express strong belief in the rights of the individual. If, however, in the face of seemingly indifferent management the union organizer is the first person to tell them this, then the grounds for union credibility may exist. The organizers will make every effort to develop a communicating relationship with your employees. This should sound familiar, because the development of such a relationship is part of your role as a supervisor.

You can be certain that most issues and incidents brought to the forefront by the union are specially selected to make management look bad. Lacking sufficient factual material, organizers frequently stage incidents intended to make the union look good and make management look foolish. The supervisor's awareness of this particular organizing tactic is critical; it is all too easy to make an inappropriate statement or incorrect decision when confronted with a trumped-up grievance or problem at an inconvenient time and under awkward circumstances (which usually includes the presence of some employee witnesses). Such matters would be rightly dealt with by administration, labor relations, or whoever else may be coordinating the institution's counterorganizing activities. However, there is a need for the supervisor to react on the spot, without making promises or commitments and without seeming to be refusing to listen to an employee. Afterward, the incident can be promptly reported to the proper persons.

▶ Unequal Positions

Under the NLRA, unions and employers do not have equal clout in the organizing process. In many respects, the union enjoys the upper hand. Under the act, an employer can commit an unfair labor practice and such charges can be brought against the organization by the union. If the NLRB, ruling on an unfair labor practice charge, upholds the union's claim, then the union may be automatically certified as a recognized bargaining agent without the necessity of a representation election. The law, however, does not work the other way around; although a union may perhaps engage in some questionable practices while organizing, for all practical purposes, there is no such thing as an unfair labor practice committed by a union. Also, as noted earlier, if the union should lose a bargaining election, it may petition for another election after 1 year has elapsed. The employer may well have to win year after year to remain union-free. However, the employer need lose only once and the union is in, permanently for all practical purposes, because decertification of a union is difficult to achieve and occurs infrequently.

▶ A Manager's Role

The guidelines pertinent to the behavior of all managers, especially first-line and middle managers, during a union organizing campaign make up a sizeable collection of what one can do (**EXHIBIT 17.1**) and what one cannot do (**EXHIBIT 17.2**). It is to

---

EXHIBIT 17.1 What the Supervisor Can Do When a Union Beckons

1. Campaign against a union seeking to represent employees, and reply to union attacks on the institution's practices or policies.
2. Give employees your opinions about unions, union policies, and union leaders.
3. Advise employees of their legal rights during and after the organizing campaign, and supply them with the institution's legal position on matters that may arise.
4. Keep outside organizers off institution premises.
5. Tell employees of the disadvantages of belonging to a union, such as strikes and picket-line duty; dues, fines, and assessments; rule by a single person or small group; and possible domination of a local by its international union.
6. Remind employees of the benefits they enjoy without a union, and tell them how their wages and benefits compare with those at other institutions (both union and nonunion).
7. Let employees know that signing a union authorization card is not a commitment to vote for the union if there is an election.
8. Tell employees that you would rather deal directly with them than attempt to settle differences through a union or any other outsiders.
9. Give employees factual information concerning the union and its officials, even if such information is uncomplimentary.
10. Remind employees that no union can obtain more for them than the institution is able to give.
11. Correct any untrue or misleading claims or statements made by the union organizers.
12. Inform employees that the institution may legally hire a new employee to replace any employee who strikes for economic reasons.
13. Declare a fixed position against compulsory union membership contracts.
14. Insist that all organizing be conducted outside of working time.
15. Question open and active union supporters about their union sentiments, as long as you do so without direct or implied threats or promises (see Shifting Ground Rules).
16. State that you do not like to deal with unions.

EXHIBIT 17.2 What the Supervisor Cannot Do When a Union Beckons

1. Ask employees about their union sentiments in a manner that includes or implies threats, promises, or intimidation in any form. Employees may volunteer any such information and you may listen, but you may ask only with caution (see Shifting Ground Rules).
2. Attend union meetings or participate in any undercover activities to find out who is or is not participating in union activities.
3. Attempt to prevent internal organizers from soliciting memberships during nonworking time.
4. Grant pay raises or make special concessions or promises to keep the union out.
5. Discriminate against pro-union employees in granting pay increases; apportioning overtime; making work assignments, promotions, layoffs, or demotions; or applying disciplinary action.
6. Intimidate, threaten, or punish employees who engage in union activity.
7. Suggest in any way that unionization will force the institution to close up, move, lay off employees, or reduce benefits.
8. Deviate from known institution policies for the primary purpose of eliminating a pro-union employee.
9. Provide financial support or other assistance to employees who oppose the union, or be party to a petition or such action encouraging employees to organize to reject the union.
10. Visit employees at home to urge them to oppose the union.
11. Question prospective employees about past union affiliation.
12. Make statements to the effect that the institution "will not deal with a union."
13. Use a third party to threaten, coerce, or attempt to influence employees in exercising their right to vote concerning union representation.
14. Question employees on whether they have or have not signed a union authorization card.
15. Use the word *never* in any statements or predictions about dealings with the union.

the individual manager's advantage to be sensitive to the limitations these requirements place on one's actions, decisions, and comments in dealings with employees. Ideally, first-line managers—the supervisors in an institution undergoing organizing pressure—should receive classroom training in these guidelines from a labor attorney or a labor relations expert.

It is also to the individual supervisor's advantage—at all times, but especially during a union organizing campaign—to know the employees in the group as individuals, and know them well. Although people cannot be stereotyped, and there are few reliable generalizations concerning employees' receptiveness to a union, it is nevertheless possible for a supervisor to make some reasonable judgments as to how certain employees might react under organizing pressure. Often the employee sympathetic to the union's cause may:

- feel unfairly treated by the organization and believe that reasonable opportunities have been denied
- feel that the organization has been unsympathetic regarding personal problems and pressures

- express a lack of confidence in supervision or administration and be unwilling to talk openly with members of management
- feel unequally treated in terms of pay and other economic benefits
- take no apparent pride in affiliation with the institution
- exhibit career-path problems, having either changed jobs frequently or having reached the top in pay and classification while still having a significant number of working years remaining
- be a source of complaints or grievances more often than most other employees
- exhibit a poor overall attitude

It is extremely important for a supervisor to know your employees' attitudes toward the institution in order to develop a sense for how well one is communicating. Ultimately, a labor union has little to offer if employees already feel that the organization is responding to their needs.

▶ Shifting Ground Rules

The lists of what the supervisor can (Exhibit 17.1) and cannot do (Exhibit 17.2) in the presence of union organizing are based on interpretations of the NLRA by the NLRB. Many of these interpretations are clear-cut and have stood the test of time regardless of the composition of the NLRB. Some, however, are not clear-cut and are likely to change as the Board's composition changes. The matter of management's questioning of employees about union sentiments and activities is the best illustration of this possibility.

For years, it has been relatively accurate to cite the so-called TIPS Rule in summarizing the most important elements of what a member of management could not do during union organizing: A manager could not Threaten, Interrogate, Promise, or Spy. (One may also encounter "TIPS" as "SPIT" or "PITS," depending on the arrangement of the four prohibitions.)

In the middle 1980s, the NLRB loosened its interpretation of interrogation to suggest that it is lawful for an employer to question union supporters about their union sentiments as long as the questioning carries with it no threats or promises and in no way interferes with or restrains the employees in the exercise of their rights under the NLRA.

The present posture on interrogation is hardly new; it had been an applied principle of labor relations for 30 years until 1980. In 1980, however, when the NLRB was dominated by the Democratic Party, the stricter interpretation of the interrogation prohibitions of the law was imposed. This stricter interpretation was reversed in 1984, when the NLRB composition changed again. However, in recent years, the composition of the NLRB has changed still further, essentially swinging Board sentiment back toward more strongly favoring unions. Thus, organizations presently coming under union organizing pressure should best observe the stricter interpretation of the interrogation prohibition.

Given its present composition, with a number of strongly pro-union activists among its members, the NLRB has been able to shape much labor organizing activity through its rule-making authority. The NLRB's recent actions seem intended to create an environment that is more conducive to union organizing and in general to revitalize the organized labor movement overall.

Managers who you find themselves caught up in a union organizing drive must pay strict attention to the institution's labor attorney and labor relations director (or whoever else may be coordinating management's counterorganizing efforts) for advice on what to do and what to avoid. Although the actions enumerated in Exhibits 17.1 and 17.2 should remain largely valid, some of them will inevitably vary in content or emphasis from one national administration to another depending on the makeup of the NLRB.

▶ The Bargaining Election

The union, often working through both external and internal organizers, will go about the business of securing sufficient employee interest to allow it to petition the NLRB for a bargaining election. Generally, the indications of such support will take the form of simple cards that employees sign to indicate interest in having an election. Employees should be aware that signing a card is not an automatic "yes" vote for union representation but rather simply an expression of interest in having an election. (Not long ago a piece of proposed legislation known as the Employee Free Choice Act could have made it possible for a union to become certified by simply obtaining a majority of signed authorization cards, but this did not become law.)

When sufficient signatures are gathered (usually half or more of the number of employees in the unit that the union is seeking to represent, although the union need have signatures from just 30% of eligible employees to legally submit its petition), the union will petition the NLRB. After what is usually a cursory investigation, the Board will sanction an election and a date for voting will be set.

Election is by secret ballot, and all employees who work in the unit the union is seeking to represent are eligible to vote. If the union receives a simple majority of the vote, it will then be certified by the Board as the legal bargaining agent for all persons who work in the unit. Although compulsory union membership is not required by law, this usually means that all persons working in the unit must eventually join the union because this particular right of the union is usually bargained for in the initial contract.

If the union fails to achieve a simple majority and various possible legal challenges do not upset the results of the election, the union will withdraw at least for a while if the vote was close or perhaps for a longer period if the results were clearly one-sided.

Keep in mind, however, that some elections are little more than formalities—many elections are lost long before the organizers ever show up. If the trend in relations between employees and management is clearly in the direction of a union, this can be difficult to reverse. Reversal may, however, be accomplished through hard work and plenty of open and honest communication.

Even if a single unit of employees is lost to a union (for instance, a union representing service and maintenance employees or one representing only licensed practical nurses), then new steps aimed at creating positive communicating relationships can still pay off. A new atmosphere can make contract bargaining easier, smooth out day-to-day labor relations matters, and help keep other bargaining units out of the institution.

▶ If the Union Wins

Soon after—and often immediately after—the union is certified as a recognized bargaining unit, negotiations will commence for an initial contract. This gives all managers, especially managers with regular working contact with union members, a whole new set of rules and regulations to observe.

The first-line managers must learn the contract inside out—learn what it says, learn what it does not say, and learn why it says what it says—and comply with it faithfully. Some contracts seem top-heavy with numerous details and exacting requirements, but one may find that some parts of the supervisory job have actually become easier because there are now hard and fast rules for some situations that were previously subject to interpretation and judgment.

Above all, be open and honest in all dealings with the union and do your best to avoid an adversarial relationship with union representatives.

The presence of a union does not mean the supervisor can back off from active communications with employees and simply wave the contract at them. Complete two-way communication remains essential in establishing and maintaining your relationships with all employees whether they are or are not represented by a union. After all, the employees work for the institution, not for the union. Generally, the union will be the employees' voice only if the employees feel they are not recognized as individuals and are not being heard by management.

▶ Decertification

As initially passed, the NLRA strongly favored unions and took considerable steps to protect employees from abuse by employers. In amending the NLRA, the Labor Management Reporting Act of 1947 (Taft-Hartley) took a more balanced approach to protecting the rights of individual employees from abuse by both employers and unions. Taft-Hartley made it possible for employees to get out from under a union that no longer seemed to serve their purposes or be acting in their best interests. This change allowed employees to remove a union when its leaders failed to meet membership expectations through a process called decertification.

A petition for decertification cannot be filed within a union's first year (its "certification year"). A newly chosen union is given this period to negotiate a contract and demonstrate what it can do for its members. A bargaining unit is allowed only one representation election, whether initial or decertification, within any 12-month period.

Management cannot be involved in initiating a move toward decertification. In particular, managers cannot volunteer information to employees about how decertification can be accomplished. They cannot tell employees that they would be treated better without the union nor can they suggest that employees generate a petition to decertify a union. Finally, supervisors must avoid behaving in a manner that is intended to encourage employees to seek decertification.

During the initiation stage, management is legally permitted only to respond to employee questions about decertification. Supervisors cannot include any encouragement to pursue decertification or any unsolicited advice on how to go about doing so.

Should a decertification effort reach the petition stage, the employer can still do little more than respond to employee questions. At this stage, however, some responses can be more specific and helpful. For instance, management can direct employees to appropriate authorities at the NRLB and can provide additional information about the decertification process as long as doing so is in direct response to employee inquiries. However, this is assistance at a minimal level because management is still forbidden to help with the wording of a petition or allow the petition to be transmitted on the organization's letterhead. Managers cannot allow employees to solicit petition signatures during working hours, or provide space for signing to occur. Management cannot provide time off for an employee to file the petition.

Once a decertification petition is filed and a decertification election campaign officially begins, management has options for its activities. Management is allowed to express its views about the presence of a union. However, these views cannot include direct or implied threats of reprisals for retaining the union or promises of rewards for removing it. At this stage of a decertification campaign, management may communicate its views to employees by letter or give comparisons of wages and benefits of union and nonunion workers to employees. They may hold meetings with employees, provided that attendance is voluntary.

Two important limitations exist. Management may not interfere with the right of employees to choose between decertification or not. Neither promises nor threats that could upset the conditions under which employees are to choose may be made.

Brief Chapter Summary

Increasing employee interest in unions frequently occurs because of a few significant management errors. Although economic issues, such as pay and benefits, are usually prominent in union demands, many of the reasons driving employees toward a union are intangible. Health care is becoming more and more of an organizing target because it is a growth industry with expanding numbers of employees while unions in industries, such as manufacturing, are losing members as manufacturing employment continues to shrink. Supervisors and managers usually find themselves in a key position when a union seeks to organize their employees, but the entire organizing process can be a minefield of legal traps and pitfalls. A union losing a bargaining election is allowed to try again with the same employer after 1 year and keep coming back until winning; the employer need lose just one election and the union is in. A union can be decertified and removed if its members are unhappy with it, but this process is difficult and decertifications do not readily occur.

Questions for Review and Discussion

1.   Why do most union demands seem to revolve around pay and benefits when we know there are a variety of reasons that can cause employees to seek representation?
2.   In a union organizing situation why might some supervisors be sympathetic toward employees as opposed to remaining solidly loyal to management?
3.   Why do you believe organizing within health care has been expanding while union membership overall has declined?
4.   Leafleting may be the first visible sign of union interest in your organization's employees. Is anything likely to have occurred before leafleting, and if so, what?
5.   Why can a union legally promise unorganized employees anything its representatives wish to promise to induce people to accept the union, but the organization's management cannot legally promise anything to induce employees to reject the union?

6. How are you going to answer the long-time employee who asks you, "Should I vote for or against this union?"
7. One of your employees voluntarily tells you about what occurred at a union meeting to which he had been invited. What can you do with his information?
8. Why do you suppose that signing a union authorization card should not be considered a vote in favor of having a union?
9. This chapter suggests that first-line supervisors are extremely important in countering a union organizing effort; if so, why is it that some organizations exclude these supervisors from counterorganizing activity?
10. Why might some supervisors believe it can sometimes be easier to manage their groups with a union in place?

🔍 CASE: The Organizer

You are the central supply supervisor in a hospital presently under union organizing pressure. The union's drive has reached the stage of signature cards. You are passing through one of the nursing units when you observe an individual who you believe is a union organizer backing one of the nursing assistants into a corner and waving what appears to be a union authorization card. The nursing assistant looks worried and in considerable distress and also appears to be physically trapped in the corner by the other party. You cannot hear what the person with the card is saying, but you believe you recognize the kind of card this person is waving and you can tell this person is speaking quite forcefully.

Describe what you would do under the following sets of circumstances:

1. You recognize the probable organizer as an employee of the hospital but belonging to a department other than your own.
2. You are reasonably certain the probable organizer is not an employee of the hospital.
3. Maybe use this?

Case: The Confrontation

Imagine you are head nurse of a medical–surgical unit that has been operating at full capacity for a number of months. Times have been hectic, so you have been pitching in on the floor much more than used to be necessary. On days when you have been short-staffed, you have been providing lunch relief personally for one or two other nurses. This practice has caused you to change your own lunchtime to the time when the hospital cafeteria is most crowded.

Today you have just gotten your lunch and are standing in the dining room, tray in hands, looking for familiar faces and open seats, when you are approached and very nearly circled by three of your staff members. One of them says to you, "We've been meaning to talk with you, but we're all so much on the run that we haven't gotten to you. Things have got to change around here. We can't keep going the way we're going. We're thinking of asking a union to come in, and we want to talk with you about it—now."

There you stand in the middle of the noisy, crowded cafeteria dining room, tray in both hands, feeling surrounded.

How do you believe you should handle this incident?

References

Fallon, L. F., & McConnell, C. R. (2014). Relations with labor unions. In *Human resource management in health care: Principles and practice* (2nd ed.). Burlington, MA: Jones & Bartlett Learning.

McConnell, C. R. (2015). Unions: Avoiding them when possible and living with them when necessary. In *The effective health care supervisor* (8th ed.). Burlington, MA: Jones & Bartlett Learning.

Note

1. Portions of this chapter adapted from: McConnell, C. R. (2015). Unions: Avoiding them when possible and living with them when necessary. In *The effective health care supervisor* (8th ed.). Burlington, MA: Jones & Bartlett Learning (Chapter 30); and Fallon, L. F., & McConnell, C. R. (2014). Relations with labor unions. In *Human resource management in health care: Principles and practice* (2nd ed.). Burlington, MA: Jones & Bartlett Learning (Chapter 19).

Glossary

Accountable Care Organizations (ACOs) Collectives of physicians, hospitals, and other healthcare providers who come together voluntarily to provide coordinated high-quality care to Medicare patients.

Acquisition The outright purchase of majority control of one organization by another organization.

Activity-based costing (ABC) ABC is a reaction to the perceived deficiencies of traditional cost management systems, which sometimes struggled to accurately determine the precise costs of production and related services.

Advance practice registered nurse (APRN) An APRN must hold a bachelor's degree in nursing or equivalent and be a licensed RN who has completed additional education at the masters or doctorate level in nursing.

Agreement Whether written or unwritten, a mutually agreed upon arrangement between two or more business entities.

Allied health Allied health professionals provide services to patients that follow the plan of care set forth from the physician or nurse responsible for the patient.

Almshouses Charitable housing for the poor and elderly who were no longer able to work.

American Medical Association (AMA) National membership organization of physicians founded in 1847 under the leadership of Dr. Nathan Smith.

Bargaining election A secret-ballot election sanctioned by the National Labor Relations Board by which the members of a specific employee group determine whether they do or do not wish union representation.

Bargaining unit A specific collective of employees a union represents; the group covered by a collective bargaining agreement.

Biomedical engineering A department in a hospital responsible for installing, maintaining, and repairing medical equipment used in the hospital.

Bundled payments Offer all-inclusive payments to hospitals, physicians, and aftercare services (care and support post-hospitalization) for a particular illness over a specified length of time for certain diagnoses and procedures treated in the hospital setting.

Center for Medicare and Medicaid Innovation (CMMI) CMMI is charged with creating, evaluating, and diffusing innovations to lower costs, provide better health outcomes, and improve patient experiences through the Medicare and Medicaid programs.

Certificate of need (CN) A program put into law in an attempt to control the cost of healthcare services by limiting the number of hospital beds in a community; CON laws are intended to ensure adequate access to health care to meet specific community needs.

Chief Executive Officer (CEO) A top-ranking manager in an organization, responsible for overall operations, fund raising, long-range planning, and relations with the board of directors. Alternate titles in use include Administrator, President, Executive Director, and others.

Chief Financial Officer (CFO) A manager with overall responsibility for all finance and accounting activities of an organization, billing, and collections from all entities involved in reimbursing for patient care.

Chief Information Officer (CIO) A manager with overall responsibility for overseeing all aspects of computer operations and ensuring that all data are entered, accessed, retained, and stored and are managed according to federal and state regulations.

Chief Operating (or Operations) Officer (COO) A manager responsible for overseeing all aspects of daily operations of an organization; a superior of all department managers and responsible for the safety and well-being of patients, staff, and visitors.

Clinical laboratory Made up of two basic divisions: clinical pathology and anatomical pathology. Clinical pathology performs laboratory tests as ordered by physicians; anatomical pathology examines tissue and other samples and performs autopsies to determine the cause and manner of death.

Collective bargaining agreement An agreement between an employer and a union that has been sanctioned as the legal representative of an employee group; a "union contract."

Completed staff work Taking a problem and recommended solutions to one's superior, rather than simply looking to the boss for help.

Consumer-directed health plan (CDHP) CHDP is an HDHP combined with a pretax savings account. In a CDHP, qualified healthcare costs (except preventive care) are typically paid first from the pretax account; when that is exhausted, any additional costs up to the deductible are paid out-of-pocket by the member (this gap is sometimes referred to as a bridge or a doughnut hole).

Core competencies Essential strengths of an organization that contribute to its success and support its competitive advantage.

Cost-containment The process of controlling the expenditures required to operate an organization, to provide a specific array of services, or to perform within the limits of a specific budget; generally, to constrain costs from increasing beyond the limits of financial resources.

Decertification A formal process by which an employee group may remove a union when it is felt that the union and its leadership have failed to meet the expectations of the membership.

Diagnostic and therapeutic imaging Diagnostic imaging and therapeutic radiology services provide patients with high-quality, cost-effective imaging and therapeutic services to aid in the diagnosis and treatment of disease.

Diploma programs Nursing education programs established and operated by various hospitals. Usually three years in duration, these were hospital-based programs that provided both academic and hands-on nursing education.

Electronic health records (EHRs) Records focusing on the total health of the patient, beyond standard clinical data collected in providers' offices and including a broader view of each patient's care.

Electronic medical records (EMRs) Digital versions of the paper charts in providers' offices, each EMR containing the medical and treatment history of each patient in one practice.

Entries to care The various means by which patients can be admitted to the hospital.

Environmental services A department in a hospital designed to provide a safe, sanitary, and comfortable environment and to help prevent the development and transmission of disease and infections.

Exclusive provider organization (EPO) EPOs are really benefits design products offered by commercial payers that use their existing health maintenance organization (HMO) or preferred provider organization (PPO) networks, or based on rental networks in the case of some self-funded plans. Benefits coverage is available only when nonemergency services are provided by the EPO's network providers.

Facility security A department in a hospital with the primary role of protecting patients, visitors, and employees from harm and keeping the hospital and its property secured.

For-profit Also referred to as proprietary; incorporated as a business, with profits from operations accruing to owners or stockholders.

Healthcare system As a term utilized through the several middle decades of the 1940s, the American Healthcare System was a loosely organized cottage industry made up of many individual providers and a number of multi-hospital groupings based on common ownership (such as religious hospital "chains").

Health Insurance Portability and Accountability Act (HIPAA) Also known otherwise as the Kennedy-Kassebaum Act, HIPAA provides for mobility of health insurance for certain employees leaving their jobs, sets forth guidelines for ensuring patient privacy, and addresses a number of other information and security issues.

Health insurer One who provides employment-based group health insurance.

Health maintenance organization (HMO)
A healthcare system that assumes both the financial risks associated with providing comprehensive medical services (insurance and service risk) and the responsibility for healthcare delivery in a particular geographic area to HMO members, usually in return for a fixed, prepaid fee. Financial risk may be shared with the providers participating in the HMO.

High-deductible health plan (HDHP)
A health insurance plan based on lower premiums and higher required deductibles than traditional plans; also a requirement for having health-savings accounts.

High-deductible health plans with savings option (HDHP/SO) Plans which are paired with accounts that allow enrollees to use tax-deferred savings to pay plan cost sharing and other out-of-pocket medical expenses not covered by the plan.

Hill-Burton The Hospital Survey and Construction Act of 1946 passed to provide federal financial assistance for the planning, construction, and improvement of healthcare facilities through financing guaranteed under the Public Health Service Act.

Hippocrates A Greek physician of the Age of Pericles, a major figure in the history of medicine, often referred to as the Father of Modern Medicine.

Horizontal mergers A horizontal merger, common in health care, occurs within the same sector of an industry; the companies involved offer the same product or service. An example of a horizontal merger is two hospitals merging into one organization.

Hospital closures Closings of hospitals driven largely by financial and reimbursement issues or by mergers or acquisitions; have affected mostly but not exclusively small and rural hospitals.

Indemnity plan A type of medical plan that reimburses the patient or provider when expenses are incurred.

Independent physician (or practice) association (IPA) An IPA is a legal entity that contracts with private physicians (both primary care physicians [PCPs] and specialists) for purposes of then contracting with health maintenance organizations (HMOs) or other payers.

Interprofessional practice Interprofessional practice is the provision of patient care by a team of healthcare professionals of several fields.

Joint operating agreement A written contract that establishes a new organization to accomplish a specific task while permitting the originating organizations to maintain their individual operating and inherent characteristics.

Joint venture An agreement between two business entities that have decided to provide specific organizational resources in order to accomplish an initiative.

"Lean"management A process-improvement methodology; an important approach to management is intended to serve customer needs, reduce waste, and ensure defect-free products or services while continuously improving processes.

Licensed practical/vocational nurse (LPN/VN) A licensed practical or vocational nurse (LPN or LVN) is an individual who has completed a state-approved practical or vocational nursing program and is licensed by a state board of nursing to provide patient care. LPN and LVN work under the supervision of a registered nurse, advanced practice registered nurse, or physician.

Managed care organization (MCO) An organization that combines the functions of health insurance, the delivery of care, and overall administration of same.

Managed care plans Plans that generally provide comprehensive health services to their members, and offer financial incentives for patients to use the providers who belong to the plan. Examples of managed care plans include: health maintenance organizations (HMOs), preferred provider organizations (PPOs), and point-of-service plans (POSs).

Medicaid A means-tested (or need-based) program that provides health insurance to low-income adults and children, and the financing and administration of Medicaid is shared between the Federal and State governments.

Medicaid impact In general, the effects of the Medicaid health insurance program, with benefits to lower-income individuals including more treatment provided, fewer financial hardships for patients, and reduced out-of-pocket medical expenses.

Medical staff Licensed physicians and dentists who are approved and given privileges to provide health care to patients in a hospital or other healthcare facility or private practice setting.

Medical staff Primarily, the physicians who are authorized to admit patients to the hospital and to treat them therein; in addition to independently practicing physicians, the medical staff may include some physicians employed by the hospital.

Merger A legal combination of two or more corporate entities into a single new corporation; occasionally, a combination of equals or near equals, but often seen as a smaller entity being absorbed by a larger entity.

Mergers A formal and legal agreement between two organizations with the goal of creating a new organization.

Not-for-profit Legal status of a corporation chartered to operate in such a way that no profit accrues to owners or stockholders; tax exempt; status of the majority of hospitals in the country.

Nursing Nursing is the art and science of caring for individuals of all ages, families, groups, or communities in all settings in which that health care may be offered.

Nursing services Comprises registered nurses (RNs), licensed practical nurses or licensed vocational nurses (LPN and LVNs), nursing assistants, and other staff; the largest hospital department, the mission of which is to ensure the delivery of quality, courteous, and considerate care.

Occupational therapist Occupational therapists treat injured, ill, or disabled patients so that optimum function of everyday activities can be achieved.

Organizational chart A visual depiction of the arrangement of the organization's departments, functions, and activities relative to each other and position of each element in the chain of command.

Organizational flattening Removal of layers of management such that a resulting organization chart appears "flatter."

Organizational structure The arrangement of departments, divisions, or functions that reflects the manner in which these elements are assembled to pursue the organization's mission and purpose.

Partnership A legal agreement between two (or more) organizations that involves cooperation to accomplish a specific initiative or set of initiatives.

Patient Protection and Affordable Care Act (PPACA) This Federal legislation includes a multitude of initiatives, from creating insurance exchanges to raising a myriad of taxes to fund a national healthcare program.

Payer Any commercial insurer or health benefits administrator that pays medical claims. This designation may include any of the following as well as others.

Pennsylvania Hospital Organized by Dr. Thomas Boyd, the Pennsylvania Hospital in Philadelphia was the first incorporated hospital in America.

Pharmacist Pharmacists dispense prescription medications to patients and provide instruction in the safe use of prescriptions.

Pharmacy The hospital department responsible for dispensing pharmaceuticals and compounding drugs as necessary and providing other diagnostic and therapeutic chemical substances that are used in the hospital.

Physical therapist Physical therapists (PTs) diagnose and treat individuals from newborns to the elderly who have medical problems or other health-related conditions that limit their abilities to move and perform functional activities in their daily lives.

Physical therapy Healthcare occupation the practitioners of which diagnose and manage movement dysfunction to restore, maintain, and promote optimal physical function and fitness and quality of life as related to movement and health.

Plant engineering and maintenance A department in a hospital responsible for addressing problems with the physical parts of the hospital or the equipment used.

Point of service (POS) A POS plan is an HMO/PPO hybrid; sometimes referred to as an open-ended HMO when offered by an HMO. POS plans resemble HMOs for in-network services. Services received outside of the network are usually reimbursed in a manner similar to conventional indemnity plans (e.g., provider reimbursement based on a fee schedule or usual, customary, and reasonable charges).

Point of service (POS) plan POS plan provides benefits coverage but with higher levels of cost sharing, including a higher deductible and coinsurance instead of a copayment.

Preferred provider organization (PPO) An indemnity plan in which coverage is provided to participants through a network of selected healthcare providers (such as hospitals and physicians). The enrollees may go outside the network but would incur larger costs in the form of higher deductibles, higher coinsurance rates, or non-discounted charges from the providers.

Registered nurse (RN) A registered nurse (RN) is an individual who has completed nursing education at the diploma, associate's degree, or baccalaureate degree level and is licensed by a state board of nursing to provide patient care.

Respiratory therapist Respiratory therapists (RT) care for patients with breathing disorders and provide treatment for a variety of respiratory diseases.

Respiratory therapy Involved in both general care and critical care, respiratory care addresses the maintenance or improvement of respiratory function (breathing) as applied by practitioners trained in pulmonary medicine and includes services such as oxygen therapy.

Span of control The breadth of responsibility that a manager can effectively fulfill, and specifically the number of employees one manager can oversee effectively.

Specialty hospitals Often physician-owned institutions, these are generally private institutions that appear to serve a favorable selection of patients and avoid charity care and emergency services.

SWOT analysis Part of the strategic planning process is to perform a SWOT (strengths, weaknesses, opportunities, and threats) analysis which consists of an evaluation of both internal (strengths and weaknesses) and external (opportunities and threats) environmental factors that can have either a positive or negative impact on the hospital's operations.

Synergy The overarching goal of a merger is to create synergy, which means the result of the cooperative effort will be greater than the single operational effect of the organizations; in everyday terms, we could say this means *one plus one equals three*.

Third-party administrator (TPA) Companies that administer benefits plans on behalf of a self-funded employers. Technically, they are not "insured," but are employee welfare benefits plans operated by an employer.

Third-party payers Refer to the payer entity (e.g., government, insurance company, or self-insured employer) involved in paying for treatment received by a patient.

Unity of command For each task to be done or each responsibility to be fulfilled, there is one person ultimately responsible.

Vertical mergers A vertical merger is one that occurs within different sectors of an industry. The organizations offer various products or services, with the goal of creating efficiencies of operations and expansion of services.

Index